FISCAL MANAGEMENT

AND

ECONOMIC REFORM

IN THE

PEOPLE'S REPUBLIC OF CHINA

by

Christine P. W. Wong

Christopher Heady

Wing T. Woo

Published for the Asian Development Bank
by Oxford University Press

HONG KONG
OXFORD UNIVERSITY PRESS
OXFORD   NEW YORK

Oxford University Press

Oxford   New York
Athens   Auckland   Bangkok   Bogota   Bombay
Buenos Aires   Calcutta   Cape Town   Dar es Salaam
Delhi   Florence   Hong Kong   Istanbul   Karachi
Kuala Lumpur   Madras   Madrid   Melbourne
Mexico City   Nairobi   Paris   Singapore
Taipei   Tokyo   Toronto

and associated companies in
Berlin   Ibadan

Oxford is a trade mark of Oxford University Press

First published 1995
Paperback edition published 1996
This impression (lowest digit)
1 3 5 7 9 10 8 6 4 2

Published for the Asian Development Bank by Oxford University Press

British Library Cataloguing in Publication Data
available

Library of Congress Cataloging-in-Publication Data

Wong, Christine, 1950–
    Fiscal management and economic reform in the People's Republic of
China / by Christine P.W. Wong, Christopher Heady, Wing T. Woo.
      p.   cm.
    Includes bibliographical references.
    ISBN 0-19-586771-8 (hb)   0-19-587837-X (pb)
      1. Fiscal policy—China.   2. Finance, Public—China.   3. Economic
stabilization—Government policy—China.   4. China—Economic
policy—1976–   I. Heady Christopher John, 1951–   .   II. Woo, Wing
Thye.   III. Asian Development Bank.   IV. Title.
HJ1401.W66   1995
338.951—dc20   95-3991
                                                                    CIP

Printed in Hong Kong
Published by Oxford University Press (China) Ltd.
18/F Warwick House, Taikoo Place, 979 King's Road, Quarry Bay, Hong Kong

Contents

List of Tables

Notes to Tables:
   "n.a."   not available
   "-"   magnitude zero

List of Figures

List of Text Boxes

Abbreviations

BAF	Budgetary Adjustment Fund
CESH	Culture, Education, Science and Health
CC	Capital Construction
c.i.f.	cost insurance freight
CICT	Consolidated Industrial and Commercial Tax
CRS	Contract Responsibility System
EBF	Extrabudgetary Funds
ETKF	Energy and Transport Key Construction Fund
f.o.b.	free on board
GBR	Government Borrowing Requirement
GDP	Gross Domestic Product
GFAF	Gross Fixed Asset Formation
GNP	Gross National Product
MOF	Ministry of Finance
PBC	People's Bank of China
PCBC	People's Construction Bank of China
PRC	People's Republic of China
SAMC	State Asset Management Corporation
SIM	Shenzhen Investment Management Company
SB	State-Owned Bank
SPTR	Separating Profits and Taxes Reform
STAQS	Securities Trading Automated Quotation System
SOE	State-Owned Enterprise
TVE	Township and Village Enterprise
UK	United Kingdom
VAT	Value-Added Tax

Glossary

adjustment income	revenues from industrial-commercial taxes, a portion of which was used to supplement local fixed revenues to cover local government expenditure under the 1980 revenue-sharing arrangements
central fixed revenues	revenues accruing solely to the central government and not shared with local governments
commodity housing	housing built for sale at market prices (for profit)
corporatize	to convert into a shareholding company
five cost factors (in housing reform)	depreciation, maintenance, management, real estate taxes and returns to investment
fenshuizhi	system of tax sharing introduced on an experimental basis in nine provinces in 1992 and nationwide in 1994 in a slightly altered form
fiscal gap	a fiscal gap is said to exist when the financial resources of a government are insufficient to provide an adequate level of service needs of the locality. This is different from the actual budget deficit which is the gap between actual outlays and financial resources.
fixed rate remittance	a fiscal contracting arrangement where the provincial remittance is a fixed percentage of shared revenues
fixed quota remittance	a fiscal contracting arrangement where the provincial remittance is a fixed amount
free riders	those seeking to enjoy the benefits without sharing the costs.

golden handshake	a large bonus payment offered, often as inducement to a departing manager or chief executive officer
government borrowing requirement	the most commonly used definition of the budget deficit.
guagou	meaning "linking up". An attempt to control labor costs by linking the rate of wage increases to productivity rises
hard budget constraint	denotes a situation where enterprises cannot expect the government to grant subsidies to cover losses that arise from mismanagement. It is in contrast to the term "soft budget constraint", popularized by Kornai (1980).
hunger for investment	the insatiable demand for investment in enterprises that do not face financial discipline, i.e., those facing a "soft budget constraint"
incremental contracting	a fiscal contracting arrangement where the provincial remittance is set to grow by a fixed rate
ligaishui	"to replace profits with taxes". A reform in 1984 that introduced income taxes to SOEs, to substitute tax payments for profit remittances.
line item cities (*jihua danlieshi*)	a program under which selected cities have acquired "line item" status. At present, nine cities have direct revenue-sharing relations with the central government, making their budgetary status equivalent to that of provinces (and the municipalities of Beijing, Shanghai and Tianjin).
local fixed revenues	revenues accruing to local governments prior to revenue sharing
monetary aggregates	measures of money supply

pay-as-you-go
pension system with no reserve funds, where current year liabilities are financed from current year receipts.

provincial level cities
Beijing, Shanghai and Tianjin municipalities which have the administrative level (and budgetary status) equivalent to a province

quota subsidies
fixed-sum transfers from the central government to poor provinces under the revenue-sharing system

rational rent
rent that covers the opportunity costs of providing housing

shared revenues
revenues which are shared between central government and local government

standard rent
rent needed to cover the "five cost factors": costs of depreciation, maintenance, management, and real estate taxes, and a 3 per cent return on investment

standard price
for housing
unit costs that cover construction costs, land acquisition costs, and compensation payments to displaced residents

three cost factors
(in housing reform)
depreciation, maintenance, management fees

shuili fenliu
"to separate profits and taxes". A reform that called for profit contracting to apply only to after-tax profits of SOEs.

soft budget constraint
denotes a situation where enterprise budget constraints can be circumvented through special tax exemptions and subsidies. Popularized by Kornai (1980).

| stock definition of the budget deficit | measures the increase in the accumulated total of government debt, including borrowing from the central bank. This is equal to the borrowing requirement (representing additions to the debt stock) minus loan principal repayments (representing reductions in the debt stock). |

tax sharing — See *fenshuizhi*. System of tax assignments whereby taxes are assigned to the central government, local governments, or shared between them.

"two funds" — Budgetary Adjustment Fund (BAF) and Energy and Transport Key Construction Fund (ETKF)

two-track pricing system — system of pricing whereby a good is sold at two (or more) prices depending on whether it is under plan allocation. Plan prices are in general lower than market prices.

voting with one's feet — to move to a location under another government administrative unit in response to differing local government policies

welfare housing (*fulifang*) — one type of housing sold at concessionary prices in Shenzhen

wool wars and silk cocoon wars — erection of provincial barriers to resource flows to protect the financial health of local enterprises and markets

Preface

Fiscal Management and Economic Reform in the People's Republic of China deals with the complex nature of the market-oriented reform process in the world's largest country. Although the focus of the study is on fiscal policy and the broader realm of public finance, because of the complex and interlinked nature of the whole reform effort, it also addresses other economywide reforms under implementation. The authors conclude that the success of the fiscal reforms will hinge crucially on enterprise reforms, financial sector reforms, price reforms, and other ongoing or planned structural reforms that promote market-based macromanagement.

The reform process in the People's Republic of China (PRC) has been gradual and incremental in contrast to reforms undertaken in the countries of Eastern Europe and the former Soviet Union. This strategy has allowed for reviewing policy reforms, assessing their impact on the economy, drawing lessons for adjusting the reform process, and framing future reform strategies. The study highlights the need for properly sequencing reforms to ensure that they are successful, gain acceptability, and avoid major economic and social disruptions.

The publication of this book comes at a time when the Communist Party has called for the early establishment of a socialist market economy and for expediting the opening up and reform process. The book will hopefully provide valuable guidance to that effort.

The study has been based on the research carried out under a grant financed by the Asian Development Bank. However, the opinions expressed are those of the authors. In undertaking the task that resulted in this book, the authors worked closely with officials from the Ministry of Finance in the PRC. The authors acknowledge the contributions of Zhu Fulin, Director of the General Planning Department; Xie Xuren, Deputy Director of the Budget Management Department; and Kang Xuejun, Division Chief and Economist of the Statistics Division, Comprehensive Planning Department. They also thank Charles McLure Jr., Senior Fellow of the Hoover Institute for reviewing the manuscript.

Within the Asian Development Bank, the project was conceived and supervised by Khaja H. Moinuddin, Assistant Chief, Development Policy Office. Bruce Murray, Manager, Programs Department (East) and Anella Munro, Economist, coordinated the publication. Jill Gale de Villa edited the text. Erlinda Chavez provided valuable secretarial assistance. Typesetting was done by Printing Section.

EIICHI WATANABE
Director
Programs Department (East)
Asian Development Bank

Executive Summary

Reforms to the economy of the People's Republic of China (PRC) since 1979 have produced considerable benefits, including a high rate of economic growth. However, the reform process is not complete and improvements in the system of fiscal management are required before the full benefits of a market economy can be realized. The requirement of improved fiscal management can only be met by improving the Ministry of Finance's capacity to analyze the economic situation, anticipate future changes and guide economic reform. This report is intended to assist the Ministry of Finance in improving these capacities.

Three major aspects of the PRC fiscal system are currently causing serious concern: (1) the decline in government revenue as a proportion of gross national product (GNP) and the resulting increase in the government budget deficit; (2) the repeated bouts of inflationary pressure followed by depressed market demand, which have highlighted weaknesses in macroeconomic management; and (3) the difficulties in central-local fiscal relations which are affecting revenue mobilization.

A key element in all three of these problems is the position of state-owned enterprises (SOEs). Their poor profitability is partly responsible for reductions in government revenue and increases in loss subsidies. The financing of their growing wage bills and their high levels of investment are partly responsible for excessive monetary growth and the associated problems of macroeconomic control. Their close relationship with local governments is an important aspect of the difficult central-local fiscal relations. Enterprise reform is therefore fundamental to the establishment of a satisfactory fiscal system.

In addition to the current difficulties, other aspects of the fiscal system need reform before the market can function properly. Most importantly, the fiscal system must encourage labor mobility so that workers move from unprofitable enterprises to new opportunities elsewhere in the economy. Reform of the pension system, unemployment insurance, and housing provision are all necessary to free workers to move. Such reforms will also assist the reform of SOEs, by making their costs more closely related to their efficiency and by making it easier to allow enterprises to go bankrupt.

THE PRC FISCAL SYSTEM IN INTERNATIONAL PERSPECTIVE

The process of reform has included substantial changes in the PRC fiscal system, and many of these changes have moved it closer to international norms. However, there are still a number of respects in which the PRC fiscal system differs from that in most other countries.

One difference is the budgetary accounting system. Enterprise subsidies are counted as negative revenues, rather than expenditure, and government borrowing (except from the central bank) is regarded as revenue. Neither of these conventions conform to international practice. This means that substantial adjustments to PRC revenue, expenditure, and deficit figures have to be made before standard economic analysis can be applied or international comparisons made.

Another difference that hinders international comparisons is the role of enterprises in providing housing, medical care, and retirement pensions. This means enterprises are responsible for a substantial amount of expenditure that is part of the government budget in other countries. However, this enterprise expenditure is not simply an accounting convention: it inhibits labor mobility and makes it difficult for the government to allow enterprises to go bankrupt.

The tax system is also different from international standards. Indirect taxes are complicated: the number of different tax rates is very high and two systems of sales tax (value-added tax [VAT] and product/business tax) coexist. Also, the PRC VAT differs in some important details from international standards. As for direct taxes, the different tax treatment of different enterprises on the basis of their ownership goes against international norms of equal treatment.

A particularly important and unusual feature of the PRC fiscal system is the practice of contracting. It is applied to the tax payments and profit remittances of enterprises and to the revenue-sharing arrangements between different levels of government. For enterprise income tax, contracts will specify that the enterprise will pay the standard tax on a fixed level of profit whether or not it is actually achieved, and a lower tax rate (often zero) on any profits above that level. For provincial governments collecting revenues that are shared with the central government, the contract will specify a sharing proportion for a basic level of revenue, but the province is allowed to keep a higher proportion of revenues above that level.

In both cases, the contract aims to increase incentives. For enterprises, it encourages greater profitability. For provinces, it rewards higher levels of tax collection. These increased incentives are obviously desirable, but are obtained at considerable cost. They reinforce income inequalities. They lead to a falling share of tax revenue, especially the central government share of tax revenue, as GNP rises. They promote macroeconomic instability by reducing the tax share in GNP during booms.

One aspect of contracting that should be highlighted is that it increases the amount of individual negotiation. Enterprises individually negotiate their tax contracts with the level of government that owns them, while different levels of government negotiate the basis of revenue sharing. This enormous amount of negotiation represents one of the most significant differences between the PRC fiscal system and those in other countries. Most other countries have developed tax and revenue-sharing systems that are governed by uniform rules that exclude, as far as possible, individual negotiations. These systems are established by law, or constitutional amendment, and enforced by courts.

The culture of individual negotiation between enterprises and the tax authorities in the PRC goes beyond the negotiation of tax contracts. It extends to granting tax exemptions from indirect taxes to individual enterprises for a variety of reasons, a practice that is very rare in the rest of the world. In other countries, tax exemptions are laid down by law in a way that minimizes individual negotiation. This is a particularly serious problem because the PRC is one of the very few countries where local governments collect taxes on behalf of the central government. Thus, local officials are granting discretionary tax exemptions that reduce the central government revenue. This naturally leads to the granting of excessive exemptions.

MACROECONOMIC MANAGEMENT

The budget deficits of 3 per cent of gross domestic product (GDP) in both 1990 and 1991 are underestimates of overspending by the state. A complete accounting should include the deficit spending of SOEs that is being financed by the central bank. This expansion of reserve money to allow appropriation of resources by SOEs has the same effect on the economy as monetization of the budget deficits. These hidden subsidies to SOEs should be made explicit and disbursed through the budget, which would oblige the state to reconsider every year the relative priority of SOE support. Taking the hidden subsidies into account, the estimated total budget deficit was as much as 6 per cent in 1988 and 1989, and 8 per cent in 1990 and 1991. This upward trend is a serious threat to macroeconomic stability.

There is an unfortunate stop-go pattern in the conduct of monetary policy, which is reproduced in the movements of the price level and GNP. The central bank, however, cannot be held responsible for the poor performance of monetary policy because it has only one instrument (bank credits) to perform the many functions assigned to it. The side effects of using monetary policy to achieve one goal often conflict with another goal; for example, between guaranteeing full employment and maintaining price stability.

Examination of the sources of reserve money growth in 1990 and 1991 reveals a potential source of "shock" in the future. The growth in foreign assets contributed 8 percentage points to money supply growth in 1990 and 9 per cent in 1991 as a result of balance-of-payments surpluses. This monetary expansion suggests that steps must be taken now to develop open-market instruments to control the money supply, to prevent the PRC from losing monetary control with the expansion of trade.

Two of the most important reasons for the poor performance of monetary policy are the great number of objectives assigned to it and the great number of departments involved in its formulation. The use of monetary policy should be limited to stabilizing the price level and the rate of nominal GNP growth; and the size and composition of the monetary policy council should be reviewed.

REFORMING THE FINANCIAL SYSTEM

There are two major institutional flaws in the central bank. First, the regional branches are under dual leadership by the head office and by the local government. Given the great interest of local governments in promoting local development, this makes a branch bank reluctant to implement a tight credit policy that is ordered by the head office. The influence of local governments over the banking system should be minimized.

The second major problem is the administrative setting of interest rates, at low levels, with the result that the central bank is under great pressure to accommodate credit demands that exceed the credit target. Freeing interest rates will not only ensure that funds go to projects with the highest rates of return, it will also give monetary authorities a timely indicator of the level of aggregate demand: an interest rate rise can be a signal that the economy is overheating.

Interest rates can be decontrolled in three phases. Phase 1 consolidates the interest rates: one interest rate for working capital loans, and one interest rate for investment loans. Phase 2 frees the interest rate for working capital, and phase 3 frees the interest rate for investment capital. The cost of this incremental approach is that monetary control will continue to be loose during the transition.

The present fiscal role of the banking system is not appropriate for a market economy. Its primary role should be limited to the intermediation of funds in a market-determined fashion. Just as SOEs are being pushed to compete in the goods markets, state-owned banks must also be pushed to compete in the financial markets. The government will have to recapitalize some of the state-owned banks before they can compete in the markets as independent financial entities.

The banks' intermediation of funds should be supplemented by other forms of intermediation: nationally integrated networks of commercial paper markets, bond markets, and stock markets. The development of such financial markets should be a high priority because it will improve the allocation of capital and give the central bank the capability to conduct open-market operations. As a first step, the government should quickly deepen the secondary markets for government papers and integrate them into a national market.

The Ministry of Finance should not intervene in the secondary market for government bonds to preserve their face value when the interest rate rises. Past interventions were financed by bank loans. When such loans caused the central bank to increase the amount of reserve money, the interventions were an unexpected source of money growth.

GOVERNMENT REVENUES

The immediate concern with government revenue is its continued decline as a proportion of GNP. The three major causes of this poor revenue performance are the reduced profitability of SOEs, the tax contracting system, and the poor revenue buoyancy of indirect taxes (especially VAT).

The reduced profitability of SOEs (as a share of GNP) is due to two factors: increased competition, which has eroded profits, and a continued rise in labor costs. These factors are unrelated to enterprise productivity, which may well have improved while financial performance has worsened.

At the same time, tax contracting has meant that enterprise income tax receipts have grown even more slowly than SOE profits. Abolition of the contracting system is therefore a high priority, and implementation of the experimental *shuili fenliu* tax system that separates profit and tax appears a step in the right direction. This experiment imposes a nonnegotiable tax rate and confines contracting to sharing after-tax profits between each enterprise and the level of government that owns it. The *shuili fenliu* system also reduces the ability of SOEs to pay back loan principal from before-tax income and moves towards a situation where the same tax rules and rates apply to all enterprises, regardless of ownership. However, even the current level of revenue is unlikely to be maintained unless the Energy and Transportation Fund contributions continue to be levied. The *shuili fenliu* also maintains the undesirable feature of each enterprise paying tax to the level of government that owns it.

The poor revenue buoyancy of indirect taxes, especially VAT, is particularly surprising. Most countries find that indirect tax revenues increase as a proportion of GNP during economic growth, and this is particularly true of VAT. The granting of individual exemptions by local tax officials is a major cause of this problem. These exemptions must be reduced if the government's revenue share in GNP is to be stabilized or increased.

In addition to dealing with the major problem of revenue loss, market distortions that are caused by the tax system must be reduced. Such reforms, by taxing all sectors of the economy and all ownership forms equally, will also reduce the current heavy dependence of government revenues on the steadily narrowing base of industrial SOEs. This can be achieved by bringing the system up to international standards in the following ways, most of which are already planned by the State Tax Bureau under the reform program announced in November 1993:

1. VAT should be applied to all goods currently covered by product tax.
2. Supplementary consumption taxes should be applied to a very restricted number of goods.
3. Foreign enterprises and joint ventures should pay the same indirect taxes as domestic enterprises.
4. VAT should give credit for taxes paid on investment goods: it should be consumption-based.
5. VAT should be extended to at least some goods that are currently covered by business tax.
6. The number of VAT rates should be substantially reduced, possibly to just one rate.
7. VAT should be administered consistently across the country, using the invoice method.
8. All enterprises should be taxed at the same rates, using the same accounting principles, not allowing loan principal repayments to be deducted before tax.
9. To ensure equal treatment of enterprises and maintain the integrity of depreciation allowances, the Energy and Transport Key Construction Fund and the Budgetary Adjustment Fund should be phased out. Care must be taken to ensure that the revenue they currently produce is collected in some other way.
10. Personal income taxes should be integrated to a greater extent.

11. The rate structure of personal income taxes should be simplified.
12. Personal income tax administration should be strengthened to allow the proper taxation of people with more than one income source.
13. Application of the resource tax should be thoroughly reviewed.
14. Local governments should be allowed some discretion in setting local tax rates.
15. The role of the investment orientation tax and the construction tax should be reviewed.

GOVERNMENT EXPENDITURE

Public expenditure has fallen as a proportion of GNP. It is difficult to make comparisons because of the different way in which pensions and housing are financed in the PRC, but the proportion of GNP devoted to public expenditure in the PRC is now similar to that in other developing countries.

Public investment in capital construction and technical updating has experienced the largest cutbacks, and is close to the level of other low-income countries. Capital construction is always an easy item to cut when there is a shortage of revenue, but the temptation to continue cutting this budget item should be resisted: it is essential to the maintenance of high rates of economic growth.

Another area that should not be cut is expenditures under the heading: culture, education, science, and health. Many areas of the country have per capita levels of expenditure in this budgetary heading that are well below the national average. Considerations of both social justice and continued economic growth imply that these areas should receive the resources to bring their expenditures closer to the national average.

The expenditure items that should be cut are administration and subsidies. Government employment has grown much faster than the industrial labor force, despite the policy of reducing the government's role in the economy. There is clearly scope for considerable economies here.

A large proportion of subsidies has been price subsidies for urban food, particularly grain. Improvements in living standards imply that these are no longer necessary, and the freeing of the urban retail price of grain in 1993 has eliminated this large and growing outlay. There are also loss subsidies to SOEs unrelated to the grain trade. Some reflect price controls, but others reflect inefficiency and government reluctance to allow enterprises to go bankrupt. Enterprise reform and further price reform are necessary for the elimination of this item.

CENTRAL-LOCAL FISCAL RELATIONS

Intergovernmental relations are a central part of fiscal reform in the PRC because of decentralized tax administration. While tax laws and tax policy are set by the central government, collection is carried out by local agents, and revenues are shared upward with the central government according to revenue-sharing agreements. Tax assignment and revenue-sharing rules are taking on growing importance as incentives for motivating local tax effort.

Intergovernmental relations have been severely strained in recent years because forces unleashed by economic reform have brought substantial changes to the division of revenues and expenditures, and because the government has managed these changes poorly. On the revenue side, fiscal decline has reduced local government revenues (after revenue sharing) from 9.8 per cent of GNP in 1982 to 9.3 per cent in 1990 despite decentralization.

Expenditure has shifted even more toward local governments. Central subsidies now outweigh remittances from the provinces, and local governments have become net recipients of transfers.

The inability of local governments to cut expenditures in line with fiscal decline can be attributed partly to the downward transfer of expenditure responsibilities, most notably for price subsidies. Rising wage costs during the reform period also sharply inflated the cost of providing government services. In 1990, price subsidies and government administration alone absorbed nearly half of local expenditures, leaving local budgets in a tight squeeze to meet the needs for social welfare, education, and investment in infrastructure.

From the local perspective, mistrust of central government intentions stemmed from the government's actions on the revenue side. Since 1980, four different revenue-sharing regimes have been introduced in attempts to stimulate local tax effort. However, their incentive effects were undermined by central actions that claimed revenues outside the revenue-sharing system.

Revenues are actually divided between the central and local governments by a two-stage process. In the first stage, the central government sets the rules on the portion of collected revenues that are set aside as central revenues. In the second stage, the rest is shared with provinces according to revenue-sharing contracts. Through the 1980s, the government repeatedly expanded the scope of central revenues, largely through expanding its claims over enterprise ownership. In addition, it repeatedly introduced new taxes or simply "borrowed" from local governments. By the 1990s, the role of formal revenue sharing has been diminished, and local confidence in the central government's commitment to revenue-sharing contracts is understandably low. From the central perspective, declining remittances from local governments have greatly reduced its ability to allocate resources and redistribute income across regions. In 1990, block grants ("quota subsidies") to poor provinces accounted for only 15 per cent of central-local transfers. The rest was split between earmarked grants and compensatory payments for enterprise ownership transfers — neither is based on needs, and they are fragmented under the control of different ministries.

The PRC fiscal system has moved toward self-financing. The dependence of local revenues on enterprises has often encouraged excessive local development and regional protectionism. Decentralized tax administration has also allowed local governments to offer tax exemptions and reductions to enterprises and has eroded the central tax base.

Dissatisfaction with the traditional revenue-sharing system is now pervasive. With commitment problems undermining incentives for local tax collection, the low buoyancy of the fiscal system is probably the result of low tax effort — every attempt by the central government to raise the revenue-GNP and the central share of total revenues has been thwarted by local governments, which anticipate that increased collections will invite imposition of a larger remittance quota in the next round.

This system of revenue sharing is also incompatible with a decentralized economy, where high remittance rates are deterrents to tax efforts, especially in rich provinces. Indeed, the differential remittance rates, combined with tax expenditure authority at the local level, have created a highly regressive tax system where enterprises in rich provinces often enjoy lower effective tax rates than those in poor regions.

ENTERPRISE REFORM

The PRC has made impressive reforms in the enterprise sector. Most prices have been freed, the bonus scheme appears to have sharpened work effort, SOEs now enjoy autonomy in their output and investment decisions, and there is a variety of ownership forms. However, as noted on page 1, enterprise reforms need to be deepened to remove the fiscal difficulties that arise from low enterprise tax revenue and high enterprise loss subsidies.

A major flaw of the present SOE system is the incentive structure for managers. In addition to facing the natural demands for higher compensation, a manager's future promotion depends on fulfilling the housing, medical, and education needs of the work force. This produces a temptation to increase the workers' living standards at the expense of profitability.

The attempt to control labor costs by linking the rate of wage increase to productivity rises has failed. Wage changes are asymmetrical, rising when efficiency rises but seldom falling when efficiency declines. In addition, noncash compensation to workers is even more difficult to control and this component has increased at the expense of profits.

Another source of financial problems is the "hunger for investment," that has led to the large increases in loans to SOEs for investment and the consequent large increases in the money supply. This high demand for investment funds stems from SOEs' desire to increase future output and hence future consumption. The problem arises because the costs of investment to the enterprises are artificially reduced by three factors: (1) the controlled low interest rates, (2) the ability of SOEs to pay back the loan principal from pre-tax income, and (3) the fact that SOE managers can rely on the government to prevent closure of the enterprise even if an imprudent investment causes large losses.

These problems of excessive consumption and investment can partly be addressed by increasing the pressure on managers to maximize profits, as discussed below. However, the solution must also include reforms in other spheres. The financial sector has to be restructured to harden the "soft" loan constraint, and the fiscal system reformed to harden the "soft" budget constraint: special tax exemptions and subsidies must be reduced.

One method of increasing the pressure for management improvement and profit maximization is to convert SOEs into joint-stock companies with the state as a stockholder in each one. The people's degree of satisfaction with an SOE's financial performance and their assessment of its economic future will be reflected in the prices of its stocks. Such transparent "voting" by the people on different enterprises in the same industry will (1) constrain the supervising ministry from introducing too many noneconomic considerations into its appraisal of management performance, and (2) generate a natural indicator for the supervising ministry to use in approving managers' and workers' compensation.

A prerequisite for the rational working of the stock market is the universal adoption of a common accounting framework that matches the analytical categories of modern economics. The present industry-specific accounting practices are, in any case, unsuitable for conducting policy analysis.

Another way of elevating profit maximization to be the primary goal of SOE managers is to set up asset management corporations to take over enterprise supervision from the ministries. Shenzhen City established the Shenzhen Investment Management Company in 1987 to oversee its SOEs. The company has set up profit-sharing arrangements with the SOEs and made managers personally responsible for part of any losses and profits. It also has the power to sell and merge SOEs and approve the dividend and bonus practices of each SOE.

The stock market approach and the asset management approach are complementary solutions. Competition among asset management companies in the regional stock markets will not only enhance the monitoring of SOE management, it will also improve the allocation of the capital stock. The government should approve the establishment of mutual funds to intensify the pressures on SOEs to improve their financial performance.

The move to profit maximization is important not only for improving the government's budgetary position, but also for increasing the efficiency of resource allocation. However, the second goal will only be achieved if competition in the goods market is also increased. The legal barriers to setting up collective, cooperative, and private enterprises, and local restrictions on regional trade should be reduced.

SOCIAL INSURANCE REFORM

Social insurance in the PRC consists of disaster relief, welfare support, retirement insurance, medical insurance, and unemployment insurance. Social insurance expenditure of urban-based enterprises has increased from 14 per cent of their total wage bill in 1978 to 27 per cent in 1987, an increase from 2 per cent to 5 per cent of GDP. Because social insurance expenditure is rising rapidly, it is important to consider how to control the upward cost trend.

The Pension System

The chief problem with the pension system is its narrow coverage and extreme fragmentation which inhibit labor mobility. The system covers only workers in SOEs and large collectives, and even then in pools specific to each enterprise. Only recently are these enterprise-specific pools being combined at the city and county level.

The pension system has weakened the fiscal position of the government in two ways. First, permanent SOE workers, who comprise the majority of the participants, do not make pension contributions. This reduces enterprise profits and government revenue. Second, SOEs with few retirees are often induced to join the city pension pools by granting them tax exemptions.

"Free riders" are a major problem with the operation of the new common pension pools: some enterprises have raised the incomes of skilled workers by retiring and then rehiring them, and some workers have retired from SOEs with full pension benefits to get new jobs with nonstate enterprises. There is a high incidence of early retirement on account of illness, which SOEs approve in order to get younger workers.

The immediate reform task is to make pensions more portable. The government should take a first step toward a national pension fund by centralizing administration at city and county levels so that job changes can be recorded easily. The contribution and benefit levels should be standardized, and the pools should be widened by eliminating the exemptions of some SOEs and extending coverage to township and village enterprises, private enterprises, and the self-employed.

The administration of the pension pool should be tightened, with rigorous examination of applications for early retirement and frequent independent auditing of management fees and the management of funds. The practice of investing entire pension funds in time deposits at banks should be discontinued, and investment in the domestic security markets should be allowed, subject to a specified maximum share of the portfolio. Pension fund managers should receive salaries tied to the performance of the investments.

The existing retirement ages are low by international standards. Retirement ages should be raised gradually by five years to ameliorate the problem of an aging population, and the retirement age for men and women should be equalized.

The base for calculating pensions should be changed from the total wage in just the last year to the average over the last three years, to reduce the incentive for enterprises to give a "golden handshake" to its retiring workers by giving large wage increases in the last year.

Unemployment Insurance

Eradicating the expectation of lifelong employment and easing labor flows between enterprises are vital to the success of enterprise reforms. Guaranteed lifelong employment ended in 1986 with the changes in regulations governing labor contracts. An unemployment insurance scheme for SOE workers was launched at the same time. In 1991, 88 per cent (70 million) of the SOE labor force was covered by this scheme.

The draw on unemployment insurance funds has been small to date, because SOEs are under great pressure to hold on to their surplus workers, receiving tax exemptions and bank loans to do so when necessary. In Chongqing in 1992, about half the SOEs were running losses, but only 1963 people were receiving unemployment benefits.

Some regions have used the unemployment fund reserves to provide loans that allow SOEs to retain their surplus labor. This practice could be more expensive than the direct payment of unemployment benefit to surplus workers and goes against the whole purpose of reform: to move workers from unproductive employment into other jobs.

The coverage of the unemployment insurance system should be increased in phases. Coverage should be extended first to temporary and seasonal SOE workers, then to workers in nonstate urban enterprises, and finally to workers in township and village enterprises.

HOUSING REFORM ISSUES

Housing in PRC cities is owned by housing bureaus, SOEs, and administrative agencies. It is provided at nominal rents. With the housing stock more than doubling during the 1980s, subsidy costs grew rapidly and may have exceeded budgetary outlays for price subsidy and for enterprise loss subsidies.

The goals of reform are to produce a system where: (1) housing provision is separated from work units, (2) rents/purchase prices will cover the total cost of providing housing, (3) fiscal subsidies for housing are sharply targeted to provide a safety net for indigent families, and (4) government involvement in housing development is confined to planning the use of urban space and to providing supporting infrastructure.

The planned pace of the current rent reform is far too slow to significantly reduce distortions in consumer choice. In addition, the provision of wage supplements to partially offset rent increases makes rent reform unattractive to local governments, since it commits them to a protracted process involving contentious negotiations over the size of wage supplements while providing little budgetary relief in the reduction of subsidy outlays.

In contrast, the program of privatization provides significant revenue incentives for local governments and work units, both to shed subsidy burdens and to raise funds for further housing development. Sales revenues will be a major financing source for wage supplements as well. Indeed, one danger is that the reform plan may have created incentives that are lopsided in favor of privatization, where local governments operating under severe budgetary pressures will find it difficult to resist the temptation to sell their housing stock to produce revenues.

Large-scale privatization of urban housing is premature under the present circumstances. The combination of very low rents and restricted property rights makes the purchase option unattractive. Even for residents willing to buy, the lack of financing often requires sellers to carry mortgages at below market rates. Furthermore, the housing units that are being produced are too large for average PRC consumers to afford.

RECOMMENDATIONS FOR FURTHER REFORM IN THE LIGHT OF THE STUDY VISITS

The experience of the three study countries — Canada, India, and the United Kingdom (UK) — and our study of the PRC can tell us about the final system to which the reforms are directed. We then move our attention to the sequencing of these reforms.

The Reform of Central-Local Fiscal Relations

Most countries have systems where revenues are clearly divided among levels of government. In addition, all three study countries devote a considerable amount of central government revenues to equalization programs that attempt to compensate local governments for differences in fiscal capacities and, in some cases, differences in need. These equalization programs can only be afforded because the central government receives most revenues — over 70 per cent in Canada and India, and over 90 per cent in the UK. It is only by adopting some system of this sort that the PRC can move towards providing equal access to basic services such as health care and education for all PRC citizens.

A larger share of revenues should be controlled by the central government. However, recentralization of revenues should not be accompanied by recentralization of control over expenditures. Provision of public goods should be decentralized to maximize efficiency. The extent of expenditure decentralization in the PRC appears to be largely correct. Thus, the recentralization of revenues should be accompanied by the introduction of equalization programs that redistribute a substantial portion of central revenues to the provinces.

The required substantial increase in central revenue should be obtained by assigning all revenues from product tax, business tax and VAT to the center. This transfer of taxes would eliminate the misallocation of resources that occurs because each province wants to establish heavily taxed industries so that it can collect a share of the high tax payments. The additional revenue accruing to the central government should be automatically redistributed to the provinces on a formula basis.

The central and local fixed incomes could stay as they are, with the exception of enterprise income taxation. That each level of government should receive income tax from the enterprises it owns perpetuates the "softness" of the current tax system and runs against the whole idea of enterprise reform. Income taxes from enterprises of all ownerships should be seen as one revenue source. It is administratively simpler for all enterprise income taxes to become central fixed revenue. However, enterprise income taxes could be made a local fixed income in order to increase provinces' incomes.

One potentially rich source of revenues for local governments is property taxes on land and buildings, over which local governments should be given autonomy in setting tax rates and defining the tax base. In other countries, this is a major source of local revenues — in Canada this accounts for 98 per cent of local revenues below the provincial level, in UK it accounts for 100 per cent.

In each study country, as in almost all countries other than the PRC, the central government collects all of its own revenues. In addition, in Canada the central government collects the provinces' income taxes on their behalf, while the Indian federal government collects all of the shared taxes. These arrangements have administrative advantages, particularly for VAT. Outside of the PRC, only in Brazil, Mexico and Germany is the VAT administered at a subnational level. Among them it has worked well only in Germany. The particular situation in the PRC makes the case for central revenue collection even stronger. At the moment, provinces have to be allowed large shares of each tax in order to motivate their tax collection efforts. But these large shares prevent the central government from collecting enough revenue to help the poorer provinces, and provide a strong motive for local protectionism. The achievement of greater revenue centralization requires, as a first step, the establishment of a national tax service that is given the clear responsibility to enforce tax laws on a uniform national basis.

Macroeconomic Management and Monetary Reform

All three of the study countries have an institutional structure that allows the identification of two separate aspects of macroeconomic management: fiscal policy and monetary policy. The institutional structure that allows this separation is the independence of the banking system, as illustrated by our three study countries. In these countries, the government may decide how much of the budget deficit should be financed by expansion of the money supply, and may try to influence interest rates, but leaves decisions about loans to the banks themselves.

This contrasts with the PRC situation, where many policy loans are made to enterprises in financial difficulties and to enterprises wanting to undertake investment. To support these policy loans, the central bank supplies the banks with credits that allow them to extend loans beyond their deposits. These central bank credits have the same expansionary effect on the money supply as credits to finance the government budget deficit. This means that the banks are effectively carrying out government fiscal policy. There is no separation between monetary and fiscal policy. The expansion of central bank credits to support these policy loans should be counted as part of the government budget deficit.

For macroeconomic stability, the reduction of this hidden deficit is just as important as the reduction of the open budget deficit. Policy lending should be conducted explicitly through the budget and not through the banking system. The banking system should be commercialized and should cease to be a fiscal agent of the government.

Another institutional requirement for the separation of monetary and fiscal policy is the existence of a market in government securities. This exists in all three study countries and allows governments to run budget deficits, in either the long term or the short term, without requiring the central bank to increase the money supply. A thriving government securities market requires that interest rates be decontrolled.

Social Security and Housing Reform

Canada and the UK have social security systems that provide retirement pensions and unemployment insurance. These systems relieve enterprises from any responsibility for their workers after they have retired. It also makes it easier for workers to be dismissed. Because pensions are not lost when workers change employers, labor mobility improves.

One problem that Canada and the UK are experiencing, along with most developed countries, is increased costs caused by an increased proportion of retired people in the population. It is important that the PRC choose a level of pension and a retirement age that it will be able to afford.

Enterprises are not responsible for housing for their workers in any of the three study countries. Housing for poor people in Canada and the UK is provided by local governments. It is clear that market economies cannot operate efficiently with housing tied to employment, as in the PRC.

Enterprise Reform

The poor financial performance of SOEs is a worldwide phenomenon, from which India suffers particularly. Because SOEs do not naturally maximize profits, an external environment that forces them to do so must be created. One way is to use the financial markets to discipline the SOEs. The method chosen by Canada and the UK in the 1980s was to privatize most of their SOEs.

The PRC government should adopt a new supervision mechanism to force the SOEs to maximize their profits. One possible method is to set up state asset management corporations (SAMCs) to "corporatize" the SOEs, control labor costs, and tie managerial compensation to the performance of investments. The effectiveness of the SAMCs could be enhanced by allowing the establishment of nonstate investment companies and selling part of each SOE to the public through stock markets. SAMCs must be motivated to act as profit-maximizing institutional investors, through performance- related pay, and must be prepared to close SOEs that have been chronically unable to cover costs, after the implementation of social security and housing reforms. Eventually, the SAMCs should in turn be corporatized and sold on the stock market.

Trade liberalization and exchange rate unification should be implemented quickly so that the deregulation of SOEs will not produce monopolies. Furthermore, the government should replace all tariff and nontariff barriers with a low uniform tariff to ensure that market forces are the primary determinant of the composition of SOEs' output.

Tax Structure

The tax structure in the study countries is more suitable for an economy with different types of enterprise ownership than is PRC's. The study countries apply equal taxation to all ownership types. They also have a much more equal tax treatment of different products and sectors. Inequalities misallocate resources and lead to a loss of revenue if highly taxed goods lose their share of national output. Many countries have moved to more broadly based taxes, such as VAT, to cover services as well as manufactured goods. They have also moved to simplify rates, and the PRC must do the same. This will be achieved by implementing the detailed tax proposals listed on pp. 7-8.

SEQUENCING OF REFORM

For the PRC, a fairly clear sequencing of reform can be recommended because the prerequisites for some reforms are already satisfied. Reforms that can be started immediately are the changes to the tax structure; the improved enforcement of tax laws, leading to a national tax service; housing and social security reform; further price reform; SOE corporatization and stock market development; the replacement of policy loans by explicit subsidies; the commercialization of banks; and the development of a market in government securities.

Once these are achieved, it will be possible to start eliminating enterprise subsidies and closing enterprises that are still not profitable because the artificial forces that could have been blamed for poor financial performance will have been removed and the social costs of unemployment will have been reduced.

The reform of central-local fiscal relations requires a simplified tax system and strengthened central control of revenue collection. The main obstacle will be the need to reach agreement on the formula that will be used to redistribute central revenues to the provinces.

Although this sequencing is required, a major problem remains: the imposition of a hard budget constraint on SOEs, in the form of bankruptcy, relies on a large number of prior reforms and therefore can be expected to take considerable time. In the meantime, attempts to collect taxes more rigorously may simply result in the need for more policy loans or (preferably) budgetary subsidies. The budget deficit may still not be brought under control. In these circumstances, the incentives will have to be increased for enterprise managers to control costs and maximize profits. It may also be necessary to start closing some enterprises that will clearly continue to make losses even after all the other reforms are carried out.

Chapter 1

Overview of the Fiscal System in the Macroeconomic Setting

Economic reforms in the People's Republic of China (PRC) have produced impressive gains in national income and living standards since 1979. However, the reform process is not complete, and several aspects of the fiscal system need reform before the full benefits of a market economy can be realized. Repeated bouts of inflationary pressure, followed by depressed market demand, have demonstrated the need to improve macroeconomic management. This requires the government to be able to control revenue, expenditure, and the money supply, which can only be done by improving the Ministry of Finance's capacity to analyze the current economic situation, anticipate future changes, and guide economic change.

This report aims to contribute to strengthening policy analysis in the Ministry of Finance, by looking at some crucial areas of reform that have important fiscal implications: tax reform, debt management, changes in expenditure patterns, enterprise reform, central-local fiscal relations, housing reform, and social security reform.

Chapter 1 provides a background to the discussion of individual topics in the subsequent chapters. It gives a brief outline of some important aspects of the fiscal system, their relation to aspects of system reform, and the linkages between the fiscal system and macroeconomic policy.

REVENUE AND EXPENDITURE TRENDS

The definitions of revenue and expenditure used in the PRC are somewhat different from those used in most other countries. Table 1.1 shows the results of modifying recent data from the Chinese

Table 1.1: The Fiscal Situation in the Reform Period

	Y Billion				Per Cent of GNP			
	Revenue		Expenditure		Revenue		Expenditure	
	Chinese Definition	"Standard" Definition	Chinese Definition	"Standard" Definition	Chinese Definition	"Standard" Definition	Chinese Definition	"Standard" Definition
1978	112.1	124.8	111.1	123.7	31.24	34.77	30.96	34.49
1979	110.3	126.4	127.4	147.0	27.66	31.69	31.94	36.86
1980	108.5	130.1	121.3	147.1	24.28	29.10	27.13	32.91
1981	109.0	130.2	111.5	140.1	22.83	27.28	23.36	29.35
1982	112.4	140.9	115.3	152.2	21.64	27.14	22.21	29.32
1983	124.9	160.7	129.2	173.0	21.50	27.66	22.25	29.78
1984	150.2	184.3	154.6	196.5	21.57	26.47	22.21	28.22
1985	186.6	229.7	184.5	236.5	21.81	26.84	21.56	27.64
1986	226.0	244.7	233.1	265.6	23.31	25.23	24.04	27.39
1987	236.9	257.6	244.8	282.5	20.96	22.79	21.67	25.00
1988	262.8	280.4	270.7	315.3	18.68	19.93	19.24	22.41
1989	294.8	326.4	304.0	363.9	18.43	20.41	19.01	22.75
1990	331.3	351.6	345.2	403.1	18.50	19.63	19.28	22.51
1991	358.3	366.0	381.4	432.4	18.13	18.52	19.30	21.88
1992	394.1	374.1	414.1	464.1	15.00	14.24	15.76	17.66

	Budget Deficit Y Billion			Budget Deficit Per Cent of GNP		
	Chinese Definition	GBR Definition	Stock Definition	Chinese Definition	GBR Definition	Stock Definition
1978	-1.02	-1.02	-1.02	-0.28	-0.28	-0.28
1979	17.06	20.60	20.60	4.28	5.16	5.16
1980	12.75	17.05	14.68	2.85	3.82	3.28
1981	2.55	9.85	5.59	0.53	2.06	1.17
1982	2.93	11.32	7.33	0.56	2.18	1.41
1983	4.34	12.29	9.54	0.75	2.11	1.64
1984	4.45	12.18	10.49	0.64	1.75	1.51
1985	-2.16	6.82	4.27	-0.25	0.80	0.50
1986	7.05	20.88	17.93	0.73	2.15	1.85
1987	7.96	24.91	19.77	0.70	2.20	1.75
1988	7.86	34.94	30.41	0.56	2.48	2.16
1989	9.23	37.53	33.40	0.58	2.35	2.09
1990	13.96	51.51	38.56	0.78	2.88	2.15
1991	23.08	66.41	n.a.	1.17	3.36	n.a.
1992	20.00	90.00	n.a.	0.76	3.43	n.a.

Notes:
(1) The "Standard" definition for revenue means subtracting borrowing from the Chinese definition, and adding in the subsidies that were counted as negative revenue. The "Standard" definition for expenditure means adding to the Chinese definition subsidies that were considered negative subsidies.
(2) The government borrowing requirement (GBR) definition of deficit is standard expenditure minus standard revenue.
(3) The "Stock" definition of deficit is GBR definition minus principal repayments.

Source: State Statistical Bureau 1992, Tables 6.1, 6.4, 6.6, 6.7, 6.11, 6.16; Ministry of Finance data; and Wong 1991, Table A2.

definitions to standard international definitions, to obtain a clearer idea of the fiscal situation and allow international comparisons. Two types of adjustment have to be made. First, government borrowing is excluded from the definition of revenue. Second, price subsidies (before 1986) and enterprise loss subsidies are added to expenditures instead of being subtracted from revenues.

As is shown in Table 1.1, these adjustments have increased the value of expenditure, because of the inclusion of subsidies. The adjustments also have also increased the value of revenue because the subsidies are no longer subtracted, an effect that is larger than the reduction caused by excluding borrowing.

The "government borrowing requirement" is the most commonly used budget deficit definition. It is equal to the difference between the revised revenue and expenditure figures, and is larger than the deficit measured by the PRC definition. This is because the modified treatment of subsidies has equal effects on the revenue and expenditure sides, while the exclusion of borrowing from the revenue side increases the measured deficit. The "stock" definition of the budget deficit measures the increase in the accumulated total of government debt, including borrowing from the central bank. This is equal to the borrowing requirement (representing additions to the debt stock) minus loan principal repayments (representing reductions in the debt stock). It is also higher than the PRC definition budget deficit.

Table 1.1 reveals a declining trend in the ratios of both revenue and expenditure to gross national product (GNP). To some extent, this decline is a natural result of the reform process. For example, many investments in capital construction are now the responsibility of enterprises and so are not financed through the government budget, while enterprises are allowed to keep a higher proportion of their profits. However, most of this transfer of responsibility had been completed by the mid-1980s, but the share of revenue in GNP has continued to decline. This has not been the deliberate aim of policy, and is causing the PRC government considerable concern.

A detailed analysis of this revenue decline is presented in Chapter 2, but some insight into the problem can be obtained by dividing total revenue into revenue derived from profit (enterprise income taxes and profit remittances) and revenue not derived from profit (such as indirect taxes):

Total Revenue/GNP = (profit revenue/profit x profit/
GNP) + (other revenue/GNP).

This decomposition shows that total revenue can decline as a result of any of three causes: (1) a reduction in the government's share of profits (the average profit tax rate), (2) a reduction in the share of profits in GNP, and (3) a reduction in the ratio of other revenues to GNP. As noted on p. 25, the reform process necessarily involved a reduction in the government's share of profits, although Chapter 2 shows how average profit tax rates have continued to decline. The reduced share of profits in GNP has also been significant, with the ratio of industrial state-owned enterprise (SOE) profits to GNP falling continuously from 21.7 per cent in 1979 to 8.5 per cent in 1990. Chapter 4 argues that enterprise reforms are needed to reverse this trend. Finally, Chapter 2 shows that a reduced ratio of other revenues to GNP has also had a role to play, at least as far as indirect taxes are concerned. This is a particular worry because most countries experience very buoyant indirect tax revenues, with revenue/GNP ratios increasing as countries grow. Therefore reform of indirect taxes is needed to prevent further revenue declines.

This fall in the share of revenue is reflected in a reduction in the ratio of government expenditure to GNP. It is interesting to compare these figures with those for other developing countries, as reported in World Bank (1988, pp. 105-120). The average share of central government expenditure in gross domestic product (GDP) is about 25 per cent in developing countries. The figure for the PRC is slightly lower and falling, a fact that is particularly surprising because Table 1.1 gives the total of central and local government expenditures (although local government expenditure is much less important in most developing countries). However, this comparison is misleading because a substantial part of social expenditure in the PRC is spent outside the budget. For example, pensions and housing are largely the responsibility of enterprises, while road maintenance and some education expenditures are covered by extrabudgetary funds. Thus, the PRC manages to spend no more than 2 per cent of its government expenditure on pensions and welfare.

The budget deficits of 3 per cent of GDP in 1990 and 1991 are not large by international standards, but they underestimate the amount of overspending by the state. A complete accounting should include the deficit spending of SOEs — the government-mandated bank loans that partially substitute for loss subsidies disbursed through the budget. This expansion of reserve money to allow appropriation of resources by SOEs has the same effect on the economy as monetization of budget deficits. Taking these hidden subsidies into account raises the consolidated budget deficit to at least 6 per cent in 1988 and 1989, and 8 per cent in 1990 and 1991 (see Box 1.1 for details). This upward trend is a serious threat to macroeconomic stability. The choice between revenue increases and expenditure reductions is always difficult and will involve social, as well as economic, considerations. Chapter 2 discusses methods of improving revenue performance and possible areas for expenditure cuts.

In addition to concern over the ratio of revenue to GNP, the PRC government has been concerned about the share of revenue that accrues to the central government. Table 1.2 shows what has been happening to the central government shares of revenue and expenditure. (Table 1.2 has not been adjusted in line with Table 1.1 because of the lack of the necessary data. It therefore follows the PRC definitions.) The central government's share of revenue has been increasing over the period as a whole, but this increase has stopped and a decline may be starting. However, the revenue shares do not give a complete picture of the resources commanded by each level of government because there is a complex system of intergovernmental fiscal transfers, which are discussed in Chapter 3. This is illustrated by the continuous decline from 1979 to 1989 of the central government's share of expenditure. This decline is causing concern.

THE OVERALL REFORM PROCESS

The fiscal reforms that are the main concern of this report are part of a more general process of economic reform. All these reforms involve a movement away from a highly centralized and controlled system towards a more market-oriented economic system.

Two major characteristics of the old system were central planning and price controls, and therefore much of the reform has

Box 1.1: Open and Hidden Deficits: Definitions and Estimates

Budget identity: Expenditure = Sources of Financing

Budget identity of fiscal authorities: $G = T + \Delta B^P + \Delta B^{CB}$ (1)

G = government expenditure (including interest payment on debt)
T = government revenue
B^P = government bonds held by (domestic and foreign) institutions, enterprises and individuals
B^{CB} = government bonds held by central bank

Budget identity of monetary authority: $\Delta B^{CB} + \Delta L = iB^{CB} + rL + \Delta R$ (2)

L = loans to SBs and SOEs extended by central bank
R = reserve money
i = interest rate on bonds issued by government
r = interest rate on central bank's loans to SBs and SOEs

In equation (2), $(iB^{CB} + rL)$ constitutes the revenue of the monetary authorities.

Definitions of deficit:
Open deficit = budget deficit of fiscal authorities = $G - T$ (3)
$\hphantom{Open deficit }= \Delta B^P + \Delta B^{CB}$ (4)

Hidden deficit = reserve money creation unrelated to financing of open deficit
$\hphantom{Hidden deficit }= \Delta L - iB^{CB} - rL$ (5)
$\hphantom{Hidden deficit }= \Delta R - \Delta B^{CB}$ (6)

Consolidated deficit = Open deficit + Hidden deficit
$(G - T) + (\Delta L - iB^{CB} - rL) = \Delta R + \Delta B^P$ (7)

Decomposition of increase in reserve money by origin:
$(G - T - \Delta B^P) = \Delta R_1$ = amount of increase in reserve money due to financing of open deficit

$(\Delta L - iB^{CB} - rL) = \Delta R_2$ = amount of increase in reserve money due to financing of hidden deficit

The contribution of the hidden budget to money growth can be derived from the equations

$$\frac{\Delta R}{R} = \frac{\Delta R_1}{R} + \frac{\Delta R_2}{R} \quad \text{and} \quad \frac{\Delta R_2}{R} = \frac{\Delta R}{R} - \frac{\Delta R_1}{R}$$

in which R and ΔR are observable, and ΔR_1 is the PRC definition of government budget deficit so that ΔR_2 can be calculated.

Box 1.1 Table: Estimated Budget Deficits[a]
(per cent of GNP)

Year	Open Deficit	Hidden Deficit	Consolidated Deficit
1988	2.48	5.14	7.62
1989	2.35	5.22	7.57
1990	2.88	7.55	10.43
1991	3.36	6.76	10.12

[a] "Hidden deficit" is defined as the expansion of reserve money in excess of the amount lent to the government for deficit financing. The "hidden deficit" is thus a part of the seignorage tax. In the consolidated budget of the entire state sector, the overall deficit is the sum of the explicit (government) deficit and the hidden (SOEs) deficit.

It must be noted that a zero consolidated deficit is not necessary for macroeconomic stability. A growing economy requires a commensurate increase in the money supply. The important point is that the hidden deficit must not cause money growth to greatly exceed (real) output growth for prolonged periods.

been concerned with decentralization and price liberalization. The decentralization has involved changing the nature of the relationships between the central government and lower levels of government and between governments and the enterprises that they own. Both of these aspects have been noted in the discussions of Tables 1.1 and 1.2. The decentralization of government functions has led to the reduced share of central government in expenditures, while the decentralization of investment decisions has led to a reduction in the share of government expenditure in GNP.

The effect of price liberalization is not captured in the revenue and expenditure statistics, but is nonetheless of great importance to the reform of the fiscal system. Under the old system of total price control, the market had no influence on the allocation of resources: this was controlled by a central plan. The tax system was then just an accounting system, with no real effects. However, price liberalization has led to a much greater role for the market in allocating resources, and taxes can distort the market mechanism. It is therefore necessary to design a tax system that

Table 1.2: Trends in Central Share of Revenue and Expenditure
(per cent)

Year	Revenue	Expenditure
1979	14	51
1980	16	54
1981	21	54
1982	23	50
1983	30	50
1984	35	48
1985	38	45
1986	41	41
1987	38	42
1988	40	39
1989	38	36
1990	41	40
1991	39	40
1992	40	41

Source: State Statistical Bureau 1993, p. 229 (Chinese Edition).

does not seriously distort the market's allocation. There have been substantial reforms of the tax system in response to its changed role but, as discussed in Chapter 2, there is more to be done to reduce unnecessary distortions.

Similarly, decentralization has necessitated reform in revenue-sharing arrangements to improve incentives for local tax collection. In the prereform system, because local expenditures were determined by the central government and weakly linked to local revenues, revenue-sharing arrangements were simply accounting procedures for financing approved expenditures. With growing autonomy at the local level, unequal revenue-sharing rates across provinces have created distortions, and poor local tax efforts have contributed to the low revenue buoyancy (see Chapter 3).

The reform of SOEs is a particularly important aspect of system reform because enterprises are responsible for most of the resource allocation decisions in the reformed economy. Also, as mentioned in previous section, the decline in profitability of industrial SOEs is a major cause of the decline in government revenue. Because of its key role, enterprise reform is discussed in detail in Chapter 4, but some points should be noted here.

Enterprise reform goes much further than the decentralization of investment decisions. The move away from central planning has meant that enterprises have had to take responsibility for almost all operational decisions, leaving the coordination of these decisions to the market rather than the central planners. For market coordination to work properly, enterprises must be responsible for their own profits and losses, otherwise they would have no incentive to respond to market forces. The process of making firms fully responsible for their own financial affairs involves distancing them from the government that owns them, so that the government does not feel obliged to cover their losses. This aspect of enterprise reform has proved to be difficult, partly because so many SOEs are unprofitable.

One important feature of PRC enterprises is the role they play in providing for the social needs of their employees. For example, they have traditionally provided their workers with heavily subsidized housing and have paid the pensions of retired workers.

This enterprise provision was satisfactory in the days of planning, when workers were expected to stay in the same job throughout their working lives, but is not suitable for a market economy for two reasons. First, it inhibits labor mobility as some of these benefits may be lost if a worker changes employer. Second, the provision makes it very difficult for the government to allow enterprises to go bankrupt, because to do so might deprive people of their homes and pensions. Thus, any real enterprise reform requires housing and social security reform. In addition, the possibility of enterprise bankruptcy raises the prospect of unemployment, as would giving enterprises the power to layoff redundant workers. This means that some form of unemployment insurance is required.

Many countries devote large amounts of government expenditure to housing and social security. It is therefore vital that the reforms in this area provide a means of generating the funds necessary for their implementation, especially in view of the already increasing government budget deficit. The fiscal aspects of housing and social security reform are the major concern of Chapter 5.

EQUITY AND EFFICIENCY IN THE FISCAL SYSTEM

The foregoing discussion of the fiscal reforms that are needed as part of overall reform concentrated on the need to ensure efficient market operation. Efficiency is an important objective, but so is equity. Most governments wish to ensure that income inequalities within their countries do not become excessive. For this reason, consideration of fiscal reform in almost all countries involves an analysis of equity and efficiency.

Equity is important in the PRC, but it is usually discussed in different terms from those used in other countries. It is not usually seen as equity between individuals, but as equity between enterprises or equity between provinces. The reason for this is that individuals have very little direct interaction with the fiscal system. Only a handful of people pay personal income tax, and the distributional impact of indirect taxes has not been a major concern because, until recently, price controls ensured that the burden of indirect taxes fell mainly on the producing enterprise. This means that individuals' standards of living depend on the financial resources of the enterprise for which they work (which determines bonuses and the quality of housing and other benefits) and the province in which they live (which determines the quality of education, infrastructure, health care and other services the government provides).

The significance of enterprise profitability in the distribution of real income between workers explains the highly differentiated indirect tax structure, which was designed largely to ensure equality between enterprises that are producing different goods. As market reforms progress, the forces of competition can be expected to equalize the profitability of different industries, and the complexity of the tax structure can be reduced. The development of an efficient personal income tax system can reduce any inequality that remains, an inequality that should reflect differences in talents and work effort. The choice of rates for such an income tax would reflect the choice between equity and efficiency (in terms of work incentives) that all countries must make.

In contrast, as explained in Chapter 3, the central government appears to be doing little to reduce inequality between provinces. To some extent, this is a result of the need to provide an incentive for provincial governments to raise their own revenues by more thorough enforcement of the tax laws. But it also reflects a lack of revenue buoyancy: if revenues grew more rapidly, the central government would have more funds that it could use to the benefit of the poorer provinces.

CONTRACTING WITH ENTERPRISES AND LOCAL GOVERNMENTS

An important and unusual feature of the PRC fiscal system is that many of the financial transfers take place on the basis of "contracts." These apply to the transfers between enterprises and the level of government that owns them, and to the transfers between different levels of government.

Contracts between enterprises and government have largely replaced the normal enterprise income tax, although the enterprise income tax still formally exists. Under these contracts, enterprises are committed to paying the standard enterprise income tax on a fixed level of profit (or handing over a fixed amount of profit) whether or not they actually achieve those profits. If its profits are below the contracted level, the enterprise is supposed to make up the difference from its own funds. If it achieves a higher level of profit, it pays a lower rate of tax (often zero) on the additional profits. The aim of this system is to strengthen the incentive for enterprises to increase their profitability, by improving efficiency and responding to the market. The aim is sensible, but the contracting system has a number of disadvantages.

First, is the issue of equity. The more successful enterprises will pay a lower proportion of their profits in tax, thus increasing the inequality in after-tax profitability. Second, partly in response to the need to limit inequality by taxing potentially more profitable enterprises more heavily, the contracts are negotiated separately between each enterprise and the level of government that owns it. This goes against the aim of distancing enterprises from government. Third, the lower rate of tax on additional profits has meant that the share of taxes in GNP has fallen. Fourth, the contracting system leads to macroeconomic instability by reducing the share of tax revenue to GNP during periods of boom, exactly when increased taxes are justified to reduce the risk of inflation. These issues are discussed in more detail in Chapters 2 and 4.

The contracting between different levels of government takes a similar form. For example, provincial governments collect revenue that is to be shared with the central government. Under contracting, there is a basic level of revenue that is shared between the province and the center, and the province can keep a higher proportion of additional revenues over this level. Many provinces have similar arrangements with lower levels of government. As with the enterprises, the idea is to provide an incentive for revenue generation; in this case it is an incentive for thorough tax collection. There are also the same problems: equity between provinces, individual negotiation, and low revenue elasticity for the central government. These arrangements are considered in Chapter 3.

THE FISCAL SYSTEM IN INTERNATIONAL PERSPECTIVE

Despite considerable progress in reform, the fiscal system in the PRC still has several features that are significantly different from the fiscal systems in most other countries. The responsibility of enterprises for social expenditures, the contracting system, and the highly differentiated indirect taxes have already been mentioned, but there are several other differences. The details are discussed in the individual chapters of this report, but a few major items are sufficiently important to highlight at this stage.

The perceived need for local government contracting arises because most of the central government's revenue is collected by local governments. This is the reverse of the situation in most countries, where the central government collects revenues that are shared with lower levels of government. The arrangements in the PRC have led to local governments granting excessive tax concessions to local enterprises, which is a major cause of the recent poor revenue performance (see Chapter 2). The contract system also prevents proper enterprise reform, by allowing individual negotiations between enterprises and government. The standardization and reduction of the exemptions must be a high priority if enterprise reform is to be achieved and if the ratio of government revenue to GNP is to be stabilized or increased.

Although local governments are responsible for collecting most of the revenue, they play no role in determining the legal tax rates. This is unusual by international standards, especially for countries approaching the size of the PRC. Most countries allow local governments some choice over the rates of local taxes.

Finally, the taxation of enterprises depends on their ownership. SOEs, urban collectives, rural collectives, private enterprises, individual household enterprises, foreign enterprises, and joint ventures are all taxed differently. This is mainly a difference in income taxation, but foreign enterprises and joint ventures pay different indirect taxes from domestic enterprises. The differential taxation by ownership is unusual and efforts are under way to reduce it and eventually eliminate it.

MONETARY POLICY AND GOVERNMENT DEBT MANAGEMENT

Strengthening monetary policy is also critical to improving the government's macroeconomic management capacity. Table 1.3 shows clearly the stop-go pattern of monetary policy. Reserve money growth went from 23 per cent in 1986 to 13 per cent in 1987, then returned to 25 per cent in 1988 and 23 per cent in 1989 before soaring to 30 per cent in 1990 and going back to 24 per cent in 1991. This stop-go pattern of monetary policy is replicated in the movements of the price level and GNP.

The central bank, however, cannot be held responsible for the poor performance of monetary policy. The poor performance came not from incompetence but from the absence of consensus in the government about the role of the central bank. The central bank has only one instrument (central bank credits) to

1. accommodate whatever portion of the government's budget, deficit upon request;
2. ensure sufficient credit to enable fulfillment of the investment plans drawn up by the state;
3. extend loans to bankrupt key enterprises to ensure continued supply of their output, and extend loans to other bankrupt large enterprises to ensure full employment; and
4. keep the inflation rate low.

Table 1.3: Balance Sheet of the Central Bank

Item	1985	1986	1987	1988	1989	1990	1991
A: Amount Outstanding (Y billion, end of period)							
Foreign Assets	14.6	14.4	25.5	28.2	40.5	82.1	140.0
Loans to Central Government	27.5	37.0	51.5	57.7	68.5	80.1	106.8
Loans to State-Owned Banks	224.9	268.2	275.6	336.4	421.0	509.1	591.8
Loans to Other Domestic Age	7.8	14.1	24.4	32.9	38.2	46.4	52.3
Other Items	-44.8	-54.8	-58.9	-56.9	-77.0	-78.9	-97.7
Reserve Money	228.4	281.9	318.2	398.4	491.1	638.7	793.1
B: Rate of Change (per cent)							
Foreign Assets		-1.2	76.9	10.8	43.5	102.6	70.6
Loans to Central Government		34.5	39.2	11.9	18.8	17.0	33.3
Loans to State-Owned Banks		19.3	2.8	22.1	25.1	20.9	16.3
Loans to Other Domestic Agents		79.2	73.8	34.8	16.0	21.5	12.7
Other Items		22.2	7.4	-3.4	35.3	2.5	23.9
Reserve Money		23.4	12.9	25.2	23.3	30.1	24.2
C: Contribution to Growth Rate of Reserve Money (percentage points)							
Foreign Assets		-0.1	3.9	0.9	3.1	8.5	9.1
Loans to Central Government		4.2	5.1	1.9	2.7	2.4	4.2
Loans to State-Owned Banks		19.0	2.7	19.1	21.2	17.9	13.0
Loans to Other Domestic Agents		2.7	3.7	2.7	1.3	1.7	0.9
Other Items		-4.4	-1.4	0.6	-5.0	-0.4	-2.9
Reserve Money		23.4	12.9	25.2	23.3	30.1	24.2
Memorandum Items							
Growth rate of narrow money (M1), %		27.9	18.5	20.0	6.3	20.1	28.2
Growth rate of broad money (M2), %		30.2	25.3	20.7	18.7	28.9	26.7

Source: International Monetary Fund, 1992.

The stop-go pattern of monetary policy was inevitable because the side effects from using monetary policy to achieve one goal may conflict with another goal of monetary policy. The most common conflict is between guaranteeing full employment and maintaining price stability.

The institutional setup of the central bank is problematic. The council that sets the annual credit plan has representatives from almost every ministry and economic agency, and this wide range of departmental interest makes it difficult to reach consensus on monetary policy, except when the macroeconomic instability is painfully severe. The upshot is a monetary policy that is reactive rather than anticipatory.

The second major institutional flaw is that the regional branches of the central bank are under dual leadership: a branch is supervised by its head office and by the local government. Since local governments provide a host of amenities to all civil servants, the staff of a branch can be very dependent on the local government for housing and medical attention. Given the great interest of local governments in promoting local development, bank branches are reluctant to implement a tight credit squeeze when ordered to do so by the head office.

A major constraint to the conduct of monetary policy is the system of administratively set interest rates. Since the interest rates have usually been set at low levels, the central bank has constantly been under great pressure to accommodate credit demands that have exceeded the credit targets. The central bank cannot set the interest rate independently of the credit target. If the interest rate is set too low for the given credit target (which has frequently been the case), then the central bank and its branches are forced either to do the politically unpleasant task of denying credit to some ministries and local governments or to revise the credit target upward. The only way out of this difficult situation is to recognize that the central bank should aim only for one target: an interest rate target or a credit target.

Examining the sources of reserve money growth in 1990 and 1991 reveals a potential source of "shock" in the future. The growth in foreign assets contributed 8 percentage points to money growth in 1990 and 9 in 1991. Foreign asset changes were a negligible source of money growth before 1990. This recent development highlights the possibility that the balance of payments will become an increasingly important cause of monetary expansion (or contraction) as the PRC continues its integration into the world economy.

The link between the balance-of-payments position and the money supply comes from the managed exchange rate regime in the PRC. For example, when there is a balance-of-payments surplus, private demand for Chinese currency (the renminbi) exceeds the private supply of renminbi in the foreign exchange market, and the People's Bank of China (PBC) has to buy foreign currencies to keep the renminbi from appreciating. This necessarily increases the amount of reserve money which PBC uses to pay for its purchases. As PBC's loans to banks and SOEs are for a contracted length of time and cannot be recalled until maturity, the only way to bring the reserve money back to its original level is for PBC to sell to the private sector an equivalent amount of treasury bonds from its portfolio. In technical terms, a balance-of-payments surplus will increase the amount of reserve money unless PBC is able to conduct open market operations to offset the expansionary or contractionary effects of its intervention in the foreign exchange market.

The large money supply growth coming from the rise in foreign reserves in 1990 and 1991 suggests that if steps are not taken now to develop open market instruments to control the money supply, the PRC may experience a loss in monetary control with the expansion of trade. The lesson of Taipei,China in the late 1980s is instructive. When Taipei,China had record balance-of-payments surpluses in the 1986-1990 period, its money supply grew by more than 30 per cent each year because its central bank lacked the technical capability to conduct offsetting open market operations.

Internal Debt Management

When economic reforms started in 1979, there was no government debt outstanding. The last issue of treasury bonds was in 1958, and it was all retired by 1974. The first government borrowing in the reform era was from abroad, Y3.5 billion in 1979 and Y4.3 billion in 1980. The first issuance of treasury bonds was in 1981, for Y4.9 billion. (The government borrowed Y7.3 billion from abroad that year, but it also retired Y6.3 billion of its external debt.)[1]

A wide range of bonds that are directly backed by the central government is available (see Table 1.4). The Ministry of Finance has issued six types of bonds: treasury bonds, fiscal bonds, state construction bonds, key construction bonds, special state

---

[1]   Exchange rates used are average exchange rates for the year.

Table 1.4: The Formal Bond Market

Bonds		Year Introduced	Amount Outstanding (end 1990) (Y billion)	Interest Rate on New Issues	
				1988	1991
State Bonds					
(issued by the Ministry of Finance)					
Treasury Bond		pre-1981	48.49		
for individuals:	3-year maturity			10.0	10.0
	5-year maturity				
for work units:	3-year maturity			6.0	
	5-year maturity				
Fiscal Bond		1988	13.72		
2-year maturity				8.0	
5-year maturity				7.5	
State Construction Bond (2-year)		1988	0.59	9.5	
Key Construction Bond (3-year)		1987	5.00		
Special State Bond (5-year)		1989	7.61		9.0
Index Bond (3-year)		1989	12.48		
State Investment Company Bond					
(issued or guaranteed by a branch of the central government)					
Key Enterprise Bond (5-year)		1987	5.41	6.0	
Capital Construction Bond (5-year)		1988	9.46	7.5	
Financial Bond		1985	8.99		
(issued by state-owned banks)					
1-year				9.0	8.5
2-year				10.0	9.2
3-year				11.0	10.0
5-year				13.0	
Local Enterprise Bond		pre-1986	9.64		
(guaranteed by local government)					
3-year maturity				13.6	9.9
5-year maturity				15.1	10.8
	Total Outstanding Bonds		121.39		

Notes:
(1) Local Enterprise Bond rates are the maximum allowed.
(2) From 1989 onward, treasury bills are sold only to individuals, and "special state bond" is the functional replacement of the treasury bill sold to work units.

Source: Data compiled from China Society for Finance 1991, Tables 10 and 33; and People's Bank of China 1991, pages 39 and 41. In the former, treasury bond is called treasury bill, index bond is called inflation-proof bond, and fiscal bond is called treasury bond. Table 10 is wrong, its data are in units of 100 million, not billion as stated.

bonds, and indexed bonds.[2] In addition, the State Planning Commission issues the capital construction bonds. The key enterprises in the electrical, metallurgical, nonferrous, and petrochemical industries issue the key enterprise bonds. Enterprise bonds are guaranteed by the supervising ministries.

Formal bond markets started in Beijing, Guangzhou, Harbin, Shanghai, and Shenyang cities in 1986; now, over 70 cities have bond markets. The Securities Trading Automated Quotation System (STAQS) links 40 domestic securities companies and trust and investment companies located in different provinces to provide a national trading network. STAQS also performs the clearance and payments functions. A PBC bureau, the State Administration of Exchange Control, regulates the issue of international bonds by Chinese enterprises.

Throughout the 1980s, treasury bonds were sold by administrative fiat and distributed by region: each province or city was allocated a portion of the treasury bonds. The provinces and cities in turn allocated purchase quotas to enterprises, specifying the breakdown between purchases by the enterprise and by individuals. The enterprises usually divided the quota for individuals between mandatory purchases (the funds for which were deducted from the workers' wages) and voluntary purchases (often enforced by moral suasion).

The 1981 issue had a 10-year maturity and carried a simple interest rate of 4 per cent per annum, with all interest payments made at maturity.[3] Since the banks were offering 6.8 per cent for 5-year deposits by households, the acquisition of these treasury bonds was clearly involuntary.

Beginning with treasury bonds issued in 1982, the state paid interest rates that were slightly higher than time deposits of equal duration for individual purchases (e.g., 8 per cent for bonds and 7.9 per cent for time deposits in 1982). For enterprise purchases, the interest rate paid continued to be lower than the equivalent

---

[2]　This terminology is from the People's Bank of China 1991. Other publications use slightly different terms. What is called "treasury bill" in the *Almanac of China's Finance and Banking 1991* is called treasury bond here. Likewise, the *Almanac* uses "Treasury Bond" for fiscal bond, and "Inflation-Free Bond" for indexed bond.

[3]　This equals a compound interest rate of 3.7 per cent. The government began redeeming 20 per cent of the bonds every year from 1986.

time deposit rate from enterprise deposits.[4] From 1982 to 1988, the gap between the bond rate paid to households and the rate paid to enterprises was 4 percentage points.

From 1981 to 1984, about Y4 billion worth of treasury bonds were issued each year, half to households and half to enterprises. From 1985 to 1987, about Y6 billion was issued annually, with two thirds going to the household sector.

1988 was a threshold year in terms of bond issue. Both fiscal and monetary policies were extremely expansionary. The expansionary fiscal policy resulted in a treasury bond issue of Y9.2 billion,[5] a state construction bond issue of Y3 billion, and a key enterprise bond issue of Y1 billion. The supply of bonds further swelled when the Ministry of Finance required the financial institutions to buy Y8 billion of capital construction bonds and Y6.6 billion of fiscal bonds.

To increase the attractiveness of these bonds, the government, in 1988, shortened their maturity from 5 to 3 years (without changing the interest rate of 10 per cent) and allowed the creation of secondary markets for government bonds held by individuals, an important institutional development.

Since the interest rate was below 10 per cent before 1986, holders of bonds issued in the 1983-1985 period would suffer a capital loss if they were to sell these bonds in the secondary market. The central government instructed the local governments and banks to intervene in the secondary market to preserve the face value of these bonds and established a Y0.3 billion fund to finance the intervention. The result was a massive rush to cash in the old bonds, and the local governments and banks spent at least Y1 billion in the intervention.

The interesting question is what portion of the funds obtained from the early redemption of pre-1988 bonds was actually used to purchase 1988 bonds. Given that the inflation rate of 19 per cent in 1988 greatly exceeded the coupon rate of 10 per cent, it is unlikely that agents would voluntarily switch from money to these bonds. In the general atmosphere of high inflation, bank runs, and panic buying sprees in July and August 1988, it is more

---

[4]   Enterprise deposit rates, until September 1988, were kept about 1.8 percentage points below household deposit rates of the same maturity.

[5]   Y2.2 billion worth of treasury bonds were retired that year.

likely that agents switched mostly from money to tangible goods – hence accentuating the ongoing inflation.

There was also substantial redemption of government bonds in the secondary market at face value in 1989 when it was clear that the big price increase in 1988 was not a one-time affair. The local governments and local banks suffered heavy capital losses from the interventions they were ordered to undertake because no central funds were allocated to them.

At the enterprise level, the diversion of funds to buy new government bond issues (with a coupon rate of 6 per cent in 1988 compared to the average 7.6 per cent for 3-year deposits) caused financial losses. There was greater unwillingness than ever to take more government papers.

The state responded to this debt management crisis in 1989 by raising the coupon rates of treasury bonds targeted at households from 10 to 14 per cent replacing treasury bonds targeted at enterprises with fiscal bonds that paid 15 per cent and issuing two bonds (indexed bonds and capital construction bonds) with floating rates that fully compensated for changes in the cost of living. Earlier in September 1988, the government had sought to halt the runs on the banks by raising the interest rates on household deposits, resetting the interest rates on enterprise deposits to equal the new household deposit rates, and indexing to the inflation rate the interest rates on (existing and new) time deposits with maturities of three years or more.

The mandatory method of bond placement and the face-value stabilization intervention undermined the purpose behind the 1981 shift from financing the whole deficit through money creation. The bond issue stemmed from the desire to reduce inflation by making fiscal policy independent of monetary policy. With bonds absorbing household and enterprise saving, an increase in government expenditure that widened the budget deficit would not cause a corresponding increase in the (reserve) money supply.

However, the mandatory method of bond placement strengthened enterprises' requests for bank loans. Enterprises claimed that the involuntary withdrawals of their working capital to purchase bonds were causing them cash flow problems. So the banking system transformed most of the deficit into money supply growth, with the enterprises acting as intermediaries.

The face-value stabilization interventions also resulted in a net increase in the high-power money supply because the local governments would cover their losses with loans from the local banks, which, in turn, received more central bank deposits.

Debt servicing has become a nonnegligible expenditure item in the government budget, reaching 14 per cent of the total in 1990 and 16 per cent in 1991. In fact, about 60 per cent of debt servicing could have been avoided if the government had issued bonds with longer maturities. Most outstanding government bonds have a maturity of only 3 years. With longer maturities, the budget deficit would not only look smaller (which confers political advantages), the government would also be spared the burden of constantly rolling the bonds over (which saves resources). Since bonds of long maturities are difficult to place in the absence of a developed bond market, this underlines the need for further financial system reforms.

Five lessons can be drawn from the post-1978 debt management experience.

The first is that there is no need to rely on administrative fiat to sell government bonds. The resentment associated with new debt issues can be avoided with the market method of allowing the interest rate to adjust to the market-clearing level, at which the public would voluntarily acquire them. The market method has the added advantage of avoiding the administrative burden of having to issue indexed bonds whenever inflation is high.

The recent decision to pay a handling fee to financial institutions such as the regional trust and investment companies and let them sell government obligations is a step in the right direction. The government should move quickly to the next stage of freeing coupon rates.

The second lesson is that the implicit taxation of enterprises from the required bond purchases at low coupon rates goes against the desire to push SOEs to become financially independent entities. It would be hard to deny subsidies to mismanaged SOEs if required bond purchases were a major reason for their losses. The decision to allow secondary trading of government bonds acquired by enterprises since 1991 is a welcome step to increase the enterprises' flexibility in the use of their funds.

The third lesson is that the government should stop intervening in secondary markets to maintain the face value of government securities. Such a commitment creates a financial loss for the local governments and local banks whenever interest rates rise. This commitment also creates an unpredictable channel for monetary expansion at the time when monetary contraction is desired. Moreover, to avoid these consequences of the commitment to maintain the face value, there is the incentive to keep interest rates at the existing level. For example, in 1988, when high inflation created popular pressures on the government to raise interest rates, the government opted to keep the rates unchanged (10 per cent for household purchases and 6 per cent for enterprise purchases) but shortened the maturity from 5 to 3 years. This introduces an inertia in monetary policy that should be avoided.

The fourth lesson is that the maturity structure of bonds is biased too much toward the short term. The administrative costs of constantly rolling over large portions of the outstanding debt can be easily avoided by issuing longer term bonds. The 3 to 5-year maturity of the construction bonds is out of sync with the earning span of the projects. The loan repayments should be spread over a longer period that corresponds to the cash flow that is generated over the life of the projects.

The fifth lesson is that the primary reason for intervention in the secondary markets should be to change the money supply to control the level of economic activity. If this is not the primary reason, then monetary and fiscal policies will not be independent of each other. Monetary policy will amplify the stance of fiscal policy, especially when the latter is expansionary.

ISSUES IN REFORMING THE FISCAL AND FINANCIAL SYSTEMS

At present, the banking system is very much a fiscal agent of the state. Through its automatic financing of budget deficits, the monetary authorities act as a tax collector for the state, collecting the inflation tax. From the biases in the system of credit rationing, the banking system is also an instrument for carrying out the national industrial policy, as well as attending to the financial needs of SOEs.

This fiscal role of the banking system is not appropriate for a market economy — the banking system's primary role must be the intermediation of funds in a market-determined fashion. The central bank should not be used to levy the inflation tax but to ensure the price stability that is required for the working of a market economy.

The hidden subsidies that SOEs have been receiving through the special loans must be ended because they erode the government's ability to control the monetary aggregates. These subsidies should be made explicit and should be disbursed through the budget. Transparency will oblige the state to reconsider every year the relative priority and the aims of the subsidies.

Interest rate controls, like price controls, are anathema to a market economy. Freeing interest rates will not only ensure that funds go to projects with the highest rates of return, it will also give monetary authorities a timely indicator of the level of aggregate demand. An interest rate rise for a given amount of reserves in the banking system can be a signal that the economy is overheating. No such information can be extracted in a regulated interest rate environment because there is always an excess demand for bank loans (even during cyclical downturns).

The freeing of interest rates will enhance control of monetary aggregates. It will resolve the conflict between the two goals of interest rate target and credit target, a conflict that has resulted in occasional large increases in the money supply.

The interest rates can be decontrolled in three phases. During phase I, the interest rates are consolidated into one interest rate for all working capital loans regardless of borrower, and preferential investment loans are eliminated. In phase 2, the interest rate for working capital is allowed to be market determined, and, during phase 3, the interest rate for investment capital becomes market determined. Incremental phasing out of interest rate controls minimizes the shock at any one time and allows economic agents to prepare for the next phase. The cost of the incremental approach is that monetary control will continue to be loose during the transition.

Just as SOEs are being pushed to compete in the commodity markets, the state-owned banks (SBs) must also be pushed to compete in the financial markets. The entry of foreign banks is desirable but they are not the quick answer to pushing banks into the market place. At a minimum, the process of dismantling the sectoral boundaries of specialized banks should be sped up.

SBs must also be restructured. Many SBs are in poor financial health if proper accounting is done. Given that half of the SOEs in Shenyang and Chongqing are running losses, for example, the portfolios of the local SB branches are likely to be saddled with many nonperforming loans.

The government will have to recapitalize some SBs before they can compete in the markets as independent financial entities. Without such prior recapitalization, the SBs with the most inherited nonperforming loans will fail, threatening not only the integrity of the financial system but also wrongly identifying "blind competition" as the cause for their collapse.

Besides financial restructuring, the government must restructure the lines of corporate responsibility in SBs. There should be a board of external directors to which the management team reports, and an external auditing body that reports to the board. The compensation scheme of the directors and management team must be closely linked to the profit performance of the bank.

There will also be the need to establish uniform banking regulations (e.g., a limit on real estate investments), a supervisory body, and (maybe) a deposit insurance scheme.

The influence of local governments in running SBs should be minimized. Local governments can set up competing banks to promote their regional objectives. Special treatment of particular regions should be given through the central budgetary process and not through the loans of SBs.

The banks' intermediation of funds should be supplemented by other forms of intermediation — nationally integrated networks of commercial paper markets, bond markets, and stock markets.

The development of such financial markets should be a high priority because it will improve the allocation of capital and give the central bank the capability to conduct open-market operations to better control the money supply. As a first step, the government should quickly deepen the secondary markets for government papers and integrate them into a national market so that it can conduct open-market operations.

Chapter 2

Fiscal Structure and Reform

Chapter 2 describes the main features of the PRC's fiscal system and the way in which it is being reformed. The system is analyzed primarily at a national level, leaving the detailed analysis of central-local relations to Chapter 3. However, the division of responsibilities between the central and local governments is so fundamental to the PRC system that some discussion of it is unavoidable.

The discussion of the fiscal system is divided into five parts: the tax system, the price control system, nontax revenues, the expenditure system, and revenue adequacy. This division is standard, apart from the inclusion of price controls, which must also be considered as part of the fiscal system because price controls act like a tax in reallocating resources between economic agents.

After the system has been described, the main points are brought together by a summary of the issues that must be addressed as reform proceeds over the next few years.

TAXES

A major reform of the tax system in the PRC was implemented in 1984, when many new taxes were introduced in response to market reforms. Thereafter other changes were introduced incrementally, but during 1988-1992 the system was relatively stable.

The 1988 tax system was thoroughly surveyed in World Bank (1990c). This section will therefore concentrate on changes that have occurred since then. However, in order to make the discussion self-contained, there will be brief descriptions of the evolution of the tax system since 1979.

The contributions of the main taxes to government budgetary revenue are shown in Table 2.1. The figures in the table have been adjusted to international conventions, as discussed in Chap-

Table 2.1: Composition of Tax Revenues

	1985	1986	1987	1988	1989	1990	1991
				Y Billion			
Indirect Taxes							
Product Tax	59.5	54.7	53.3	48.1	53.0	58.1	62.9
Value-Added Tax	14.8	23.2	25.4	38.4	43.1	40.0	40.6
Business Tax	21.1	26.1	30.2	39.8	48.7	51.6	56.4
CICT[a]	0.5	0.6	0.8	1.5	2.1	3.3	n.a.
Total Indirect Tax	95.9	104.6	109.7	127.8	146.9	153.0	159.9
Enterprise Income Taxes							
SOE Income Tax	51.4	52.4	50.5	51.4	51.9	54.3	57.1
SOE Income Adjustment Tax	8.2	7.2	5.8	5.6	6.4	6.1	5.7
SOE Profits	4.4	4.2	4.3	5.1	6.3	7.8	7.5
ETKF[b]	14.7	15.7	18.0	18.6	20.2	18.5	18.8
BAF[c]	n.a.	n.a.	n.a.	n.a.	9.1	13.1	13.9
Total SOE Receipts	78.7	79.5	78.6	80.7	93.9	99.9	102.9
Other Enterprises	10.0	10.0	10.5	10.5	12.6	12.2	n.a.
Total Enterprise Tax	88.7	89.5	89.1	91.2	106.5	112.1	102.9
Total Revenue	229.7	244.7	257.6	280.4	326.4	351.6	366.0
				Per Cent of GNP			
Indirect Taxes	11.2	10.8	9.7	9.1	9.2	8.6	8.1
SOE Receipts	9.2	8.2	7.0	5.7	5.9	5.6	5.2
Enterprise Tax	10.4	9.2	7.9	6.5	6.7	6.3	5.2
Total Revenue	26.8	25.2	22.8	19.9	20.4	19.9	18.4

Notes:
(1)   Consolidated Industrial and Commercial Tax (CICT)
(2)   Energy and Transport Key Construction Fund (ETKF)
(3)   Budget Adjustment Fund (BAF)

Source: China Statistical Yearbook 1991,CFS 1989,1992.

ter 1. The individual items will be discussed in their respective sections, but it is worth noting that indirect taxes have contributed over 40 per cent of budgetary revenue for the past few years. Meanwhile the net contribution of enterprise income taxes and profit remittances has fallen from 36 per cent to 28 per cent of budgetary revenue.

Table 2.1 shows steady declines in revenue from the major taxes as a proportion of GNP. This is one of the issues that will be addressed in the discussion of individual taxes.

Indirect Taxes

Table 2.1 shows the revenue raised from the four indirect taxes. Product tax applies to goods and business tax to services. They are both traditional turnover taxes that are levied on the total output of an enterprise and do not make any allowance for taxes paid on inputs. The only exception to this is the business tax on wholesaling, which is applied only to the gross trading margin of the enterprise. However, even here, the treatment of inputs is not the same as it would be under value-added tax (VAT).

Product tax and business tax have a much larger number of tax rates than turnover taxes in market economies. All market economies have some differentiation of indirect tax rates, usually designed to allow high taxation of alcohol, tobacco, and gasoline. The PRC applies high taxes to these goods, but also has a great deal of differentiation among other goods.[6]

The existence of a large number of tax rates is a characteristic of centrally planned economies with price controls. The taxes are designed to absorb the difference between the controlled market price and the cost of production. As this difference varies among goods, each has to have its own individually calculated tax rate. Thus, in the 1980s, Czechoslovakia had separately specified taxes for about 1500 categories of goods.

---

[6]   Another difference from turnover taxes in market economies is that the tax rate is expressed as a proportion of the final selling price instead of the pretax price. This has no fundamental importance, but it is important in making international comparisons of tax rates. For example, the 60 per cent product tax rate on grade A cigarettes means that for every Y100 of final sales, the enterprise receives Y40 and the government receives Y60. In other countries, this would be regarded as a tax rate of 150 per cent.

In a centrally planned economy, these highly differentiated tax structures have little effect. But in a market economy, where the pattern of production is determined by the forces of supply and demand, these taxes distort the economy. For this reason, Czechoslovakia reduced the number of its tax rates to three soon after it adopted a market economy, and has recently further simplified the taxes. As the PRC has allowed more and more goods to be sold at free market prices and has allowed enterprises to choose their levels of production, these tax differences can no longer be seen as a device to absorb the difference between controlled market prices and costs of production. Instead, the taxes are affecting the balance of demand and supply in the market, altering prices, and distorting resource allocation.

Many countries with traditional turnover taxes have realized their disadvantages: the cascading of taxes[7] and the creation of an incentive for unnecessary vertical integration. They have therefore taken steps to alleviate these problems by giving some sort of allowance for taxes paid on inputs into production. Frequently, this has involved a change to VAT, as has been done by the European Community. The PRC is also following this route but is not following international practice: for example, the PRC continues to express tax rates as a proportion of the final sales price.

First, and most strikingly, the PRC is introducing VAT gradually. This is done by taking industries whose goods are subject to product tax one by one and converting them to VAT. Thus, all goods are subject to either product tax or VAT, but not to both at the same time. The effect of this gradual change on the relative revenues from product tax and VAT can be seen in Table 2.1 (although the figures for 1990 constitute an exception (see p. 53). Most countries introduced VAT in one step, applying it immediately to all the relevant goods. In some countries, VAT was first applied to the manufacturing sector and then extended to services. But no other country has introduced it one group of goods at a time.

---

[7]   Cascading of taxes occurs when a tax is levied on the sale of a good that is subsequently used as an input into the production of another good. The price of the second good will then reflect the tax paid on the input, in addition to any tax directly levied on its own sale. This happens with product tax, but is avoided with VAT as any tax paid on inputs is refunded to the purchaser.

This gradual introduction of VAT is consistent with the general PRC approach of introducing change slowly. It has had the advantage of preventing revenue loss that might have occurred as a result of a sudden change in the tax system. However, the coexistence of product tax and VAT has also had disadvantages. For example, it is virtually impossible to calculate exactly the credit that should be given for taxes on inputs that are still subject to product tax, because of the cascading.

The gradual introduction of VAT may also be partly responsible for the fact that the necessary administrative changes have not taken place: VAT is not being administered in a consistent manner across the country and a proper invoice system has not been introduced. Several aspects of VAT administration lack consistency. For example, some tax offices only gave credit for taxes paid on inputs at the time they are actually used, while others followed the international practice of giving the credit as soon as inputs are purchased. Also, some tax offices applied a composite rate for input credits, while others attempted to calculate the input credit exactly, even when multiple rates were involved, making use of invoices when these were available.

The second difference is that there is an unusually large number of VAT rates: 12. This is the result of the large number of product tax rates and the gradual introduction of VAT. To both maintain revenue and prevent an increase in the tax burden of industries, the VAT rate for each industry has been calculated to raise approximately the same revenue as the old product tax. Thus, the market distortions caused by the multirate product tax have not been removed by introducing VAT. Also, the existence of many VAT rates has added enormously to the difficulty of its administration, particularly because of the absence of an invoice system.

These difficulties are due to end in 1994 as a result of the recent decision to move to only two rates of VAT: a basic rate and a low rate for items such as agricultural inputs and basic foods. This will be accompanied by extending VAT to cover all industry (thus eliminating product tax), wholesaling, and retailing.

The simplified VAT structure will still allow the application of high taxes to alcohol, tobacco, gasoline and about 20 luxury items through the use of supplementary consumption taxes outside the VAT system. This will conform to international practice (although the number of goods involved is larger than usual), and implies that enterprises that purchase these goods as inputs will not be given an allowance for the supplementary tax. In contrast to the standard argument for giving allowances for taxes paid on inputs, no allowance is given because part of the purpose of the supplementary tax is to discourage the use of these goods.[8]

The third difference from international practice is that VAT has not been applied to the service sector. VAT will be extended to wholesaling and retailing. However, the considerable advantages to extending VAT to a more substantial part of the service sector include (i) preventing bias in favor of services and the (relatively rich) people who tend to consume them most heavily, (ii) preventing cascading in transactions between the manufacturing sector and the service sector, and (iii) allowing the tax rates on services to be the same as those on manufacturing, ensuring that the government will not lose revenue as a result of changes in the structure of the economy.

Fourth, the PRC VAT does not give allowances for taxes paid on investment goods. In other words, the PRC VAT is gross product VAT. Some other countries use a gross product VAT,[9] but the European Community and most other VAT-using countries have chosen the consumption-based version. The disadvantages of the gross product VAT are that it discourages investment and it places a heavier tax burden on more capital-intensive industries.

In the PRC's current situation, discouragement of investment may seem beneficial. However, the current high levels of investment are partly the result of a number of distortions elsewhere in the tax and financial systems. These distortions will have to be eliminated in the move to an efficient market economy, and then a gross product VAT might inhibit desirable investments. Also, the heavier tax burden placed on capital-intensive industries by the current PRC VAT was stated by the State Tax Bureau as a reason for not extending VAT to rail transport. The move to a consumption-based VAT would make it easier to extend VAT more widely in the economy.

---

[8]   This is certainly the case for taxes on gasoline, which can be seen as a charge for the costs of pollution and congestion that motor vehicles impose on society. It hardly applies to alcohol and tobacco taxes because enterprises are unlikely to purchase significant quantities of these products.

[9]   Some countries also operate an income-based VAT, where credit is allowed on capital goods as they depreciate.

A change from the current gross product VAT to a consumption-based VAT would need to be planned with care. However, much can be learned from the experience of countries that changed to VAT from traditional turnover taxes that included investment goods. They did not refund the tax paid on the existing capital stock of enterprises. However, they did have transitional arrangements that reduced the incentive for enterprises to postpone their investments until after the introduction of the allowances for taxes paid on investment goods. Details are given in Tait (1988, pp. 182-5), but the most frequent approach was to give partial allowances for investment goods during a transitional period.

In addition, a change to a consumption-based VAT would require an increase in the average nominal rate of VAT if revenue is to be maintained. However, this would be fairly easy to achieve as part of the reduction in the number of different rates.

Finally, the experience of revenue growth from VAT in the PRC has differed from that in most other countries. Most countries have found VAT to be a very buoyant source of revenue, and experienced increases in the ratio of VAT revenue to GNP. Table 2.1 shows the recent PRC experience. VAT revenue did grow from 1986 to 1989, but partly because of the gradual shift from product tax to VAT (total indirect tax receipts fell as a proportion of GNP), and in 1990 the VAT revenue actually fell.

There are several possible explanations for the poor performance of indirect tax revenue in general, and VAT revenue in particular. First, exports are zero rated for VAT and so the improvement of the balance of trade in 1990 could have reduced VAT revenue. However, export rebates in VAT increased by only Y3 billion from 1989 to 1990 (from Y12.218 billion to Y15.151 billion). This is equal to the fall in VAT revenue between those two years, and so can only be a complete explanation of the fall if there was no increase in imports or domestic production of goods subject to VAT. This is inconceivable, as GNP increased by 5 per cent. Second, the highly differentiated structure of indirect taxes could produce reductions in revenue performance if the pattern of production and consumption moves away from the more heavily taxed goods. Unfortunately, the detailed data that would be required to estimate the impact of this possible explanation are not available.

However, a third possible explanation is tax exemptions. Local tax offices provide exemptions from, or reductions in, enterprises' indirect tax liabilities on a very large scale. Regulations allow provincial tax bureaus to grant exemptions of indirect taxes up to Y30,000 per application, and this authority is routinely delegated downward to subprovincial tax bureaus. These exemptions are often granted to enterprises simply because they are new, because they are in financial difficulties or because they are investing in technical improvements. They are not confined to enterprises in or near special economic zones. They are typically granted by tax officials at low levels of government, without control by higher levels, and the practice appears to be growing as decentralization proceeds. Such increasing exemptions would affect VAT revenue particularly, as shown in Table 2.1, because the main product tax revenues come from well-established producers of highly profitable goods such as tobacco and alcohol.

The harmful consequences of this system of granting exemptions for enterprise reform are discussed in Chapter 4, but Table 2.1 suggests that the system may also have serious revenue implications. A fundamental weakness in the PRC fiscal system is that the ability to grant tax exemptions is vested with local officials, but the local government only bears some of the cost of the exemption. The reason for this is that indirect tax revenue is shared between the level of government that collects it and higher levels of government. If the share of the collecting government agency is substantially less than one, that agency does not have a strong enough incentive to deny applications for tax exemption.[10]

Consider the example of a local government that wants local enterprises to grow rapidly to create employment opportunities and improve the local standard of living. It will be tempted to allow indirect tax exemptions for enterprises in its jurisdiction. These exemptions will not cost the local government very much because part of the revenue will have to be shared upwards. Also, the exemptions will increase enterprise profits and so in-

---

[10]   If the PRC used the invoice system for collecting VAT, such exemptions on intermediate goods would not lose revenue: the revenue lost from the seller would be balanced by reducing the tax credit to the purchaser. However, in the PRC, the tax credit can be claimed by the purchaser without showing that tax was paid by the seller, and so there is a revenue loss.

crease enterprise income tax receipts and, possibly, the income from various local charges. Finally, the exemptions may attract resources (workers, managers) from other areas, thus increasing the local tax base.

Thus, the local government will lose little, and may even gain, from granting indirect tax exemptions. However, higher levels of government will lose. They will not gain from the increased enterprise income tax receipts, which are typically not shared upwards. Also, the higher levels of government will not gain much from the increase in the local tax base, even for indirect taxes, because part of the increase will be a transfer of resources from other areas, where the resources would have been taxed anyway.

Consequently, there is a conflict of interest in granting exemptions between local governments and higher levels of government, and even between different local governments that are competing to attract resources. Such conflicts of interest occur in many countries. What is unusual about the PRC is that so much decision-making power over major taxes is controlled by local government, while local officials are supposed to apply tax regulations that are made at the center. The difficulty is that the formal rules do not take account of the discretion that local tax officers can create for themselves in almost any country.

Many countries prevent that discretion from being used in the interests of local government by using a national, centrally managed, tax service to collect taxes. One exception is Germany, which is similar to the PRC in having provincial governments collect revenue that is shared with the center. However, the German system does have very strict controls to ensure that the tax laws are applied uniformly throughout the country. If the PRC is to prevent a continual decline in its tax revenue, it will have to take determined action to prevent widespread granting of tax exemptions. At the very least, it must establish a centrally controlled auditing system to monitor the granting of exemptions, calculate budgetary costs and ensure uniform application.

The revenue from consolidated industrial and commercial tax is small because it is now only levied on the products of joint ventures and foreign enterprises. It is a turnover tax that used to be applied to the output of all enterprises before domestic enterprises were made subject to product tax, business tax, and VAT in 1984. Thus, the existence of the consolidated industrial commercial tax is something of an anomaly and product tax, business tax, and VAT will be extended to all enterprises within a few years. This is welcome, as it equalizes the tax treatment of enterprises and allows fair competition.

Enterprise Income Taxes

As Table 2.1 shows, SOEs make the largest contribution to enterprise income tax receipts. The current system of SOE taxation is the result of a number of changes since the early 1980s. Before the start of the reform process, enterprises remitted their profit to the government, retaining only what was necessary to pay workers' bonuses and finance social facilities. In 1984, this was replaced by a system of enterprise income taxation. Large and medium- sized enterprises paid 55 per cent of their profits in tax, while small enterprises were subject to a progressive tax scale. Enterprises that were particularly profitable were subject to an additional enterprise income adjustment tax. The rate of the additional tax depended on the enterprise's profitability in 1983. Not all enterprises were subject to this new system: a few continued to make direct profit remittances.

Apart from the existence of the adjustment tax, the enterprise income tax system differed in two important ways from equivalent tax systems in other countries. First, tax payments are made to the level of government that owns the enterprise, which has implications for enterprise reform that are discussed in Chapter 4. Second, the repayments of the principal on loans is allowed as an expense for tax purposes.[11] Thus, investments that are financed by loans are very attractive for enterprises, and an investment that would be unprofitable before tax may be profitable after tax. The Tax Bureau has realized this disadvantage and its removal is part of the experimental system of "separating profit and tax," which is described in Chapter 4.

The enterprise income tax system has been modified by the contract system, which was introduced nationwide in 1987 after a number of experiments. Under this system, enterprises contract to pay taxes on a specific level of profits, whether or not they

---

[11]   However, because repayment patterns are rigid, enterprises are prevented from taking out a series of loans, each to repay the previous one, and claiming each repayment as an expense for tax purposes.

are actually achieved. The enterprises are then subject to a lower (or even zero) rate of tax on profits above that level. The contracted levels are usually based on previous years' profits, plus some expected growth. Most SOEs, and also most urban collective enterprises, are currently under the contract system.

The aim of the contract system was to increase the incentive for enterprises to become more profitable. However, there are two major disadvantages. One is that the contracts are individually negotiated and so subvert the process of enterprise reform (see Chapter 4). The second is that revenue growth from enterprise contracts would only keep pace with general economic growth if the contracted profits were set to grow at a sufficiently high rate.

The revenue consequences of contracting are shown in Table 2.1, where both SOE income tax and SOE profits (which includes the adjustment tax) are mainly delivered under the contract system. This shows that the total of income tax and profit remittance was almost constant from 1986 to 1989, despite a general increasing trend of SOE profits over the period (from Y134 billion in 1986 to Y177 billion in 1989).

Such poor revenue performance must be attributed in part to the low rate of revenue growth specified in the tax contracts, but is also partly caused by the failure of enterprises to fulfill the contract if their profits are lower than expected. During 1987-1991, profit shortfall by contracting enterprises led to a revenue loss of Y5.1 billion. All of this should have been made up from enterprise resources; in fact, only Y1.9 billion (or 37 per cent of the loss) was paid, leaving the government with a revenue shortfall of Y3.2 billion. An additional factor is the granting of exemptions from enterprise income tax, for the same sorts of reasons as exemptions from indirect taxes.

In effect, the contract system has worked to reward enterprises that perform better than expected, but does not fully penalize those that perform worse. Such asymmetry can only lead to continual revenue loss. If this process is to be stopped, the government must ensure that a substantial part of the enterprise income tax revenue is not subject to contracting and that exemptions are minimized. The first aim is achieved by the separation of profit and tax experiments (see Chapter 4), but the second requires improvements in the control of tax officials.

In July 1992, the State Council issued a decree on the management of SOEs that, among many other provisions, allows SOEs
a drawback of 40 per cent of the enterprise income tax they have
paid on profits that they reinvest. They are also allowed more
scope in choosing how they depreciate their fixed assets. The aims
and precise implementation of these two changes are not yet clear.
However, it is clear that they will both increase the incentive for
enterprises to invest, and the first change will reduce the relative advantage of using loan finance over retained earnings. Also,
the drawback will reduce government revenue in the short run.
However, in the longer term, the additional investment may
increase the tax base sufficiently to partially offset the revenue
loss or even reverse it.

In addition to paying income taxes, SOEs contribute to the
Energy and Transport Key Construction Fund (ETKF). The contribution, which is a 15 per cent charge on the sum of after tax
profits and depreciation, is nominally not a tax, but paid out of
"after tax profits." However, the contribution effectively raises
the rate of enterprise income taxation and has been included as
part of SOE receipts in Table 2.1. The contribution is particularly
anomalous, as it is applied to depreciation as well as after-tax
profits. The contribution is clearly a device to capture some of
the money that enterprises still hold after paying their taxes.

Since 1989, in an attempt to counteract the falling budgetary revenues, SOEs have also had to contribute to the Budget
Adjustment Fund, which is levied at a rate of 10 per cent on the
same base as the ETKF.

The taxation of other enterprises is much more straightforward: there is not the issue of paying tax to the level of government that owns the enterprises (as they are not state owned), and
there has not been the extensive experimentation of the SOE
income tax. The enterprises can be divided into different groups:
urban collectives, township and village enterprises (TVEs), individual household enterprises, private enterprises, joint ventures,
and foreign enterprises. Each category has a set of tax rules and
rates.

The only really significant revenue raiser is the income tax
on urban collectives and rural collective TVEs, with a revenue
of Y11 billion in 1990. Although many of these enterprises are
involved in tax contracting, along the lines of the SOEs, the treat-

ment of loans is different. All interest and principal are allowed deductions on bank loans for working capital, while 60 per cent is allowed for loans for technical transformation and none for capital construction loans. Urban collectives pay taxes on the same progressive rate structure as small SOEs (rising from 10 per cent to 55 per cent). TVEs only pay a 20 per cent tax.

The individual household enterprise income tax raised about Y1 billion in 1990. The rules for loan interest and principal deductions are similar to those for collective enterprises, but the rate structure is slightly different (rising from 7 per cent to 60 per cent). There is also a surcharge of 10-40 per cent on annual profits over Y50,000. The private enterprise income tax is similar in design, but that only raised Y52 million in 1990.

The income taxes on joint ventures raised Y308 million and those on foreign enterprises raised Y396 million in 1990. These businesses are taxed more lightly than domestic enterprises, except TVEs. The tax on equity joint ventures is particularly interesting as it is the model on which the planned unified enterprise income tax system is going to be based. The tax rate is 33 per cent and it is applied to a fairly standard tax base, allowing deductions for interest payments but not loan principal repayment. The rate is reduced to 15 per cent in special economic zones, and at least Shenzhen has anticipated the future unified enterprise income tax by applying it to all enterprises in the zone.

This application of different rates of tax to different bases for different types of enterprise distorts the economy by preventing equal competition. There are plans to unify the enterprise income tax system on the model of the equity joint venture. The unification is to be welcomed in principle, but there is not yet enough evidence to show that it can be achieved without substantial revenue loss (see Chapter 4).

Personal Income Taxes

The two personal income taxes raised a combined total of only Y1 billion in 1990, and are therefore not shown separately in Table 2.1. Such a small revenue from personal income taxes is natural for a country with the per capita GNP of the PRC. However, the reform process is beginning to produce an increase in income inequality and a rise in income levels, thereby increasing the role for an income tax. Therefore, the design of this tax should be reviewed before it is applied to a substantial number of people.

The original personal income tax was introduced in 1980 and has an exemption level of Y800 per month, a level that is so high that it could apply to very few PRC citizens and therefore can be thought of as applying only to foreigners. A progressive seven-rate tax schedule (from 5 per cent to 45 per cent) is applied to income above this level. The personal income adjustment tax was introduced in 1986, and applies only to PRC citizens. It has a more modest exemption level of Y400 per month and has a five-rate progressive tax schedule (from 20 per cent to 60 per cent). Both taxes have additional provisions for the treatment of nonwage income.

The existence of two different personal income tax systems is somewhat unusual by international standards, as is the separate tax treatment of individual household enterprises (whose taxation is described Enterprise Income Taxes, page 56). Most countries subject their own citizens and foreigners to the same personal income tax, perhaps allowing different deductions. They also apply that same tax to the profits of unincorporated businesses (the equivalent of individual household enterprises). The State Tax Bureau is therefore planning to bring these three taxes closer together, as well as reduce the rates and extend their base to include retirement incomes and the incomes of agricultural households.

These proposals include the application of a common five-step progressive scale for both personal income taxes but different exemption levels: Y3,000 per month for foreigners and Y400 per month for PRC citizens. The individual household enterprise income tax is planned to have an exemption level equivalent to that of the personal income tax for PRC, Y4,800 per year, but have its own progressive scale (from 5 per cent to 40 per cent).

These reforms are welcome, especially the broadening of the tax base. However, it is not clear why they have not gone further. In particular, it would seem natural to apply the same tax rates for personal income tax and individual household enterprise income tax. Also, the proposed reforms do not sufficiently reflect the reduction in the use of multirate progressive tax schedules in other countries. Both theory and experience show that tax schedules with one or two marginal tax rates can be just as strongly redistributive as schedules with five or more rates. In the United Kingdom, almost all taxpayers pay the same standard rate of income tax, but the system is progressive because of the substantial exemption level. Such simplified rate schedules also make administration much easier. For example, it allows accurate tax withholding for taxpayers with more than one income source, something that the current PRC system cannot manage. Simplified schedules would also make it much easier to integrate the taxation of income from capital, including capital gains, into a genuine global income tax.

Also, the increase in the exemption level for foreigners seems hard to justify, even though it is simply restoring the US dollar value of the exemption at the time the tax was introduced. Foreign nationals, and the companies that pay them, have adjusted to the eroded value of the exemption. To restore its full value is simply a transfer from the PRC government to the foreigners, or (more probably) their employers. The attractions given to foreign companies are already considerable and the proposed increase appears to be a waste of money, although a small one.

It is difficult to apply uniform exemption levels across the country because of differences between regions in the extent of food and housing subsidies, and the cost of living more generally. For example, in Shenzhen the high cost of living has led to an increase in the tax threshold for the PRC to Y700 per month. Wage reform, housing reform and subsidy reduction must spread throughout the country before a uniform income tax can properly be applied.

Minor Taxes

The PRC has a considerable number of other taxes. An idea of their relative revenue importance can be gained from the revenue raised in 1990 (see Table 2.2). In addition, the government receives repayments on capital construction loans (Y2.2 billion) and a modest amount of fines (Y635 million).

The basic characteristics of the taxes are reported in World Bank (1990c), with the exceptions of stamp tax, banquet tax and the special taxes on liquor and tobacco. The following descriptions draw heavily on that source.

Table 2.2: Revenue from Minor Taxes (1990)

Tax	1990 Revenue (Y billion)	Tax	1990 Revenue (Y billion)
Customs Duties	15.9	Special Fuel Tax	1.1
Urban Construction	9.2	Bonus Taxes	1.0
Agricultural Taxes	8.8	Stamp Tax	0.985
Construction Tax	3.8	Salt Tax	0.835
Urban Land Use Tax	3.1	SOE Wage Adjustment	0.340
Resource Tax	2.2	Banquet Tax	0.004

Source: World Bank (1990c).

Customs duties are levied on most imports and a few exports. Import duties are levied as a proportion of the cost insurance freight (c.i.f.) price, at rates varying from 3 per cent to over 100 per cent. Imports are also subject to product tax or VAT on the duty-paid price, according to the same rates as domestic products. Export duties are levied as a proportion of the free on board (f.o.b.) price, at rates varying from 10 per cent to 60 per cent. These apply to a very limited range of goods, mainly minerals and rare foods. Exports of manufactured goods are zero rated for VAT, and so exporters receive refunds for VAT that was previously paid on goods they export.

Urban construction tax is a local surcharge on the indirect taxes paid by enterprises. The base is the amount of indirect taxes paid, and the rate is usually 7 per cent in municipalities, 5 per cent in counties and 1 per cent in townships. There is a plan to switch the base of this tax from turnover taxes to profit taxes.

Agricultural taxes are based on the value of grain[12] that is usually harvested. The tax per unit land area therefore varies between localities, depending on the fertility of the land. It is, however, not a tax on land values as it is only based on grain yields and so does not take account of the suitability of the land to grow vegetables and other high value crops. Agricultural households are not liable to personal income adjustment tax.

---

[12] Referred to as the "Urban Maintenance and Construction Tax" in World Bank (1990c).

The proportional contribution by the agricultural tax to revenue is clearly smaller than agriculture's share of national income. However, this is appropriate because most agricultural households have an income that is substantially below that of nonagricultural households. For that reason, the reduction in the implicit tax represented by the grain procurement policies (discussed in Price Control, p. 67) should be welcomed. Also, it is disturbing to hear reports that agricultural households are being subject to a range of local charges that are outside the budget, and of dubious legality. Other methods of local finance must be found, so that these charges can be eliminated.

The *construction tax*[13] is 10 per cent on construction undertaken outside the state investment budget, typically financed from enterprise extrabudgetary funds. It is designed to curb investment that is not regarded as important by the planners. Investments with clear social value (such as energy and transport facilities, medical facilities, and schools) are exempt. The fundamental purpose of the tax is to strengthen the planners' control, and it should therefore be removed as the PRC moves towards a market-oriented economy.

Revenue from the *urban land use tax* has grown considerably. This shows the revenue potential of charging for the use of natural resources (in this case land), and it is hard to understand why some areas, for example Shenzhen, do not apply the tax.

The other charge for natural resources is the *resource tax*, which started in 1984 and is currently applied to coal, oil, natural gas, and iron ore. The tax will be extended to include metallic and nonmetallic minerals as well as forest and water resources. This extension should be beneficial in raising revenue, especially as a tax on resource rents is nondistortionary. However, the current method of calculating and levying the tax is not entirely satisfactory: it is actually levied in proportion to output, although the law says that the tax should be based on the profits from sales. The current system levies different charges on output for different enterprises, and so distorts the allocation of output between

---

[13]   This is referred to as the "Extrabudgetary Construction Tax" in World Bank (1990c).

enterprises. It would be worthwhile to devise a new system for charging for natural resources, taking account of the experiences of other resource-rich countries.

In other countries, natural resource revenues are seen as a payment for resources that are owned by the state, rather than as a tax that is aimed at equalizing profits. The most common form of payment is a royalty: a charge per unit of resource extracted, which is the same for all enterprises, expressed either as a specific amount or as a percentage of its market value. Some countries have an excess profits tax, either alone or in addition to the royalty. Both methods suffer from the disadvantage that the government is not collecting the full value of the resource; for example, they are not able to capture the extra value that some coal mines have because they are particularly easy to operate. In principle, this problem could be solved by competitive bidding for the right to use particular resources. This approach is used in some countries, including the United States of America. However, such a system can only be implemented in an economy without price controls, and where there are a reasonable number of competitors who will bid for each resource. The identification of an appropriate system for the PRC would require detailed consideration of the industries using natural resources and the markets in which they operate.

The *special fuel tax* is levied on enterprise consumption of crude and heavy oil, in an attempt to encourage the use of coal. The use of this tax indicates that the PRC government believes that the relative prices of coal and oil are not correctly set. The belief is hard to evaluate, as both coal and oil prices are still subject to considerable controls. However, the need for the special fuel tax will be reduced as coal and oil prices become more market determined, and there are plans to eliminate this tax when VAT is extended to cover these products.

Bonus taxes are levied on bonuses that exceed four months' wages. Those who receive a bonus of between four and five months' wages are taxed at 20 per cent, those who receive between five and six are taxed at a marginal rate of 50 per cent (on the portion of the bonus which exceeds five months' wages), those between six and seven are taxed at a marginal rate of 100 per cent, and those over seven are taxed at a marginal rate of 200 per cent. This tax is clearly aimed at controlling bonus payments, in order to control the distribution of income and maintain the financial health of enterprises. The *SOE wage adjustment tax* has a similar purpose, and taxes wage increases that exceed 7 per cent in a year. The tax is 20 per cent for increases between 7 and 13 per cent, 50 per cent for increases between 13 and 20 per cent, 100 per cent for increases between 20 and 27 per cent and 200 per cent for higher increases.

As explained in Chapter 4, the lack of a "hard budget constraint" for enterprises gives rise to a situation where they tend to give excessive pay increases. There is therefore a case for continuing bonus and wage adjustment taxes until enterprises are more thoroughly reformed. However, the taxes are not being completely effective in holding down pay and there are plans to eliminate them.

Salt tax has a history that goes back much further than any other taxes.[14] Currently, it is levied on salt producers and marketing agencies at rates ranging from Y50 to Y160 per ton, depending on the type of salt and the type of producer. There are plans to eliminate this tax.

One new tax since 1988 is the *investment orientation adjustment tax*, which was introduced in 1991. This is a tax on investment in fixed assets, and is designed to encourage certain areas of investment while discouraging others. The tax is therefore similar in intent to the construction tax. Investments in priority sectors are tax free, while investments in areas to be discouraged are taxed at 30 per cent. Investments in areas that are neither encouraged nor discouraged are taxed at 5 per cent. Of the revenue from the tax, 30 per cent goes to the central government, and the remaining 70 per cent is kept by local government. The idea of this new tax is to supplement the direct planning controls on investment, directing investment funds to where they are thought to be most urgently needed. The effects of the tax have not been studied.

---

[14]   Easson and Li (1987, p. 435) state that it dates at least to the Qin dynasty (221-207 B.C.).

The justification for the investment orientation adjustment tax, as for the planning controls that it supplements, is that the current market system is not allocating resources properly. For example, we were told of the need to prevent investment in industries where there is excess capacity. In the short run, such a tax has an obvious appeal. But, in the long run, it is better to look for the cause of the problem than simply to treat a symptom: there must be some distortion in the financial system if enterprises wish to invest in industries that already have too much capacity.

Central Versus Local Government Tax Revenue Base

The central government share in total revenue is reported in Table 1.2. Tax assignments have changed numerous times since 1980. In 1993, the central government received all the income from customs duties, the special fuel tax, and SOE income taxes from centrally owned enterprises. The local governments received all the income from the SOE income taxes for the enterprises they owned, all other enterprise and personal income taxes (except a small part of the foreign enterprise income tax), bonus taxes, wage adjustment tax, stamp tax, banquet tax, construction tax, salt tax, agriculture tax (except a small amount of the farmland use tax), urban construction tax (except a small sum), and resource tax (except a small sum). The revenues from the indirect taxes (product tax, VAT, business tax, consolidated industrial and commercial tax) were shared between the central and local governments, as was the urban land-use tax. These tax assignments are subsumed under revenue-sharing arrangements, which are explained in more detail in Chapter 3.

Although local governments receive substantial revenues from the taxes that are assigned to them, there is still a sense in which it is not their tax base: they are not allowed to choose the tax rate. In almost all countries, local governments have the power to choose the rates of local tax. The range within which they are able to choose the rates is often limited and the tax base is often not very large. Nonetheless, this rate-setting power gives the local government an ability to respond to local needs and circumstances. At the moment, there are reports that local governments in the PRC are levying extra-statutory charges (particularly on farmers) on a fairly arbitrary basis in order to meet local financing requirements. The granting of explicit tax-setting powers for a local tax would produce a fund raising source that is legal, transparent and fairer.

PRICE CONTROL

Price controls are similar to taxes because they redistribute income between economic agents. However, while taxes redistribute income from taxpayers to the government, price controls redistribute income from the seller of a good to its buyer. Only when the government is the buyer does the price control generate government revenue. Conversely, the government can transfer income to buyers by selling goods below cost.

The major price-controlled item that the government buys is grain. The difference between the procurement price and the free market price is just like a tax on producers. However, the grain system does not yield net revenue to the government because the benefit of the low prices is passed on (such as the costs of transport, storage, and processing) directly to the urban residents who consume the grain, as an implicit subsidy together with other subsidy elements.

A second area of price control is the sale of nonagricultural products to consumers. World Bank (1990c) estimated that these price controls reduced the retail price index by about 7 per cent.

Finally, there are price controls on some transactions between enterprises. These price controls are only applied to transactions that are subject to planning. Additional outputs and inputs are traded at market prices. This produces a two-track pricing system under which an enterprise's profitability can be influenced by the proportions of its inputs and outputs that are bought and sold under the plan. The importance of these price controls for enterprise profitability were estimated in a joint World Bank-Development Research Center project, using data from 1987 and reported in Heady (1992). As an example, raising the controlled price of coal to the market price (an increase by a factor of about 2.5) would have increased the rate of profit on capital in the coal industry from -1.4 per cent to +5.2 per cent. At the same time, it would have reduced the rate of profit on capital in the electricity industry from 5.3 per cent to 2.7 per cent, and in rail freight from 8.9 per cent to 8.0 per cent.

Changes in Price Control

Price reforms started in 1979 and accelerated from 1984 to 1988, with the introduction of the two-track pricing system and the removal of price controls from some consumer goods. The inflation in 1988-1989 led to the reintroduction of some price controls. However, modest price reforms continued in 1989-1991.

By the end of 1991, only 20.9 per cent of retail commodities were sold at list prices, 10.3 per cent at guidance prices, and the remaining 68.8 per cent at market prices. For industrial materials the figures were 36 per cent at list prices, 18 per cent at guidance prices, and 46 per cent at market prices. Also, the proportion of agricultural procurement at market prices had risen to 58 per cent, with 20 per cent purchased at guidance prices that were very close to market prices. In addition to the reduction in the scope of price controls, the difference between list prices and market prices was reduced by a series of increases in list prices for cotton, edible oil, tobacco, coal, grain, oil, rail transport, electricity, lumber, and many industrial products.

Price reform accelerated anew in 1992-93. By mid-1993, grain prices had been completely freed in 1800 counties in 27 provinces. Only three provinces have retained the use of grain coupons: Hainan, Ningxia, and Tibet.[15] The retail prices of other agricultural products are also being decontrolled. Subsidies are declining for other agricultural sales, including pork, everywhere except Beijing. The most significant area of price control for consumers is housing (see Chapter 5).

Price control for industrial materials has also been reduced. The number of such goods subject to price control has been substantially reduced. However, coal and steel are still subject to price controls on their plan quantities. Less than 40 per cent of coal is sold at a list price which is about 65 per cent of the market price; while 25 per cent of steel is sold at a list price which is about 70 per cent of the market price. Meanwhile, oil is still completely controlled, but with two prices, one five times as high as the other.

---

[15] China Daily, 19 May 1993, page 3.

Regional Impact

The system of price controls has an impact on the distribution of income between regions. Regions will gain from the controlled-price purchases and will lose from controlled-price sales. The data that are required to calculate these gains and losses include proportions of sales and purchases of each good at controlled prices for each province, but unfortunately they are not available.

All that can be done is to identify the provinces that produce particularly large quantities of price-controlled goods (judged from output figures in the *China Statistical Yearbook 1991*).[16] This procedure is subject to two sources of error. First, provinces differ in the proportion of the outputs of particular goods that are sold at list price: a province that produces a large amount of a good subject to two-track pricing may not be selling a large amount of it at list price. Second, provinces will differ in the proportion of their list price sales that are made to other provinces. For example, a province might produce a large amount of controlled-price coal, but use it all in producing electricity within the province, thus suffering no aggregate loss.

Major products that are subject to price control are coal, oil, electricity, and steel. The provinces with large production of these items are shown in Table 2.3. Liaoning appears on all four lists, and so there must be a strong presumption that it has lost from price control, despite the qualifications discussed above. Heilongjiang, Sichuan, Hebei, and Shandong all appear twice, and so it is quite likely that they also are losers. However, the possible errors involved are so great as to prevent any firmer conclusions.

NONTAX REVENUES

Some nontax revenue sources have already been mentioned in this Chapter: domestic debt, loan repayments, and fines. Also, it could be argued that direct profit remittances of SOEs and the contributions to the ETKF and the Budgetary Adjustment Fund

---

[16]   State Statistical Bureau 1991.

**Table 2.3: Major Provinces Producing Products
Subject to Price Control**
(declining order of importance)

Coal	Oil	Electricity[a]	Steel
Shanxi	Heilongjiang	Shandong	Liaoning
Henan	Shandong	Liaoning	Shanghai
Heilongjiang	Liaoning	Jiangsu	Hubei
Sichuan			Sichuan
Hebei			Hebei
Jianxi			Beijing
Liaoning			

[a]   There is not very much differentiation between provinces.

are not really taxes, although such an argument is hard to sustain. However, two other sources of revenue have not been discussed so far in this Chapter: foreign debt and extrabudgetary funds (EBF).

The PRC's foreign borrowing has been modest in comparison to many developing countries. Its debt repayments (principal and interest) in 1990 amounted to Y6.8 billion, only 0.4 per cent of GNP. The money raised by foreign loans in 1990 was Y17.8 billion, continuing a steady increase of about Y3 billion, each year since 1986. This amount is about 1 per cent of GNP and just over 5 per cent of government revenue.

The decline in the budgetary share of GNP during the reform period was accompanied by rapid growth in EBF, which have grown to rival the size of the budget itself. In 1990, they totalled Y271 billion, or 15.6 per cent of GNP. Most of the growth in EBF resulted directly from shifting funds from budgetary to extrabudgetary channels, the major components of which are enterprise-retained profits and depreciation funds. The other components of EBF comprise revenues from surcharges and users fees levied by administrative agencies and local governments. In 1990, the enterprise share of EBF was 76 per cent, administrative agencies 21 per cent, and local government 2 per cent. The details and evolution of EBF are treated in Appendix I.

Given that EBF belong to SOEs and government agencies, a question that is often raised is whether they should be counted as part of government. In fact, whether and how to include EBF significantly affects our interpretation of the state of subnational finance. The common perception is that these funds have grown excessively, at the expense of budgetary control, and that they are primarily under local control. This notion is fuelled by official statistics showing over 60 per cent of both extrabudgetary revenues to be under local control. In fact, these impressions are caused by the large size of enterprise funds, and the division of these funds along the lines of subordinate relationships, such that funds retained by centrally owned enterprises are classified as "central," and funds belonging to locally owned enterprises are "local."

For determining government size, it is necessary to divide EBF into a fiscal portion (belonging to local governments and administrative units) and an enterprise portion (belonging to SOEs). An expanded definition of "government" includes both budgetary and fiscal EBF, but excludes enterprise funds, because the latter belong, at least in principle, to increasingly autonomous SOEs and are not available for financing government operations. This definition overestimates the size of government somewhat, since some administrative agencies engage in activities that are not really "government," such as hotels and restaurants run by government agencies. With the data currently available, however, a finer division is not possible. Adding fiscal EBF to the budget only increases the size of budgetary revenues by 3.7 per cent of GNP, and expenditures by 2.4 per cent.

In terms of the central-local division, the inclusion of fiscal EBF enlarges the local share, since fiscal EBF are highly concentrated at the local level: in 1990 the local share was Y51.6 billion, or 89 per cent of the total.

EXPENDITURE

The total size of public expenditure, and its central local division, was discussed in Chapter 1. This section concentrates on the composition of expenditure, as shown in Table 2.2. SOE loss subsidies are included in expenditure, in line with the modifications made to the data in Table 1.1.

It is interesting to compare the composition of PRC public expenditure with that of other developing countries, as reported in World Bank (1988, pp. 105-120). Low income developing countries spend on average 16 per cent of total expenditure on investment, 33 per cent on current consumption (wages and goods and services), and 39 per cent on subsidies and transfers.

Investment covers both capital construction and technical updating. The PRC used to spend a substantially higher proportion on these items than other low income countries. However, the proportion has now moved very near the average of low income countries. Table 2.2 does not give a number for current consumption, so this item cannot be compared with low income developing countries. However, the sum of pensions and welfare and price and SOE loss subsidies can be compared with the figure for subsidies and transfers in low income developing countries: the PRC spent a total of 22.2 per cent in comparison to 39 per cent. However, this comparison is misleading because PRC enterprises take responsibility for items that are part of government expenditure in other countries, particularly pensions and housing.

The most noticeable trend in the composition of public expenditure is the reduction in the proportion of budgetary expenditure that is spent on capital construction, although there is anecdotal evidence that this has been partly offset by extrabudgetary investment. The reduction may be a reflection of continued system reform, with the decentralization of investments to individual enterprises. However, it may well be a reaction to the declining revenue share of GNP: most countries find that capital construction is a relatively easy item of expenditure to cut, although such cuts can have serious implications for long-term development in the economy. Clearly further cuts in government capital spending will jeopardize economic growth if infrastructure investments fail to keep pace with demand, exacerbating existing bottlenecks in energy and transport supply. The Latin American fiscal austerity experience in the 1980s distinctly shows that cuts in government spending can have long-term consequences when capital shortage ultimately constrains growth.

No items of expenditure have seen their share grow as much as that of capital construction has been reduced. However, expenditures on (1) culture, education, science, and health and (2) administration have both experienced modest increases. These activities are clearly potentially valuable recipients of public funds, but the increased proportion of expenditure on administration is worrying: it suggests a lack of proper control of the bureau-cracy. Government employment has grown faster than the indus-trial labor force despite the policy of reducing government con-trol of the economy. Personnel increases occurred even in depart-ments that experienced drastic reductions in responsibilities, such as the price and planning bureaus. Guangdong Province's recent measures to disband a number of government departments, in-cluding the commercial bureau, are worthy of emulation by other provinces.

Another area in which government expenditure can be cut is price and SOE loss subsidies. Most of the price subsidies are for urban food, as is a substantial part of the SOE loss subsidies: the subsidies to grain departments have grown at an enormous rate (from Y4.5 billion, in 1986 to Y20.4 billion, in 1990). How-ever, the retail price adjustments for grain in 1991 and 1992 should have reduced these subsidies considerably.

There are also considerable SOE losses outside grain depart-ments. Some of these reflect price controls and can be expected to decline as price controls continue to be lifted. However, some reflect enterprise inefficiency and the reluctance of government to allow enterprises to go bankrupt. Thus enterprise reform, together with price reform, is important if enterprise expendi-ture is to be controlled and eventually reduced.

Table 2.2 shows that debt servicing has grown to a significant proportion of government expenditure. This reflects the growing stock of government debt, both internal and international, and rein-forces the importance of keeping the budget deficit under control.

REVENUE ADEQUACY

The question of whether current government revenues are ad-equate can be addressed in two parts: Is the revenue adequate for the current level of expenditure? and Is the current level of expenditure adequate?

As explained in Chapter 1, the level of the deficit is not a worry in itself. What is a concern is that the deficit is continuing to rise, even as a proportion of GNP. It is now only slightly smaller than the level of investment in capital construction, an item of expenditure that can reasonably be financed by debt. Also, debt

Table 2.4: Government Budgetary Expenditure

	1979	1980	1981	1982	1983
			Y Billion		
Total Expenditure	146.99	147.12	140.08	152.24	172.98
Capital Construction	51.47	41.94	33.06	30.92	38.28
Technical Updating	7.20	8.05	6.53	6.90	7.87
Agriculture	9.01	8.21	7.37	7.99	8.67
CESH	13.21	14.63	17.14	19.70	22.35
Pensions and Welfare	2.21	2.03	2.17	2.14	2.40
National Defense	22.27	19.38	16.80	17.64	17.71
Administration	5.69	6.68	7.09	8.16	10.22
Price Subsidies	7.92	11.77	15.94	17.22	19.74
SOE Loss Subsidies	11.68	14.08	12.64	19.69	23.99
Debt Service	0.00	2.86	6.29	5.55	4.25
			Per Cent of Total Expenditure		
Total Expenditure	100.00	100.00	100.00	100.00	100.00
Capital Construction	35.02	28.51	23.60	20.31	22.13
Technical Updating	4.90	5.47	4.66	4.53	4.55
Agriculture	6.13	5.58	5.26	5.25	5.01
CESH	8.99	9.94	12.23	12.94	12.92
Pensions and Welfare	1.50	1.38	1.55	1.41	1.39
National Defense	15.15	13.18	11.99	11.58	10.24
Administration	3.87	4.54	5.06	5.36	5.91
Price Subsidies	5.39	8.00	11.38	11.31	11.41
SOE Loss Subsidies	7.95	9.57	9.02	12.93	13.87
Debt Service	0.00	1.94	4.49	3.65	2.46
			Per Cent of GNP		
Total Expenditure	36.76	32.91	29.35	29.32	29.78
Capital Construction	12.87	9.38	6.93	5.95	6.59
Socal Expenditure	3.86	3.73	4.05	4.21	4.26
Administrative Expenditure	1.42	1.49	1.49	1.57	1.76
Total Subsidies	4.90	5.78	5.99	7.11	7.53
National Defense	5.57	4.34	3.52	3.40	3.05
Debt Service	0.00	0.64	1.32	1.07	0.73

Notes:
(1) CESH stands for Culture, Education, Science, and Health.
(2) Social Expenditure = CESH+Pensions and Welfare
(3) Total Subsidies = Price Subsidies + SOE Loss Subsidies

Source: State Statistical Bureau 1991 and 1992; and Wong 1991.

1984	1985	1986	1987	1988	1989	1990	1991
			Y Billion				
196.46	236.55	265.56	282.49	315.31	364.00	410.98	430.41
48.89	58.38	67.18	62.81	63.34	62.58	72.56	73.97
11.18	10.34	12.99	12.49	15.10	14.63	15.39	18.08
9.59	10.10	12.43	13.42	15.87	19.71	22.18	24.36
26.32	31.67	37.99	40.28	48.61	55.33	61.73	70.80
2.52	3.12	3.56	3.74	4.18	4.96	5.50	6.73
18.08	19.15	20.08	20.96	21.80	25.15	29.03	33.03
13.73	14.36	18.24	19.55	23.94	28.48	33.35	37.58
21.83	26.18	25.75	29.46	31.68	37.36	38.08	37.38
19.99	25.89	32.48	37.64	44.65	59.98	65.76	51.02
2.89	3.96	5.02	7.98	7.68	7.24	19.04	24.68
			Per Cent of Total Expenditure				
100.00	100.00	100.00	100.00	100.00	100.00	100.00	100.00
24.89	24.68	25.30	22.24	20.09	17.19	17.66	17.2
5.69	4.37	4.89	4.42	4.79	4.02	3.74	4.2
4.88	4.27	4.68	4.75	5.03	5.42	5.40	5.7
13.40	13.39	14.31	14.26	15.42	15.20	15.02	16.4
1.28	1.32	1.34	1.32	1.32	1.36	1.34	1.6
9.20	8.10	7.56	7.42	6.91	6.91	7.06	7.7
6.99	6.07	6.87	6.92	7.59	7.82	8.11	8.7
11.11	11.07	9.70	10.43	10.05	10.26	9.27	8.7
10.18	10.94	12.23	13.32	14.16	16.48	16.00	11.9
1.47	1.67	1.89	2.83	2.43	1.99	4.63	5.7
			Per Cent of GNP				
28.22	27.64	27.39	25.00	22.41	22.76	23.23	21.68
7.02	6.82	6.93	5.56	4.50	3.91	4.10	3.73
4.14	4.06	4.29	3.89	3.75	3.77	3.80	3.90
1.97	1.68	1.88	1.73	1.70	1.78	1.88	1.89
6.01	6.08	6.01	5.94	5.43	6.09	5.87	4.45
2.60	2.24	2.07	1.85	1.55	1.57	1.64	1.66
0.42	0.46	0.52	0.71	0.55	0.45	1.08	1.24

repayments are starting to rise quickly. Clearly these trends cannot be allowed to continue. The considerable reduction in the ratio of tax revenue to GNP must be reversed if large and painful cuts in government expenditure are to be avoided.

The assessment of the adequacy of public expenditures is much more difficult. A comparison with other developing countries given in Chapter I showed that the PRC devotes a smaller-than-average proportion of GNP to public expenditure, but the comparison was shown to be misleading. What is more significant is that the share of capital expenditure within public expenditure is now down to the level of other developing countries. It cannot be allowed to fall further, and arguably should rise, if infrastructure needs are to be met. This can only be achieved by reducing other areas of public expenditure or increasing revenue.

Another important indicator is the continued fall in public expenditure as a proportion of GNP. Most countries experience a rise in the proportion of public expenditure to GNP as they develop. In the PRC, of course, there has been a deliberate policy of reducing government expenditure as part of system reform. However, the share of public expenditure has continued to fall, even after most of the enterprises have become responsible for their own investments. That public expenditure is being held back by the inadequate revenue performance is confirmed by a general feeling in the central government and many local governments that revenue is inadequate.

A further indication of revenue inadequacy is the inequality in public expenditure per head in different provinces. In 1990, the average provincial expenditure per head on culture, education, science, and health was Y46 billion but it varied from a low of Y28 billion in Henan to highs of Y128 billion in Shanghai and Y148 billion in Beijing. Such inequality in basic services is quite remarkable, and in most countries would provoke a call for increased central government support for these expenditures in poorer areas. That support for a clear need (how can children in Henan need less education than those in Shanghai?) is not forthcoming is evidence of the tight financial situation in which the central government finds itself. One possible (and rather conservative) measure of revenue inadequacy would be the amount of money needed to raise the expenditure of below average provinces to the current average.

ISSUES

Chapter 2 identified a number of issues that must be addressed if the continuing fiscal reforms are to succeed. Some relate to the immediate problem of the falling ratio of tax revenue to GNP, while others are concerned with bringing the tax system into line with best international practices and with the requirements of a socialist market economy.

Two major causes of the poor revenue performance of the PRC tax system have been identified: the contracting system and the granting of tax concessions. The first problem is being addressed by the experiments in separating profit and tax, but tax concessions appear to be out of control. It is essential that measures are taken to restrict this practice, which erodes revenue and misallocates resources. A third cause of the poor revenue performance is the declining profitability of SOEs (see Chapter 4).

This Chapter has also identified areas of concern in the pattern of expenditure. Expenditure on administration and subsidies should be cut, while that on capital construction and equalization of provincial resources should be increased.

Fifteen additional items relate to bringing the tax system up to standard.

1. VAT should be applied to all goods currently covered by product tax.
2. Supplementary consumption taxes should be applied to a very restricted number of goods.
3. Foreign enterprises and joint ventures should pay the same indirect taxes as domestic enterprises.
4. VAT should give credit for taxes paid on investment goods: it should be consumption-based.
5. VAT should be extended to at least some goods that are currently covered by business tax.
6. The number of VAT rates should be substantially reduced, possibly to just one rate.
7. VAT should be administered consistently across the country, using the invoice method.

8. All enterprises should be taxed at the same rates, using the same accounting principles, not allowing loan principal repayments to be deducted before tax.
9. To ensure equal treatment of enterprises and maintain the integrity of depreciation allowances, the ETKF and the Budgetary Adjustment Fund should be phased out. Care must be taken to ensure that the revenue they currently produce is collected in some other way.
10. Personal income taxes should be integrated to a greater extent.
11. The rate structure of personal income taxes should be simplified.
12. Personal income tax administration should be strengthened to allow the proper taxation of people with more than one income source.
13. Application of the resource tax should be thoroughly reviewed.
14. Local governments should be allowed some discretion setting local tax rates.
15. The role of the investment orientation tax and the construction tax should be reviewed.

The State Tax Bureau is already planning action on a number of these points, particularly points 1 - 3 and 5 - 10. However, the remaining points should be thoroughly considered in the light of international experience.

These changes would eliminate the use of the tax system as an instrument of industrial policy, which is appropriate as the PRC economy becomes more market oriented: the market mechanism should allocate resources with as little distortion from the tax system as possible. The past practice of using indirect taxes for industrial policy will become ineffective, as well as undesirable. As the PRC reduces its restrictions on international trade, VAT's effect on the pattern of industrial production will disappear; the VAT is levied on imports and rebated on exports, so it is really a tax on consumption rather than production.

Industrial policy in future should take place through the expenditure side of the budget, rather than through taxation. All countries undertake public expenditure that is aimed at promoting industrial growth. The provision of education and physical infrastructure, such as roads and railways, are essential. However, these expenditure policies should be aimed at promoting industry in general, not specific sectors. Experience in other countries suggests that governments are not good at deciding which industries are worth supporting. The rates of growth of individual sectors should be left for the market to determine.

Chapter 3

Central-Local Fiscal Relations

This chapter examines central-local fiscal relations in the PRC. An unusual feature of the Chinese fiscal system had been identified in Chapter 2: while tax laws and tax policy are set by the central government, taxes are collected by agents at the local level and shared upward with higher levels of government according to revenue-sharing rules. Because of this decentralized tax administration, tax reform cannot be separated from reform in intergovernmental fiscal relations. Revenue-sharing arrangements also have a direct impact on reforms in the SOE sector, and vice versa, since tax revenues are apportioned among governments partially according to ownership of enterprises. In the course of reform, not only are tax signals playing an increasing role in influencing resource allocation, tax assignment and revenue-sharing rules are also taking on growing importance as incentives (or disincentives) for local tax collection.

Debates over the intergovernmental division of revenues and expenditures are heated in the PRC because of the sharply conflicting interpretations of recent trends. At the simplest level, the opposite trends shown in the central share of revenues and expenditures can, and do, give rise to opposing interpretations on whether central control is waning (Table 1.2, p. 30). The debates also reflect differing views of the appropriate degree of fiscal decentralization, how revenues should be divided between the central and local governments, and what the appropriate roles should be for the different levels of government. Finally, the disagreements also stem partly from the difficulty of sorting through the multiple strands of intergovernmental transfers, many of which are not reflected in budgetary statistics.

Sorting out the different numbers and opposing arguments requires a careful examination of the whole picture of central local interaction that includes all the components of financial flows. The discussion is divided into six parts. Section one presents the

current situation of subnational finance in the PRC, beginning
with the institutional setup. (In this chapter, "local" and
"subnational" refer to all governmental units at the provincial
level and below.) Section two examines central-provincial revenue-sharing arrangements as well as transfers outside of the
revenue-sharing framework to highlight the complex and
multistranded financial interaction between the central and local governments. Section three examines subprovincial finance.
Section four discusses expenditure assignments across levels of
government and their evolution in the reform period. Section five
analyzes the incentive effects of the whole fiscal system to explain local government behavior. Section six discusses the reforms
proposed for 1994 and the issues remaining in improving central-local fiscal relations.

THE CURRENT STATE OF SUBNATIONAL FINANCE

Government administration in the PRC is divided into five levels: (1) central; (2) provincial, with 27 provinces and the 3 municipalities of Beijing, Tianjin, and Shanghai, which have provincial
status; (3) prefectural, with 151 prefectures and 185 prefectural
level cities; (4) county, with 1,903 counties and 279 county-level
cities; and (5) township, with 56,000 townships and towns, and
city districts (see Figure 3.1). Fiscal administration largely corresponds to the governmental structure, with two new changes
introduced in the 1980s. First was the introduction of "line item
cities" (*jihua danlieshi*).[17] Since 1984 nine cities have gradually
acquired direct fiscal relations with the central government, making
their budgetary status equivalent to that of provinces (and Beijing,
Shanghai, and Tianjin municipalities). These nine cities are

---

[17]   The *jihua danlieshi* reform program sought to facilitate urban development by elevating the administrative status of selected large cities to that of provincial units.
Under the planning regime, cities with "line item" status would receive higher
priority in the allocation of funds and materials. In the reform period, even though
the plan allocation of materials has declined in importance, this status is important in terms of credit allocation and budgetary considerations in revenue-sharing negotiations. In the original design of "line item cities" reform, it was envisioned that all such cities would have provincial level budgetary status. However, because of opposition from provincial governments, only 9 (of 14) have this
status.

Figure 3.1: Government Structure in the PRC

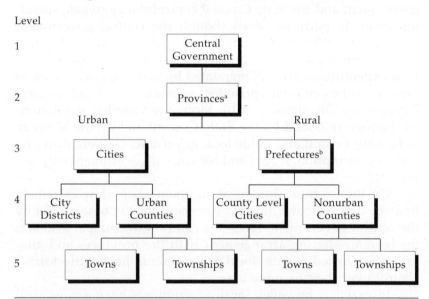

a Includes Beijing, Shanghai and Tianjin municipalities.
b In some provinces, the administration unit of prefectures has been eliminated, and rural counties are directly under city administration. Some examples are Guangdong, Hainan, Jiangsu, and Liaoning Provinces.

Chongqing, Dalian, Harbin, Ningbo, Qingdao, Shenyang, Shenzhen, Wuhan, and Xiamen. Consequently, the number of "provincial level" budgetary units increased to 39. The second addition was that, in response to the rapid growth and diversification of rural economies, the government decided in 1985 to set up fiscal administration at the township level. Previously, fiscal administration extended downward only to the county level. By 1992, nearly 47,000 offices had been set up, covering 96 per cent of townships and towns.

Formally, budgetary power exists at every level of government, since the constitution calls for local governments to formulate budgets, that must be approved by the people's congress of the same level. In practice, local autonomy in budget formulation is more limited than implied by the constitution. First, since the consolidated national budget (which includes local government budgets) must be approved at the national level, the central government and the State Council control the aggregate spending level. In addition, even though the central government announced in 1980 that it would no longer stipulate individual expenditure items in local budgets, some major components of local expenditures are still mandated by national policy, such as price subsidies and enterprise loss subsidies (see Central-Local Expenditure Divisions, p. 110). Moreover, detailed regulations are frequently issued by the State Council and by the Ministry of Finance to limit and guide local government expenditures on social consumption, wages and bonuses of government employees, etc.

On the revenue side, local autonomy is by law extremely limited. Policies governing tax rates and the tax base are set by the central government. Since the central government also sets the revenue-sharing arrangement with the provinces and allocates earmarked grants, local governments have little formal control over their revenue base.

In practice, however, local governments have a good deal of control over effective tax rates and the tax base through their administration of tax policy. As noted in Chapter 2, under enterprise contracting, local governments can set the effective rates of taxation on profits for local enterprises. Even over indirect taxes (which are shared with the central government), provincial governments have authority to grant temporary exemptions of up to Y30,000 per application for enterprises in financial difficulty, and this authority is often delegated to subprovincial levels. In recent years, local governments have made liberal use of their authority to offer tax holidays and reductions. Not only has this been a growing source of leakage that has contributed to fiscal decline, it has also resulted in tax environments that vary greatly across provinces—the richer provinces with lower revenue retention rates are more likely to be generous with exemptions, resulting in lower effective tax rates for their enterprises than for those in poor provinces.

In fact, the appropriate degree of fiscal decentralization depends on the relative weights the government assigns to central control versus provincial autonomy. Through most of the 1980s, the trend in the PRC was toward increasing local autonomy in fiscal management. Given the country's large size, and given the large populations in the provinces and subprovincial units (on average, provinces have over 30 million people, and prefectures 3.4 million), a substantial degree of local autonomy seems both necessary and desirable. It is also consistent with the reform program's objective of increasing flexibility and responsiveness by turning over economic decision making to lower level units.

On the other hand, the need for effective macroeconomic stabilization requires greater central control over fiscal policy. First, the direct linkage between local SOEs and local budgets provides a strong incentive for local governments to promote local development, especially in industry. This has long been a source of overheating in the PRC economy. Moreover, the ability of local governments to use tax and spending policies to aid local enterprises may have negative externalities on other regions, when the tax and spending policies take on forms of protectionism and anticompetitive behavior. These externalities reduce the benefits of fiscal decentralization.

Other institutional features in the PRC also argue for curbing the degree of fiscal decentralization. For example, the institutionalized immobility of the population, where the mechanism of "voting with one's feet" is not available either to limit local government action or to equilibrate demand and supply of public goods at the margin. An immobile population, large regional income disparities, and the absence of personal income taxation all point to the need for the central budget to play a significant equalizing role. The continuing role of planning and administrative prices in the PRC economy also requires the fiscal system to have a strong central component that can counteract and offset the redistributive effects of plan-directed exchange at nonmarket prices. While most of these institutional features will be gradually altered or eliminated in the process of reform, their presence argues for caution in the sequencing and coordination of reforms and decentralization.

CENTRAL-PROVINCIAL REVENUE SHARING

Revamping central-provincial revenue-sharing schemes has been a major focus of the reform effort, and the PRC government has tinkered continuously with the revenue-sharing formulas to try to improve incentives for revenue mobilization and budget management at the local level. Since 1980, four major revenue-sharing systems have been used, with many regional variations, culminating in fiscal contracts that have been applied to the majority of provinces and cities since 1988 (see Appendix II for details of revenue-sharing reforms in the early 1980s). These contracts stipulate a target revenue-sharing base, on which a fixed share or quota is remitted. Above this base figure, the marginal retention rate is typically much higher, up to 100 per cent. (Box 3.1 discusses the major contract types and offers the detailed terms for each province in 1992.) In 1992 a new experimental system of Tax Sharing (*fenshuizhi*) was introduced in nine provinces and cities (see Appendix III). In November 1993, the Ministry of Finance announced that tax sharing will be introduced in all provinces in 1994 (see Issues in Intergovernmental Fiscal Relations, page 133). This represents another attempt at dividing revenues to motivate local tax effort while ensuring sufficient and growing revenues for the central government.

Throughout the 1980s, incentives for local tax effort were improved in each successive scheme for revenue sharing, as marginal retention rates were continually raised. However, these favorable incentive effects were also continually undermined by the frequent changes in revenue-sharing regimes, as well as by the numerous transfers that took place outside the revenue-sharing contracts.

First, revenues are actually divided between the central and local governments in a two-stage process. In the first stage, the central government sets the rules on the portion of collected revenues that are set aside as central revenues, and only the rest goes into the pool that is shared with provinces according to revenue-sharing formulas or contracts. Through the reform period, by repeatedly expanding the scope of central revenues, the central government effectively reduced its dependence on revenue sharing from below and undermined the incentive effects intended in the revenue-sharing contracts.

Under the decentralized system of tax administration, virtually all revenues except customs duties in the PRC are collected by local agencies. Once collected, revenues are divided into three portions: "central fixed revenues," "local fixed revenues," and "shared revenues." Beginning with fiscal reform in 1980, this division among central, local, and shared revenues has been by source and by ownership of enterprises. Under the 1980 system (see Appendix II), "fixed revenues" at each level were comprised primarily of remitted profits from "own" enterprises—central fixed revenues came from central enterprise profits, and provincial fixed revenues came from provincial enterprise profits. Tax revenues were also divided by type and origin and designated as central, local, or shared. Central taxes at that time included customs duties and indirect taxes collected by the Ministry of Railroad. Local taxes included minor taxes such as the agricultural tax, salt tax, and income taxes on collective enterprises.

Under the 1980 system, revenue sharing between the central and provincial governments was confined mostly to setting the portion of "adjustment income" that provinces were to retain. The sharing formula was set for each province to allow the sum of local fixed revenues and retained adjustment income to provide just sufficient funds to cover local expenditures, which were in turn pegged to 1979 levels as base figures. Shared income came from turnover taxes (then called the industrial-commercial tax), which was the dominant tax source and produced over 85 per cent of tax revenues, or over 40 per cent of budgetary revenues (of which 45 per cent came from enterprise profit remittances). For a few revenue-rich provinces such as Liaoning, where local fixed revenues alone exceeded the approved provincial expenditure level, the provincial retention rate on shared income was set at zero, and the central government also shared the local fixed revenues.[18]

Since 1980, many changes have been introduced to the definition and composition of central fixed, local fixed, and shared revenues. Through the successive changes in revenue-sharing systems, however, two basic features have been retained. First, central fixed revenues are not subject to revenue sharing, so that whatever is designated as central revenues is excluded from the pool of revenues to which revenue-sharing formulas are applied. Second, enterprise incomes, whether in the form of remitted profits or direct tax revenues (after 1984), continue to be divided among governments by ownership. Through the reform period, the portion of revenues designated as "central revenues" rose from

---

[18] See Wong 1992 for revenue-sharing rates for selected provinces under that system.

Box 3.1:   Variants of Revenue-Sharing Contracts

Fiscal contracting was introduced to most provinces in 1988. In 1992 five variations were applied (see Box 3.1 Table).

- Under "basic sharing," the province retained a fixed proportion of all revenues. Basic sharing was applied to Anhui, Shanxi and Tianjin where the retention rate ranged from 46.5 per cent in Tianjin to 87.6 per cent in Shanxi (Bahl and Wallich 1992). In 1992, Tianjin had moved to the tax-sharing system, leaving only Anhui and Shanxi.

- The most popular contract type was "basic sharing with growth," which was applied to ten provinces and cities. Under this type, provinces retained a fixed proportion of revenues up to a specified target figure that is based on the actual 1987 revenue plus a stipulated annual growth. Revenues in excess of this target were retained entirely by the province. For example, Chongqing Municipality's contract under this scheme called for the city to retain 33.5 per cent of all revenues up to the level of 1987 revenues plus an annual growth of 4 per cent. City officials estimated that the city was able to retain an extra Y50 million per year during 1988-1989, when the city's revenues grew in excess of 4 per cent per year.

- The "fixed quota delivery" was the contract form originally applied to Fujian and Guangdong in 1980. This was considered the most favorable for provinces, because it specified a nominal remittance quota, with no annual adjustments, so that growing revenues would translate into rapidly declining remittance rates (as a result of the zero remittance rate on incremental revenues). In 1988, Heilongjiang, Shandong and Shanghai won fixed quota contracts while Guangdong was moved to a less favorable type of contract.

- "Fixed quota with growth" contracts specified a nominal remittance for the first year, with the remittance quota adjusted upward each year by a specified rate. This form applied to Guangdong (with the remittance quota set to grow at 9 per cent per year) and to Hunan.

- Fourteen provinces (including Fujian) were placed on "fixed quota subsidies," which specified a nominal subsidy each year, with no growth adjustments.

When contracting was first introduced, there was a sixth contract type, "incremental sharing," under which provinces retained a fixed proportion of revenues up to the base figure, with a higher retention rate on incremental revenues. In 1988, "incremental sharing" was applied to Dalian, Qingdao and Wuhan cities. In 1992, since all three cities had enrolled in the tax-sharing experiment (*fenshuizhi*), this type of contract no longer applied.

Among the contract types offered to provinces with surplus revenue, there was a substantial range in marginal retention rates, from 100 per cent beyond the specified revenue growth range in "fixed quota delivery" and "basic sharing with growth" contracts, to as low as 25 per cent for provinces/cities under "incremental sharing" (Wuhan). On the whole, marginal retention rates were high under these contracts, a feature that contributed to further reducing revenue buoyancy after 1988. At the same time, contracting had eroded the fiscal position of deficit provinces, since all previous revenue-sharing schemes had built-in growth adjustments in their subsidies.

Box 3.1 Table: Central Local Revenue-Sharing Contracts, 1992

City/Province	Basic Sharing	Basic Sharing with Growth		Fixed Quota to State (Y100 m)	Fixed Quota with Growth		Fixed Quota Subsidy (Y100 m)
		Basic Retention Rate (%)	Contracted Rate of Increase(%)		Initial Amount to State (Y100 m)	Contracted Annual Rate Increase (%)	
Shanxi	87.6	—	—	—	—	—	—
Anhui	77.5	—	—	—	—	—	—
Henan	—	80.0	5.0	—	—	—	—
Hebei	—	70.0	4.5	—	—	—	—
Beijing	—	50.0	4.0	—	—	—	—
Harbin	—	45.0	5.0	—	—	—	—
Jiangsu	—	41.0	5.0	—	—	—	—
Ningbo	—	27.9	5.3	—	—	—	—
Shanghai	—	—	—	105.0	—	—	—
Heilongjiang	—	—	—	3.0	—	—	—
Shandong	—	—	—	2.0	—	—	—
Guangdong (inc. Guangzhou)	—	—	—	—	14.1	9.0	—
Hunan	—	—	—	—	8.0	7.0	—
Inner Mongolia	—	—	—	—	—	—	18.4
Xinjiang	—	—	—	—	—	—	15.3
Tibet	—	—	—	—	—	—	9.0
Guizhou	—	—	—	—	—	—	7.4
Yunnan	—	—	—	—	—	—	6.7
Qinghai	—	—	—	—	—	—	6.6
Guangxi	—	—	—	—	—	—	6.1
Ningxia	—	—	—	—	—	—	5.3
Hainan	—	—	—	—	—	—	1.4
Gansu	—	—	—	—	—	—	1.3
Shaanxi (inc. Xian)	—	—	—	—	—	—	1.2
Jilin	—	—	—	—	—	—	1.1
Fujian	—	—	—	—	—	—	0.5
Jiangxi	—	—	—	—	—	—	0.5

Source: Ministry of Finance.

14.3 per cent of the total in 1979 to over 40 per cent in 1990 (see Figure 3.2), as a result of the introduction of new central taxes and fees such as the special taxes on tobacco and liquor, the Energy and Transport Key Construction Fund, the Budget Adjustment Fund, and recentralization of key enterprises in the automotive, power, nonferrous metals, and coal industries. In other words, the portion of total revenues to which revenue sharing is applied has fallen from 85.7 per cent to less than 60 per cent. (Even netting out debt incomes, which accrue entirely to central revenues, the central portion has risen from 11.5 per cent to 34 per cent of the total during 1979-1990.)

Even in the second stage (after setting aside central revenues), revenue-sharing contracts govern only one of several sets of financial flows between the central and local governments. The main components of these flows are schematically presented in Figure 3.3, which shows four downward flows and four upward flows. At the center are revenue transfers (C_1 and L_1) under the

Figure 3.2: Stage One Division of Revenue
(before revenue sharing)

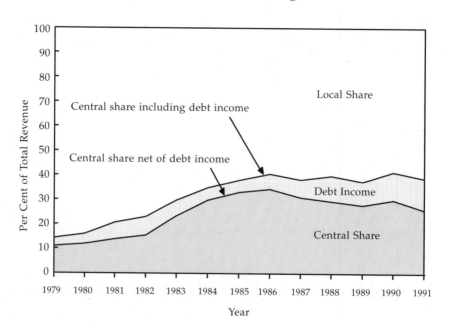

fiscal contracts negotiated between the central and provincial governments. With five line item cities represented, Table 3.1 shows that 21 provinces and cities remitted revenues to the central government, while 14 provinces received quota subsidies under fiscal contracting. In addition, seven "line item cities" remitted an annual surplus; Hubei and Sichuan Provinces eliminated their remittances after the transfer of Wuhan and Chongqing to "line item" status.

In addition to the remittances under fiscal contracts (component L_1 in Figure 3.3), provincial transfers to the central government include special taxes that accrue to the central government L_2. These include two special taxes on cigarettes and one special tax on liquor that were introduced in the middle to late 1980s to draw back revenue from sectors where prices were raised sharply, boosting profits. These taxes remain outside the regular system of revenue sharing.

Figure 3.3: Intergovernmental Financial Flows

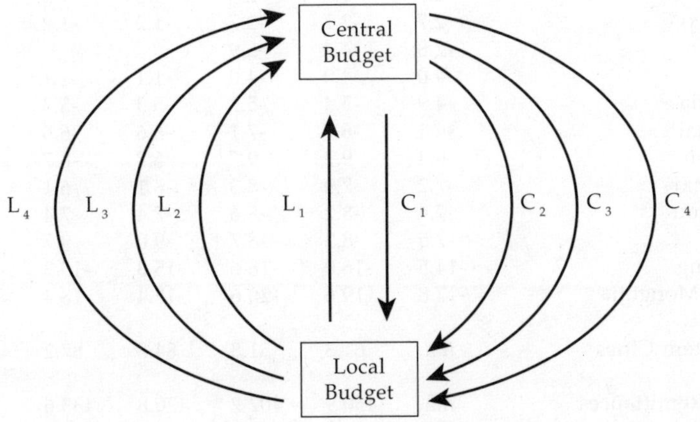

Local-Central Transfers:
L_1 = remittances under fiscal contracts
L_2 = special taxes
L_3 = compensatory payments
L_4 = "loans" to central government

Central-Local Transfers:
C_1 = quota subsidies under fiscal contracts
C_2 = earmarked grants
C_3 = compensatory payments
C_4 = final account subsidies

Table 3.1. Contracted and Earmarked Transfers by Province
(Y100 million)

Province/City[a]	Contracted Transfers (Local to Center)					
	1985	1986	1987	1988	1989	1990
Shanghai	138.1	133.7	124.1	105.0	105.0	105.0
Jiangsu	50.8	55.1	59.2	62.0	65.1	65.9
Liaoning	38.9	19.5	30.8	22.6	23.4	24.2
Tianjin	26.7	30.1	31.0	21.6	20.1	18.9
Shandong	26.2	12.9	0.8	2.9	2.9	2.9
Zhejiang	25.2	29.5	28.5	24.2	25.8	27.5
Beijing	25.2	28.8	30.3	29.0	30.1	31.3
Hubei	15.1	16.7				
Hebei	13.2	13.5	15.1	15.9	16.6	17.3
Henan	8.9	9.9	7.3	12.1	12.7	13.3
Guangdong	7.8	7.8	7.8	16.4	17.8	17.2
Sichuan	6.2	6.7				
Anhui	5.7	6.6	7.2	8.6	9.8	10.1
Hunan	4.5	5.4	6.1	8.6	9.2	9.8
Heilongjiang	3.1	3.4	1.4	3.0	3.0	3.0
Shanxi	0.6	0.7	0.8	4.3	5.0	5.3
Fujian	-2.4	-2.4	-2.4		-0.5	-0.5
Jiangxi	-2.4	-2.4	-2.4	-0.5	-0.5	-0.5
Gansu	-2.5	-2.5	-2.5	-1.3	-1.3	-1.3
Shaanxi	-2.7	-2.7	-2.7	-1.2	-1.2	-1.2
Hainan	-2.8	-4.4	-5.9			
Jilin	-4.0	-4.0	-4.0	-1.1	-1.1	-1.1
Hingxia	-4.9	-5.4	-5.7	-5.3	-5.3	-5.3
Qinghai	-6.1	-6.7	-7.1	-6.6	-6.6	-6.6
Yunnan	-6.4	9.3	-9.7	-6.7	-6.7	-6.7
Guangxi	-7.2	-7.9	-8.3	-6.1	-6.1	-6.1
Guizhou	-7.4	-8.2	-8.6	-7.4	-7.4	-7.4
Tibet	-7.5	-8.3	-8.7	-9.0	-9.7	-9.9
Xinjiang	-14.5	-16.0	-16.6	-15.3	-15.3	-15.3
Inner Mongolia	-17.8	-19.6	-20.6	-18.4	-18.4	-18.4
Line Item Cities	n.a.	61.3	51.8	84.8	87.2	n.a.
Total Remittances	n.a.	450.9	402.2	420.8	433.6	n.a.
Total Subsidies	-85.7	-85.9	-99.0	-81.6	-84.4	-86.1
Net Transfers[b]	n.a.	365.0	303.2	339.2	349.3	n.a.

a   In order from largest to lowest contracted transfers in 1985.
b   Positive numbers in this row represent net remittances from local governments to the central government.

Source: Ministry of Finance.

Earmarked Transfers (Center to Local)						
1985	1986	1987	1988	1989	1990	Province/City[a]
2.9	3.0	5.4	6.6	7.2	7.7	Shanghai
10.4	14.5	14.4	13.4	12.9	13.1	Jiangsu
9.2	8.5	11.2	12.7	15.4	14.7	Liaoning
6.1	6.0	3.0	3.4	3.7	4.0	Tianjin
9.3	13.6	14.1	14.7	16.0	16.3	Shandong
5.2	7.6	8.6	7.9	8.3	8.9	Zhejiang
6.4	7.7	9.7	10.4	14.6	13.0	Beijing
9.3	12.4	10.9	10.4	11.9	12.8	Hubei
7.1	9.6	11.1	11.3	12.0	12.9	Hebei
9.8	15.0	12.6	12.3	12.3	13.6	Henan
7.2	13.9	16.2	13.7	13.8	12.4	Guangdong
12.0	17.4	17.9	17.0	17.7	19.2	Sichuan
8.4	13.1	11.6	11.3	10.3	10.8	Anhui
6.3	10.6	10.4	9.8	10.4	11.5	Hunan
8.7	14.5	13.2	13.0	13.5	13.9	Heilongjiang
8.2	8.5	8.6	7.5	7.7	8.3	Shanxi
3.2	4.9	6.1	6.1	5.9	7.0	Fujian
5.5	8.7	9.2	8.3	8.7	9.8	Jiangxi
5.4	6.2	7.2	6.3	6.5	7.4	Gansu
5.6	7.5	7.4	7.2	6.8	7.6	Shaanxi
			1.8	3.3	3.0	Hainan
6.9	11.4	14.6	14.4	13.8	12.0	Jilin
1.9	2.4	2.9	2.6	2.6	2.6	Hingxia
1.7	2.1	2.6	2.2	2.3	2.8	Qinghai
5.2	8.0	8.1	8.8	9.3	8.8	Yunnan
4.9	8.2	9.4	9.1	7.9	7.8	Guangxi
3.4	4.8	5.2	5.0	5.1	5.3	Guizhou
2.8	1.3	1.4	1.2	2.4	2.4	Tibet
4.9	6.5	6.8	7.2	7.1	7.4	Xinjiang
5.2	6.5	8.6	8.3	8.4	8.2	Inner Mongolia
n.a.	9.7	9.6	9.6	10.3	n.a.	Line Item Cities
n.a.	264.0	277.8	273.3	288.0	n.a.	Total Subsidies

The third component of provincial transfer (L_3) comprises compensatory payments to the central government for enterprises that have been transferred to local management. The most recent examples include the decentralization of electronics enterprises and ports to local management. In addition to its contracted remittance, for example, Liaoning Province made a compensatory payment of Y15 million to the central government in 1990 for taking over management of a port. These compensatory payments are transitory—whenever revenue-sharing contracts are renegotiated, these payments are factored into the base numbers, and the financial flows are shifted from L_3 to L_1.

The fourth component (L_4) represents ad hoc, involuntary loans to the central government, which are counted as local remittances, rather than debt income in budgetary accounts. These "loans" totalled Y7 billion in 1981, Y4 billion in 1982, Y9 billion in 1987, and over Y2 billion in 1990 (Chen Rulong 1988, p. 311.); they have never been repaid, and were in each case turned into additional remittances ex post facto.[19] The loans are in addition to the periodic compulsory purchases of state treasury bonds, which were distributed on a regional basis (by province) but purchased by SOEs and individuals.

On the right side of Figure 3.3 are four channels of central transfers to provincial governments. Aside from the quota subsidies under revenue contracts (C_1), the central government makes earmarked grants (C_2) to provinces for specific uses. These include appropriations for capital construction projects; price subsidies for grain, cotton, and oil; social relief; aid for natural disasters; subsidies for building large-scale flood and drought prevention projects; and special subsidies for health and education for poor and border provinces. Their sums for 1985-1990 are presented on the right side of Table 3.1.

The third component of central transfers to provinces comprises compensatory payments (C_3) for local enterprises that have been transferred to central ownership, to make up for lost revenues that no longer accrue to local budgets. Like their counterpart on the upward flows from the provinces, these compensatory payments are also short term, to be replaced by the next round

---

[19] In the provinces these are sarcastically referred to as "extra contributions" to the state.

of adjustments in the revenue-sharing contracts. The fourth component is final account subsidies (C_4), which are occasional transfers made to cover local budget deficits. For example, Sichuan Province received Y250 million in final account subsidies in 1985 and Y580 million in 1990.

These multiple flows upward and downward obscure the budgetary process and the resources available at each level of government. At the central level, total resources available are the sum of central fixed revenues, provincial remittances, special tax remittances, local compensatory payments for enterprise transfers, and "loans" to the center; minus the sum of quota subsidies to poor provinces, earmarked grants, compensatory payments for enterprise transfers, and final account subsidies. Of these, only two components (C_1 and L_1) are governed by the revenue-sharing contracts.

This recitation of the many components of financial flows shows the intergovernmental fiscal interaction to be far more complex than previously understood. It also helps to explain the heatedness of the debate over whether the PRC fiscal system is too centralized or too decentralized. The central government's concern with its declining share in total revenues is reflected in the summary statistics presented in Table 3.2, which show total remittances from surplus provinces declining in the presence of rapidly growing local revenue collections, so that the aggregate remittance rate fell from about 34 per cent in 1985 to about 22 per cent in 1989.

Table 3.2: Aggregate Remittance Rates, 1986-1991

	1986	1987	1988	1989	1990	1991
Remittances from Surplus Provinces[a] (Y100 million)	450.9	402.2	420.9	433.6	n.a.	490.3
Remittance Rate (%)	33.6	27.5	26.6	23.5	n.a.	22.2

a Including "line item cities".

Source: Table 3.1 and Ministry of Finance.

The trend toward a diminishing role for contractual transfers is confirmed on the aggregate level at the bottom of Table 3.1, where the totals for contractual transfers declined from 1985 to 1990, while earmarked subsidies grew absolutely and relatively. Table 3.3 presents the breakdown of central transfers to the provinces in 1990, showing that quota subsidies to poor provinces accounted for less than 15 per cent of the total, while earmarked grants comprised over 50 per cent, and compensatory payments over one third. Together, figures in these tables provide a stark illustration of one of the central government's severest budgetary problems: its diminished ability to redistribute income. Faced with declining receipts but growing subsidy outlays, the central budget had turned from being a net recipient to being a net donor of funds by the late 1980s. Moreover, among the three components of central transfers to local governments, only quota subsidies are straightforwardly based on needs, while earmarked grants and compensatory payments have large entitlement elements. In fact, nearly 90 per cent of the earmarked grants were absorbed by price subsidies for grain, cotton, and oil in 1990 (26.8 out of Y30 billion total), which were targeted at the relatively prosperous urban populace.

By looking at the whole picture of intergovernmental transfers, it is also possible to appreciate the local perspective and understand why the revenue-sharing arrangements failed to stimulate revenue collection—the apparently favorable incentives embedded in the agreements were continually undermined by the central government's actions "outside the revenue-sharing system." By claiming a growing share of total revenues in the first stage of revenue division through the introduction of new taxes and by expanding its claim over enterprises, the central government significantly reduced the revenue-sharing incentives in the second stage. The recentralization of profitable, growing enterprises has been unpopular, and local complaints of inadequate compensation are widespread. (A common complaint is that the central government compensates only for the present revenues foregone, but not for the expected growth in revenues accruing from the enterprises.) The frequent changes in revenue-sharing arrangements, despite prior commitments to multiyear contracts, also eroded incentives for tax effort. Moreover, as shown in Figure 3.3, the multiyear revenue sharing contracts, even when

Table 3.3: Estimated Breakdown of Central-Local Transfers, 1990

	Y Billion	% of Total
Quota Subsidies under Fiscal Contracts (C1)	8.6	14.4
Earmarked Grants (C2)	30+	50+
Compensatory Payments and Final Account Subsidies (C_3, C_4)	20+	34+
Total	59.6	100.0

Source: Wang Bingqian budget report 1990; Ministry of Finance.

not violated, apply to only one component of remittances (or subsidies). All the other components remain negotiable, mostly on a year-to-year basis. Given the repeated central "borrowings," local confidence in the central government's commitment to revenue-sharing contracts is understandably low.

Indeed, the whole tangled web of intergovernmental fiscal relations can be illustrated with the case of Guangdong Province, which is a favorite target for those who hold the view that the central government has given up too much revenue. With its remittance set at a lump sum during 1980-1987, the province was able to keep a rising share of its rapidly growing revenues, which grew from 73 per cent in the first year of revenue contracting in 1980, to 92 per cent by 1987. Not only are the central government's declining resources directly attributable to such fall offs in contributions from the richest provinces (including Shanghai), but people who live in provinces with comparable per capita income and revenues perceive it as unfair when their provinces remit much higher portions of their revenues to the central government. For example, Jiangsu retained only 45 per cent, and Zhejiang 61 per cent of their revenues in 1987, even though both had per capita incomes very close to those in Guangdong.[20]

---

[20] In 1978, per capita income in Jiangsu was about 12 per cent higher, and in Zhejiang about 12 per cent lower, than that of Guangdong. In the reform period, all three provinces have had similarly above-average growth performance (Ma 1992).

Table 3.4: Central-Provincial Financial Transfers, Three Cases
(Y million)

Province and Item	1980	1985	1987	1990
Guangdong Province				
Total Remittance	1,086	1,690	1,874	5,204
Under Revenue Sharing (L_1)	1,000	778	778	1,830
Special Remittance (L_2)	86	342	310	412
Enterprise Transfers (L_3)	n.a.	570	151	2,662
Loans (L_4)	n.a.	–	635	300
Earmarked Grants (C_2)	n.a.	717	1,622	1,241
Net Province-Center Transfer	n.a.	978	252	3,963
Liaoning Province				
Total Remittance	6,138	3,897	5,332	5,649
Under Revenue Sharing (L_1)	5,930	3,890	4,733	5,201
Special Remittance (L_2)	208	7	43	213
Compensation for Decentralized Port (L3)	–	–	38	15
Loans (L_4)	n.a.	n.a.	518	220
Earmarked Grants (C_2)	n.a.	920	1,117	1,474
Net Province-Center Transfer	n.a.	2,977	4,215	4,175
Sichuan Province				
Total Remittance	590	670	n.a.	1,205
Under Revenue Sharing (L_1)	n.a.	610	n.a.	1,050
Special Remittance (L_2)	n.a.	60	n.a.	100
Loans (L_4)	n.a.	n.a.	400	55
Total Central Subsidies	310	1,560	n.a.	2,910
Earmarked Grants (C_2)	310	1,200	n.a.	2,080
Final Account Subsidies (C_4)	n.a.	250	n.a.	580
Others	n.a.	100	n.a.	240
Net Province-Center Transfer	280	(890)	n.a.	(1,705)

a   Includes depreciation.

Source: World Tables 1991.

In Guangdong's defense, provincial officials argue that the favorable lump sum revenue-sharing contract was partially off-set by the agreement that the province would finance most of its own investments, as a result of which Guangdong received fewer earmarked grants for capital construction than other provinces. Moreover, aside from the quota remittances, the province made numerous contributions to the central budget that were not part of the revenue-sharing system. During 1987, for example, the contracted remittance of Y778 million constituted only 30 per cent of the Y2.64 billion the province turned over to the central government, which included a Y635 million "loan" to the center, earmarked remittances of Y310 million, Y452 million in compensation for enterprise transfers, Y314 million in new "tax payments" on extrabudgetary funds, and Y151 million in customs receipts. These multiple remittances are shown in Table 3.4 for Guangdong, Liaoning, and Sichuan provinces.

SUBPROVINCIAL FINANCE

Revenue-sharing arrangements involve only two administrative levels at a time. Given that there are five administrative levels (Figure 3.1), there are four levels of revenue sharing. Table 3.5 shows the structure of provincial administration. The normal pattern is that the first level of revenue sharing occurs between the central and provincial governments, the second between the provinces and prefectures (or prefectural level cities), the third between prefectures and counties, and the fourth between counties and townships. However, exceptions abound. In Jiangsu, the province signs revenue contracts directly with the counties, minimizing the fiscal role of prefectural cities. In Hebei, the province introduced a program modelled on the "line item cities" reform, which elevated nine counties to direct revenue-sharing arrangements with the province. In Guangdong, the province has direct contracts only with three minority counties that receive annual subsidies.

These variations can be taken as evidence that provincial governments have substantial power to set revenue-sharing rules within their regions. In addition, revenue sharing at the subnational levels also follows the same two-stage process as described earlier for central-provincial revenue sharing, and the province can set the scope of "provincial fixed revenues" and exclude them from revenue sharing in the second stage. In Hebei, for exam-

Table 3.5: Subnational Administrative Units
(end-1992)

Provincial Unit	Number of Prefectures	Number of Prefectural Level Cities	Number of Counties	Number of County Level Cities	Number of City Districts
National	148	191	1,848	323	662
Beijing			8		10
Shanghai			6		14
Tianjin			5		13
Anhui	6	10	60	8	35
Fujian	3	6	52	12	17
Gansu	9	5	67	8	10
Guangdong	0	20	72	6	41
Guangxi	8	5	76	7	21
Guizhou	7	2	72	8	6
Hainan	0	2	15	2	3
Hebei	8	10	122	17	34
Heilongjiang	4	10	52	17	63
Henan	5	12	103	15	39
Hubei	6	8	47	23	28
Hunan	6	8	77	19	26
Inner Mongolia	8	4	71	13	16
Jiangsu	0	11	44	20	42
Jiangxi	5	6	73	11	15
Jilin	2	7	25	16	18
Liaoning	0	14	33	11	56
Ningxia	2	2	16	2	6
Qinghai	7	1	37	2	4
Shaanxi	6	4	85	8	14
Shandong	5	12	70	28	37
Shanxi	6	6	91	9	18
Sichuan	10	11	164	15	40
Tibet	6	1	76	1	1
Xinjiang	13	2	70	15	11
Yunnan	15	2	113	10	4
Zhejiang	2	9	46	20	20

Source: State Statistical Bureau 1993, p. 3.

ple, to stem the decline in the province's share of revenues after the transfer of most SOEs to cities, since 1987 the province has claimed a portion of turnover taxes (product taxes, value-added taxes, and business taxes) for provincial fixed revenues. Under an early version of the "tax sharing" program that was introduced nationwide in 1994, turnover taxes were set aside from other tax revenues in six of the province's nine prefectural cities. These revenues were shared separately, with the province claiming 30-60 per cent, with a different rate for each city. For the provincial capital of Shijiazhuang, for example, the city retains 50 per cent, which goes into the pool for second stage sharing with the province.

In the second stage of revenue sharing, subprovincial contracts closely mirror the form of central-provincial contracts, reflecting their changes through the 1980s. With the adoption of fiscal contracting at the central-provincial level in 1988, contracting also became widespread in subprovincial arrangements. This comes in three basic variations: fixed rate remittance, fixed quota remittance, and "incremental contracting" (where the remittance is set to grow by a fixed rate). The latter two types of contracts have been popular, especially during the high-growth years of 1987-1988; these are the forms adopted in both Guangdong and Sichuan provinces for revenue-surplus cities (see Box 3.2). The four levels of fiscal contracts for Hebei Province are presented in Box 3.3.

The adoption of the experimental tax sharing system in nine provinces in 1992 necessitated a new round of adjustments in subprovincial arrangements to reflect the changes in the scope of revenue accrual to each level. This appeared to have affected the base figures for revenue sharing, but left the contract forms largely unchanged. In Liaoning Province, for example, where the province was expected to shift from remitting a surplus to receiving an annual subsidy of Y884 million from the central government under the new terms, the province's revenue contracts with the cities (excluding Shenyang and Dalian) called for the province to give a total of Y270 million in subsidies to three deficit cities, and to receive remittances from the other nine cities, with an annual incremental growth of 2.9-5 per cent.

**Box 3.2: Subprovincial Revenue-Sharing Contracts in
Sichuan and Guangdong Provinces**

Sichuan

Sichuan Province's revenue-sharing contract with the central government
calls for a quota subsidy to the province of about Y200 million a year,
with an annual growth factor of 5 per cent. The province has 217 counties under 21 cities and prefectures. At present, four types of revenue
contracts are applied to the cities and prefectures:

• Developed areas (eight cities) must remit a fixed amount (quota remittance) with growth adjustment of on average a little over 6 per
  cent. For Chengdu the growth adjustment is set at 6.5 per cent. Each
  city's quota remittance is set equal to the gap between its own revenues and approved expenditures. If revenue growth falls short of
  the target, the city has to make up the difference with its own funds.
  Total remittances of these eight cities are over Y2 billion a year.

• Areas in the mid-range of development (five prefectures) have a quota
  remittance with no growth. The five prefectures remit "several tens
  of millions" of yuan each year to the province (Sichuan Provincial Fiscal
  Department).

• Poor areas (five prefectures) receive quota subsidies with no growth
  adjustment. The prefectures receive "several tens of millions" of yuan
  a year from the province.

• Poor minority areas (three autonomous prefectures) receive quota subsidies with incremental growth. In 1987, they received annual growth
  adjustments of 10-12 per cent a year. These were reduced to 2 per cent
  in 1988, but were raised again to 5 per cent in 1992. Total subsidies
  now amount to over Y400 million a year. These prefectures have a
  population of 5 million, spread over 300,000 square kilometers.

Chongqing Municipality no longer has any direct budgetary relationship with the province since joining the "tax-sharing system" in 1992.

Vertical Distribution of Revenues

Data on the vertical distribution of revenues across administrative levels is difficult to obtain, since statistical reporting follows
the two-level revenue-sharing set-up. At each level, it appears

The city had become independent of the province in 1984, with its own direct budgetary relationship with the central government. However, until July 1992, the city remitted 10.7 per cent of its revenues to the province, and another 55.8 per cent to the central government (under a contract that called for the city to remit 66.5 per cent of its revenues up to the base figure). Under the "tax-sharing system", the city will make its entire remittance to the central government, severing its ties to the province altogether. (One result of this severance is that Chongqing no longer receives grain from the province at the state transfer price, as in the past. Instead, the city will have to pay a price that is halfway between the state price and the negotiated price. This difference is said to cost the city Y0.03 more per jin (Y160/ton) for the 600 million jin (300,000 tons) supplied by the province each year, or Y18 million. In turn, the central government will give a quota subsidy of Y202 million to Sichuan Province, with a growth of 5 per cent per year. Even though Chongqing's budget no longer passes through the province, it continues to be included in provincial budgetary statistics.

Guangdong

Guangdong's revenue contract with the center calls for the province to make a quota remittance of Y1.41 billion in the base year 1987, with an annual growth of 9 per cent. The province's contracts with its 19 cities fall into four types as applied in Sichuan:

- the five richest cities pay quota remittance with annual growth of 5-9 per cent,
- cities in the mid-range of development pay quota remittance with no growth adjustment,
- deficit cities receive a quota subsidy with no growth adjustment, and
- the three minority counties receive a quota subsidy with an annual growth adjustment.

  As is the case of Chongqing, while Shenzhen Municipality has no budgetary interaction with the province, the municipality's budgetary figures continue to be included in provincial budgetary accounts.

that information is collected only for itself and the level below, so that at the central level, the Ministry of Finance collects data on the central-provincial division of revenues and expenditures, and at the provincial level, data exists for the provincial-prefecture division.

Box 3.3: Four Levels of Fiscal Contracts in Hebei

Level I. Provincial contract with the central government.
In 1988 Hebei was assigned a base remittance quota of Y1.52 billion, with
an annual increment of 4.5 per cent. In 1991 the provincial remittance
was Y2.02 billion.

Level II (A). Provincial contract with Shijiazhuang.
In Hebei, provincial fixed revenues include 30 per cent of turnover taxes
from the four centralized ministries (petroleum, petrochemical, power,
and nonferrous metals), business taxes of banks and insurance companies, the direct tax revenues and profit remittances of provincial-owned
enterprises, and 70 per cent of resource tax revenues. Hebei officials report
that the first three items yield about Y500-600 million per year net of
loss subsidies. Resource taxes yield another Y100 million or more.
  City fixed revenues comprise the 13 local taxes, the urban maintenance
and construction tax, pollution fees and the water resource tax. Shared
revenues include direct taxes and profit remittances of city-owned enterprises, turnover taxes, collective enterprise income taxes, the construction tax and agricultural taxes.
  In 1988 Shijiazhuang's base remittance quota was set at Y384 million,
with an annual increment of 5.5 per cent. In 1992 Shijiazhuang remitted
about Y500 million under the contract. In addition, 50 per cent of the
city's turnover tax revenues were set aside as provincial fixed revenues,
under the tax-sharing arrangement introduced in 1987.

Level II (B). Provincial contract with Xinji City.
Counties normally have revenue-sharing arrangements with prefectures/
cities. As one of the nine "line item county cities", however, Xinji has a
direct budgetary link with the province, bypassing the prefectural level.
Placed under fiscal contracting in 1986, Xinji was assigned a remittance
quota of Y27.41 million, with an annual increment of 5.5 per cent. Its
remittance was Y35.91 million in 1992.

  In 1991, aggregate statistics show that, before revenue sharing, the provincial level (including Beijing, Shanghai, and Tianjin)
collected 22.3 per cent of total revenues, the prefecture level (including prefectural level cities) 40.1 per cent, the county level
22.9 per cent, and the township level 14.9 per cent. On the expenditure side, the provincial level spent 30.8 per cent, the prefectural level, 28.3 per cent, the county level 30.1 per cent, and
the townships 10.8 per cent (Ministry of Finance 1992a, p. 151).

Level III (A). Shijiazhuang's contracts with its six city districts.
Each district has a base remittance quota with an annual increment of
6.5 per cent.

Level III (B). Shijiazhuang's contracts with its four suburban counties. Each
county has a contract with a base remittance quota and an annual increment of 7.5 per cent. The higher incremental growth in their remittance
quotas is justified by the fact that the counties are excluded from the
provincial tax-sharing arrangement, and therefore will have higher buoyancy in their revenue base.

Level IV. Xinji's contract with Nanzhiqiu Township.
Through the late 1980s, townships received increasing budgetary autonomy. They have fixed expenditure assignments (to cover agricultural
expenses and water conservancy, basic education, health and welfare).

In 1986-1988, Nanzhiqiu had a fixed rate revenue-sharing contract with
Xinji that allowed it to retain 11 per cent of total revenues up to the revenue
base, and 80 per cent of excess revenues. The revenue base was set at
Y656,000, and the remittance base was set at Y584,000.

During 1989-91 the township was on a contract that fixed quotas for
revenues and expenditures, with a 90 per cent retention rate on excess
revenues. The "base numbers " were fixed at Y925,000 for revenues, and
Y267,000 for expenditures.

In 1992 the township was placed on a three-year contract, with a fixed
remittance quota of Y1.275 million. The remittance quota will increase
by 8 per cent in 1993 and 9 per cent in 1994. In addition, the new "special agricultural products tax" introduced in 1989 is treated separately
outside the revenue-sharing base. Eighty per cent of the revenues from
this tax go to the city, with the township retaining only 20 per cent.

City Finance

Sources of revenue at the city level include its shares of sales and
profits taxes on all city enterprises, collectives and private businesses; revenues from the urban maintenance and construction
tax; some minor local taxes; and user charges and fees levied by
public utilities. City governments have the right, jointly with the
price bureaus, to set fees for public utilities, though the use of
this right appears to be limited (World Bank 1990b).

Because of the industry-centered structure of taxation in the PRC (see Chapter 2), most revenues are produced in cities, where industries are concentrated. Table 3.6 shows per capita revenues to be highly correlated with city size. Across provinces, the degree of urbanization is an important determinant of revenue capacity. In Sichuan Province, Chongqing and Chengdu cities produce 39 per cent of all revenues; all cities together produced 49.8 per cent of total revenues, whereas the province produced 23.6 per cent and counties 27.8 per cent (*Sichuan Jingji Nianjian* 1986).

More importantly, cities have traditionally provided revenue surpluses that help to finance other levels of government. The

Table 3.6: Per Capita Revenues by City Size, 1991

Category	Population (millions)	Yuan
National Average		311.8
Cities, by size of population		
over 2 million		1,043.3
1-2 million		711.4
0.5-1 million		566.3
0.2-0.5 million		354.7
< 0.2 million		148.0
Selected Cities		
Shenzhen	0.43	5,953.5
Shanghai	7.86	1,752.7
Dalian	2.42	1,200.3
Guangzhou	3.62	1,196.1
Tianjin	5.09	1,055.2
Beijing	7.05	973.1
Chongqing	3.01	880.4
Shenyang	4.58	644.7
Chengdu	2.84	573.5
All "Costal Cities"	28.74	1,154.3
All "Line Item Citie	34.76	888.0
All Provincial Capit	48.38	706.1

Source: State Statistical Bureau 1992, pp. 672-682.

1991 budgetary statistics for Guangdong show that the 19 cities produced 66.6 per cent of all revenues but accounted for only 34.4 per cent of all expenditures, providing a large surplus for financing expenditures at the provincial and county levels, as well as remittance to the center. This is the cause of the great resentment felt by many provinces toward the "line item cities" reform, since the loss of a single large city can plunge a province into subsidy status, as happened in Hubei and Sichuan.

County Finance

The PRC's 2271 county level units (including county-level cities) had total revenues of Y73.6 billion or 25 per cent of total national revenues in 1989. An average county had revenues of Y31.35 million although there were 95 counties with revenues in excess of Y100 million (Liu and Xia 1991). Nationwide, in 1989, more than half of all counties depended on subsidies from higher levels to cover approved expenditures. In Hebei province 70 per cent of all counties had deficits in 1991 (*Hebei Jingji Tongji Nianjian* 1992, pp. 579-601). Anecdotal evidence indicates that fiscal resources are very tight at the county level, and the situation has deteriorated. This is because the bulk of county budgets are absorbed by salaries of government personnel and minimal operating costs of government offices, both of which have grown rapidly in the reform period. In Gansu Province, for example, where three-fourths of the 85 counties depend on subsidies to cover costs, 80 per cent of all expenditures at county governments go to personnel costs (*Caizheng* 1991).

Township Finance

There are over 50,000 township level financial units, each with an average of four staff members (Zhang Hongbing 1990). Because of their newness, many township fiscal offices are not entirely independent of the county offices. In many areas, township budgets are embedded in county budgets, where township revenues from shared taxes are reported simply as a county expenditure under the category of "others" (*Caizheng* 1990).

The Role of Township and Village Enterprises

Throughout the reform period, TVEs have been the most dynamic sector in the Chinese economy, growing at an average annual rate of 23.3 per cent in gross income, or 27.5 per cent by gross output value. By 1991, they numbered 19.1 million enterprises, with 1.44 million collectively owned enterprises at the township and village levels, and 17.6 million individually owned, private, or joint urban rural enterprises. Together they employed 96.1 million workers and, as shown in Table 3.7, produced gross income of Y655.6 billion (State Statistical Bureau 1992).

TVEs are by far the dominant source of revenue in the rural PRC. In 1990 they paid Y27.55 billion in taxes, more than three times the total agricultural tax of Y8.8 billion. Their 1989 tax payment of Y27.25 billion accounted for 37 per cent of all fiscal revenues at and below the county level. In some counties they are the major tax producers, especially in suburban counties ringing urban areas. Table 3.8 shows the budgetary breakdown of a suburban county in Beijing, where TVEs account for about half of total revenues. Table 3.9 presents the accounts of three townships in the county, where the size of the TVE sector is the primary factor separating a rich township from a poor one.

Table 3.7: Township and Village Enterprises
(Y billion)

Year	Gross Income	Total Taxes	Income Taxes	Profits
1978	43.14	2.20	0.74	8.81
1980	59.61	2.57	0.79	11.84
1982	77.18	4.47	1.25	11.55
1984	126.82	7.91	2.63	12.87
1986	222.36	13.73	3.86	16.10
1988	423.22	23.65	5.96	25.92
1990	521.86	27.55	5.71	23.27
1991	655.60	33.38	6.81	28.47

Source: State Statistical Bureau 1992, p. 390.

The growth of TVEs has strengthened township and county budgets, increasing the county's share in the consolidated provincial budgets. In Anhui, this share rose from 35 per cent in 1978 to over 40 per cent in 1987. Related to this, townships have become net revenue producers: in 1987 townships produced revenues of Y1.01 billion but spent only Y870 million, while the province was on the whole in net deficit status (*Anhui Tongji Nianjian* 1988).

Because of their revenue potential, TVEs are the natural focus of efforts to expand local revenue bases. Many provinces have taken an active approach to helping deficit regions become self-

Table 3.8: Revenue Composition of a County Budget[a]
(Y10,000)

Item	1985	1986	1987	1988	1989
Total Revenues	8,345	9,890	11,744	14,474	17,253
of which: Township Revenues	-	6,896	6,483	8,423	9,340
As Per Cent of Total (%)	-	69.7	55.2	58.2	54.1
1. Enterprise Incomes	(302)	(123)	76	38	-
by Sector:					
Industry	435	350	257	219	-
Construction	12	9	8	8	-
Transport	8	5	3	3	-
Agricultural Machinery	29	32	37	-	-
Commerce, Grain	(975)	(745)	(583)	(516)	-
Materials	130	145	166	101	-
Others	55	76	182	217	-
Education and Health	4	5	7	5	-
2. Tax Revenues	8,557	9,660	11,356	14,210	-
of which:					
Industrial and Commercial	8,276	9,326	10,999	13,846	-
Agricultural Tax	280	333	350	332	-
Real Estate Registration	1	1	-	-	-
Farmland Occupation Tax	-	-	6	32	-
3. Other Incomes	38	301	261	190	-
4. Earmarked Revenues	52	52	51	60	-
5. Loss Subsidies for SOEs	-	-	-	23	-

[a] The sample is a county in suburban Beijing.

Source: Sun, Wang, Yao, and Yamamoto 1991, p. 92.

Table 3.9: Revenues of Three Townships in a Suburban County
(Y'000)

Item	Township A 1988	Township A 1989	Township B 1988	Township B 1989	Township C 1988	Township C 1989
Total Revenues	10,961	12,060	39,097	61,254	2,536	2,336
of which: Agriculture	1,754	2,801	6,986	9,641	219	253
1. Budgetary Revenues	8,570	7,601	1,010	13,075	2,334	2,083
a. Township Share	n.a.	n.a.	n.a.	n.a.	738	624
b. Special Agriculture and Forestry Products Tax	76	76	190	232	191	223
c. Agriculture Tax	4	0	32	149	28	30
d. Slaughter Tax	0	0	4	4	0	0
e. Industrial/Commercial Tax	8,163	7,362	10,611	12,207	2,089	1,808
Business Tax	1,510	1,482	1,338	1,070	486	588
VAT	1,531	2,245	2,928	4,639	678	716
Product Tax	661	107	1,557	830	153	33
Income Tax	4,461	3,529	4,787	5,667	773	471
f. Urban Construction Tax	75	0	70	140	0	0
g. Real Estate Tax	89	101	0	0	0	0
h. Farmland Occupation Tax	107	0	5	7	0	0
i. Personal Income Adjustment Tax	15	21	0	147	3	0
j. Stamp Tax	0	0	0	80	0	0
k. Vehicle Tax	26	32	91	108	0	0
l. Other Taxes	13	9	7	2	23	22
2. Extrabudgetary Revenues	98	420	585	753	179	215
Education Surcharge	98	420	585	753	179	215
3. Self-Raised Revenues	2,293	4,038	27,502	47,425	23	38
a. Contract Fees	150	260	20,520	38,490	0	0
Farmland	150	260	381	1,277	0	0
Fish ponds	0	0	480	560	0	0
TVEs	0	0	15,159	30,093	0	0
Other Contract Fees	0	0	4,500	656	0	0
b. Various Collection Incomes	0	0	0	0	0	0
c. Various Fees	2,143	3,778	6,982	8,935	53	43
Land Management and Town Construction	0	9	0	0	0	1
Transport	95	130	588	743	12	13
Education	463	1,022	0	0	0	0
Management Fees from TVEs and Trading	0	80	120	164	0	0
Agricultural Production Fees Paid to Collectives	1,524	2,465	5,899	7,419	0	0
Water Fees	24	25	45	46	0	0
Electricity	100	130	345	368	0	0
Mechanized Plowing Fees	440	550	1,210	1,981	0	0
Chemical Fertilizer, Seeds	960	1,760	4,299	5,024	0	0
Social Security and Civil Affairs Fees	45	53	95	100	41	29
Others	17	20	280	510	0	0
d. Various Contributions	0	0	0	0	-30	-5

Source: Sun, Wang, Yao, and Yamamoto 1991, p. 104.

sufficient. For example, in the mid-1980s, Hubei Province adopted the method of giving deficit prefectures and counties a one-time, lump-sum subsidy to finance investment in revenue growth, equal to three years' fiscal subsidies. The recipients are expected to become fiscally self-sufficient within three years, at which point they stop receiving subsidies, and even begin remitting a small surplus to the provincial budget (Shen 1985 and World Bank 1992a, Annex 3.3). In Gansu the provincial five-year and ten-year plans contain numerical targets for turning deficit counties into self-sufficient ones *(Caizheng* 1991).

Governments at the county and township levels depend heavily on tax revenues, and on extrabudgetary resources pro-

---

Box 3.4: Types of Taxes on Township and Village Enterprises

Taxes

1. Income Tax

2. Turnover Taxes   Product Tax
                                          Value-Added Tax
                                          Business Tax

3. Tax Surcharges and   Urban Maintenance
        Minor Taxes   and Construction Tax
                                          Lathe Use Tax
                                          Collective Enterprise Bonus Tax
                                          Construction Tax

Nontax Levies

1. Contracted Profits   Quota
                                          Over-Quota

2. Management Fee

3. Ad Hoc Charges and Fees   Pension Contributions
                                          Culture-Education
                                          Land-Use
                                          Road-Building

4. "Voluntary Contributions" and Loans

Source: Adapted from Oi 1992.

vided by TVEs to finance local development and other government expenditures—in Jiangsu, for example, the province has imposed a mandatory contribution of Y120-180 per worker in TVEs to finance agricultural investment. Altogether, that TVEs in the province turn over 65-75 per cent of their pretax profits to local governments in the form of taxes, profit, remittance, fees and contributions. Nationwide the average share contributed is estimated to be 53 per cent, and 35-45 per cent in Guangdong and Shandong provinces (World Bank 1991). One survey found that TVEs in Hunan Province are subjected to over 100 types of fees, paid to more than 60 administrative units and agencies (Furusawa 1990). Box 3.4 lists taxes and levies paid by TVEs in a Shandong County.

CENTRAL-LOCAL EXPENDITURE DIVISIONS

The way expenditure assignments are divided among levels of government is considered of fundamental importance in the efficient provision of public goods. According to the decentralization theorem, "each public service should be provided by the jurisdiction having control over the minimum geographic area that would internalize benefits and costs of such provision" (Oates 1972). This is expected to lead to the most efficient supply because it brings decision making closer to the users for greater accountability and fiscal responsibility. Local provision is likely to cater better to local tastes and needs; it eliminates multiple layers of jurisdiction, and it enhances interregional competition and innovation (Shah 1991). However, these advantages are reduced when the public services have to cover a large area because local provision would lead to undersupply. The advantages are also offset by the possible loss of economies of scale, where local provision would result in higher unit costs of service (including higher administrative overhead costs). Because of such trade-offs, the optimal level of provision depends on the innate characteristics of the public goods themselves. Table 3.10 shows the conceptual basis of expenditure assignment for some major types of public goods.

Available data on intergovernmental expenditure divisions shows that the PRC conforms for the most part to this division

Table 3.10: Conceptual Basis of Expenditure Assignment

Expenditure Category	Service Responsibility	Provision of Service	Comment
Defence	F	F	Benefits/costs national in scope
Foreign Affairs	F	F	"
International Trade	F	F	"
Environment	F	S,L	"
Currency, Banking	F	F	"
Interstate Commerce	F	F	"
Immigration	F	F	"
Unemployment Insurance	F	F	"
Airlines and Railways	F	F	"
Industry and Agriculture	F,S,L	S,L	Significant interstate spillovers
Education	F,S,L	S,L	Transfers in kind
Health	F,S,L	S,L	"
Social Welfare	F,S,L	S,L	"
Police	S,L	S,L	Primarily Local Benefits
Highways	F,S,L	S,L	Some roads with significant interstate spillovers, others primarily local
Natural Resources	F,S,L	S,L	Promotes a common market

F = Federal; S = State; L = Local

Source: Shah 1991.

of labor as well as to international practice (Shah 1991). However, the expenditure divisions are an imperfect guide to intergovernmental divisions of responsibility because the level of service provision does not always coincide with the level of expenditure. For some services, while the administration or expenditure occurs at the local level, funding is provided by the central level. One example is price subsidies for grain, oil, and cotton, which were transferred to local administration in 1985, but most of the funding is still provided from the central budget. Similarly, while local budgets accounted for about 45 per cent of total budgetary expenditures on capital expenditure in 1978, approval and funding for investment were at that time largely determined by central plans. In contrast, the share of capital spending has shifted in the reform period to the point where the central government accounted for three fourths of total budgetary investment in the 1990s, but local governments have far greater autonomy and responsibility for local investment and are widely perceived to be playing a more active role in local development.

Another caveat to bear in mind when interpreting PRC budgetary data is that public expenditures are undercounted, as noted in Chapter 1. Throughout this discussion of expenditures and their major components, adjusted data will be used whenever possible to include enterprise subsidies. (Budgetary accounting in the PRC continues to treat enterprise loss subsidies as negative revenue, rather than as an expenditure.) A more intractable problem is that many social services, such as subsidized housing (see Chapter 5), pensions, child care, and even schooling, are at present provided by SOEs and administrative agencies. Even though the costs of providing these social services are ultimately borne by the budget, through reduced profits and taxes, they are not included in the government budget.

Even given these limitations, a detailed examination of intergovernmental expenditure assignments in the PRC is nevertheless necessary to understanding intergovernmental fiscal relations. In fact, a central problem is that, through the process of reform, expenditure responsibilities have become increasingly mismatched with revenue assignments.

This has been a serious problem for local governments because through the reform period, the locus of expenditures shifted progressively toward lower levels of government, with the aggregated local share rising from 53 per cent of the total in 1978 to over 60 per cent in 1990 (Table 3.11). Within the local sector, expenditures also appear to be shifting downward from the provincial level to cities and counties. This trend can be attributed to a number of factors, including a downward transfer of expenditure responsibilities in the process of decentralizing reform, a changing structure of costs that has affected local expenditures more heavily, and a changing role for the budget that altered the roles of all levels of government.

The government appears to have paid scant attention to restructuring the division of functions and expenditure responsibilities among levels of government through the reform period. Instead, with decentralization as the guiding principle, fiscal reform concentrated on reducing the central government's role in managing local budgets and turned its attention to revamping revenue divisions.

In the absence of a conscious effort to rethink the division of functions among government levels, their prereform roles have largely prevailed. In the prereform division of labor, the central government manages the overall economic development program, making capital investment decisions, managing external balances and national defense. Local governments are in charge of local administration and the provision of social services including education, health, and welfare.

Given this general division of labor, expenditures can be expected to shift toward local governments in the process of reform. First, the reform program called for the government to reduce its role in direct economic management. Accordingly, the government has sharply curtailed budgetary outlays on capital construction, transferring investment responsibilities, along with financial resources, to the enterprise and banking sectors. Second, the program adopted a more open stance toward the rest of the world, which in turn allowed defense expenditures to be scaled back. Third, reforms also called for transferring some of the social costs borne by SOEs, such as the provision of pensions, welfare, health care, and housing, to the private and public sectors. This has required some increases in government expenditure on social services. Finally, the reform process has allowed wages to rise, significantly raising the cost of providing government services and social welfare.

These changes can be seen in the third panel of Table 2.2, p. 62 where capital construction expenditures (the broad category including working capital, technical transformation, and geological prospecting) fell from 12.9 per cent of GNP in 1979 to 3.7 per cent in 1991. National defense fell from 5.6 per cent to 1.7 per cent, while social expenditures, administration and price subsidies together rose from 7.3 per cent to 7.7 per cent of GNP. These changes generally favored a reduction in central government outlays but raised local outlays, since the first two broad changes were primarily central responsibilities, while the last three are primarily local responsibilities.

This intergovernmental division of labor and expected trends are confirmed by data in Table 3.11 (Part C), which show central expenditures concentrated in capital construction and national defense, which comprised 45 per cent and 28 per cent, respectively, of the total in 1978, and 31 per cent and 19 per cent in 1991. In contrast, local expenditures on these two components together comprised only 8 per cent of the total in 1991, while culture,

Table 3.11: Central and Local Budgetary Expenditures, 1978-1991

	1978 Central	1978 Local	1988 Central	1988 Local	1989 Central	1989 Local	1990 Central	1990 Local	1991 Central	1991 Local
Part A					*Yuan Billion*					
Total	56.6	66.1	121.3	193.9	133.3	230.6	158.3	244.8	173.3	257.0
Capital Construction	25.2	20.0	47.8	14.5	46.3	16.3	54.2	18.4	53.5	19.2
Working Capital	1.7	4.1	0.7	0.3	0.8	0.5	0.8	0.3	0.7	0.3
Technological Upgrading and R&D	2.1	4.2	4.8	10.3	5.2	9.5	5.5	9.9	6.1	12.3
Geological Prospecting	0.6	1.4	3.2	0.0	3.3	0.0	3.6	0.0	3.8	0.0
Industry, Transport and Commerce	1.0	0.8	1.3	2.6	1.3	3.2	1.4	3.3	1.5	3.7
Agriculture	0.2	7.5	1.5	14.4	1.7	18.1	2.2	20.0	2.2	22.0
Culture, Education, Science and Health	1.3	10.0	6.1	42.5	6.4	49.0	7.2	54.6	7.8	62.1
Social Relief and Welfare	0.0	1.9	0.0	4.1	0.0	4.9	0.0	5.5	0.1	6.7
Defense	16.1	0.7	21.6	0.2	24.9	0.2	28.8	0.2	32.7	0.3
Government Administration	0.4	4.5	3.9	20.0	4.5	24.0	5.7	27.2	6.4	31.6
Government Debt Service	0.0	0.0	7.7	0.0	7.2	0.0	19.0	0.0	24.6	0.0
SOE Losses	4.5	7.1	15.3	29.3	22.8	37.1	21.0	36.9	23.6	27.4
Price Subsidies	0.0	0.0	3.6	28.1	3.8	33.5	4.0	34.1	5.0	32.1
Others	3.5	3.9	3.8	26.6	5.1	34.3	4.9	33.9	5.3	39.3
Part B				*Central and Local Percentage Share for each Expenditure Category*						
Total	46.1	53.9	38.5	61.5	36.6	63.4	39.3	60.7	40.3	59.7
Capital Construction	55.8	44.2	76.7	23.3	74.0	26.0	74.7	25.3	73.6	26.4
Working Capital	29.3	70.7	70.0	30.0	61.5	38.5	72.7	27.3	70.0	30.0
Technological Upgrading and R&D	33.3	66.7	31.8	68.2	35.4	64.6	35.7	64.3	33.2	66.8
Geological Prospecting	30.0	70.0	100.0	0.0	100.0	0.0	100.0	0.0	100.0	0.0
Industry, Transport and Commerce	55.6	44.4	33.3	66.7	28.9	71.1	29.8	70.2	28.8	71.2
Agriculture	2.6	97.4	9.4	90.6	8.6	91.4	9.9	90.1	9.1	90.9
Culture, Education, Science and Health	11.5	88.5	12.6	87.4	11.6	88.4	11.7	88.3	11.2	88.8
Social Relief and Welfare	0.0	100.0	0.0	100.0	0.0	100.0	0.0	100.0	1.5	98.5
Defense	95.8	4.2	99.1	0.9	99.2	0.8	99.3	0.7	99.1	0.9
Government Administration	8.2	91.8	16.3	83.7	15.8	84.2	17.3	82.7	16.8	83.2
Government Debt Service	-	-	100.0	0.0	100.0	0.0	100.0	0.0	100.0	0.0
SOE Losses	38.8	61.2	34.3	65.7	38.0	62.0	36.2	63.8	46.3	53.7
Price Subsidies	-	-	11.4	88.6	10.2	89.8	10.5	89.5	13.5	86.5
Others	47.3	52.7	12.5	87.5	12.9	87.1	12.6	87.4	11.9	88.1

Part C

					Per Cent of Total Expenditure					
Total	100	100	100	100	100	100	100	100	100	100
Capital Construction	44.55	30.26	39.40	7.48	34.75	7.07	34.24	7.52	30.86	7.47
Working Capital	3.01	6.20	0.58	0.15	0.60	0.22	0.51	0.12	0.40	0.12
Technological Upgrading and R&D	3.71	6.35	3.96	5.31	3.90	4.12	3.47	4.04	3.52	4.79
Geological Prospecting	1.06	2.12	2.64	0.00	2.48	0.00	2.27	0.00	2.19	0.00
Industry, Transport and Commerce	1.77	1.21	1.07	1.34	0.98	1.39	0.88	1.35	0.87	1.44
Agriculture	0.35	11.35	1.24	7.42	1.28	7.85	1.39	8.17	1.27	8.56
Culture, Education, Science and Health	2.30	15.13	5.03	21.91	4.80	21.25	4.55	22.30	4.50	24.17
Social Relief and Welfare	0.00	2.87	0.00	2.11	0.00	2.12	0.00	2.25	0.06	2.61
Defense	28.45	1.06	17.81	0.10	18.69	0.09	18.20	0.08	18.86	0.12
Government Administration	0.71	6.81	3.21	10.31	3.38	10.41	3.60	11.11	3.69	12.30
Government Debt Service	0.00	0.00	6.35	0.00	5.40	0.00	12.00	0.00	14.19	0.00
SOE Losses	7.90	0.00	n.a.	n.a.	n.a.	n.a.	n.a.	n.a.	n.a.	n.a.
Price Subsidies	0.00	0.00	2.97	14.49	2.85	14.52	2.53	13.93	2.88	12.49
Others	6.19	5.90	3.13	13.72	3.83	14.87	3.10	13.85	3.06	15.29

Part D

					Per Cent of GNP					
Total	15.77	18.42	8.67	13.87	8.44	14.61	9.10	14.07	9.31	13.81
Capital Construction	7.02	5.57	3.42	1.04	2.93	1.03	3.11	1.06	2.87	1.03
Working Capital	0.47	1.14	0.05	0.02	0.05	0.03	0.05	0.02	0.04	0.02
Technological Upgrading and R&D	0.59	1.17	0.34	0.74	0.33	0.60	0.32	0.57	0.33	0.66
Geological Prospecting	0.17	0.39	0.23	0.00	0.21	0.00	0.21	0.00	0.20	0.00
Industry, Transport and Commerce	0.28	0.22	0.09	0.19	0.08	0.20	0.08	0.19	0.08	0.20
Agriculture	0.06	2.09	0.11	1.03	0.11	1.15	0.13	1.15	0.12	1.18
Culture, Education, Science and Health	0.36	2.79	0.44	3.04	0.41	3.10	0.41	3.14	0.42	3.34
Social Relief and Welfare	0.00	0.53	0.00	0.29	0.00	0.31	0.00	0.32	0.01	0.36
Defense	4.49	0.20	1.54	0.01	1.58	0.01	1.66	0.01	1.76	0.02
Government Administration	0.11	1.25	0.28	1.43	0.29	1.52	0.33	1.56	0.34	1.70
Government Debt Service	0.00	0.00	0.55	0.00	0.46	0.00	1.09	0.00	1.32	0.00
SOE Losses	1.24	1.97	1.09	2.10	1.44	2.35	1.21	2.12	1.27	1.47
Price Subsidies	0.00	0.00	0.26	2.01	0.24	2.12	0.23	1.96	0.27	1.72
Others	0.98	1.09	0.27	1.90	0.32	2.17	0.28	1.95	0.28	2.11

Note: The breakdown of central and local figures for SOE Loss in 1978 are estimated from the average of the same data from 1988 to 1991.

Source: Ministry of Finance. The Local Expenditures include the Earmarked Transfers from the Central Government.

education, and health absorbed 24 per cent; administration 12.3 per cent; and price subsidies 12.5 per cent in budgetary accounts.

THE MAJOR COMPONENTS OF LOCAL EXPENDITURES

Price Subsidies

In Table 3.12, regrouping expenditures by major categories shows price subsidies to be the largest component of local budgets, absorbing 25 per cent to over 30 per cent of the total during 1986-1990. These numbers differ from budgetary statistics provided by the Ministry of Finance, which show expenditures on "price subsidies" to be only Y38.1 billion in 1990, of which Y34.1 billion was borne by local governments (absorbing 14 per cent of local expenditures). This is because budgetary numbers refer only to what is paid out under the category of "price subsidies," and exclude payments to enterprises to cover losses "due to (price) policy." This recalculation attempts to include all budgetary costs of compensations for losses or profits foregone as a result of government pricing policy. To be comprehensive, the accounting should include all compensations in the form of explicit budgetary appropriations, tax concessions, or reduced profit remittance obligations in enterprise contracts. The true extent of price subsidization is impossible to measure with available data.

In budgetary statistics, "price subsidies" did not even appear as an expenditure category until 1986. Previously, the cost of appropriations for price subsidies were simply netted out from the revenue side in order to balance budgetary ledgers. Even after 1985, the coverage of subsidies remained divided between "price subsidies" and subsidies for enterprise losses, with the latter still counted as negative revenues. Because of the incomplete coverage, budgetary figures on price subsidies are understated. Through the 1980s, as enterprise losses grew in grain trading and in the coal and oil extraction industries, so did the degree of underestimation of subsidies in budgetary statistics—for 1990, the budgetary Y38.1 billion was only 40 per cent of the total for subsidies and enterprise losses (Table 3.13).

Table 3.12: Recalculated Local Expenditures
(per cent)

	1986	1987	1988	1989	1990
Capital Construction	13.15	9.82	8.01	6.76	7.06
Technical Transformation	5.02	4.32	4.54	3.43	3.31
Makeshift Building	0.48	0.39	0.38	0.34	0.29
Geological Prospecting	0.01	0.01	0.01	0.01	0.01
Science and Technology	0.89	0.82	0.66	0.63	0.66
Working Capital	0.22	0.12	0.13	0.19	0.13
Agricultural Support	3.36	3.69	3.72	4.51	4.74
Agriculture and Fisheries	4.18	4.10	3.58	3.23	3.25
Industry, Transport, Commerce	1.54	1.36	1.32	1.35	1.32
Urban Maintenance	4.55	4.53	4.29	4.35	4.11
Urban Employment Placement	0.25	0.20	0.15	0.12	0.11
Culture, Education, Health	21.26	21.53	20.75	20.24	21.03
Science	0.39	0.88	0.80	0.74	0.77
Other Administration	3.15	3.60	2.62	2.84	3.23
Welfare Assistance	2.32	2.37	2.10	2.11	2.18
Militia	0.13	0.13	0.11	0.10	0.01
Air Defense	0.00	0.00	0.00	0.00	0.00
Administrative Overhead	9.10	9.34	10.14	10.27	11.05
Price Subsidies	15.90	16.59	14.45	14.36	13.62
Others	3.97	5.39	4.86	5.75	5.06
Special	0.96	1.30	2.50	2.78	3.22
Enterprise Loss Subsidies	9.20	9.51	14.87	15.91	14.75
Total Subsidies	25.09	26.10	29.32	30.27	28.37
Development	28.06	24.58	22.54	20.94	21.08
Administration	17.97	18.40	17.66	17.69	18.85
Social	23.83	24.11	23.01	22.47	23.32

Notes: Total Subsidies = items 19+22
   Development = items 1-7+10+13
   Administration = items 8+9+14+18
   Social = items 11+12+15

Source: Ministry of Finance.

Administrative Costs

The cost of government administration is also impossible to calculate precisely with available budgetary data because personnel costs are spread over several categories. In recent years, under calls to reduce administrative overhead, more administrative costs

Table 3.13: Price Subsidies and Enterprise Loss Subsidies
(Y100 million)

	1986	1987	1988	1989	1990	1991
Total Subsidies	582.26	671.03	763.28	972.43	959.68	884.01
Central	200.91	262.43	189.20	265.74	249.80	286.66
Local	381.35	408.60	574.08	706.69	709.88	597.35
SOE Loss Subsidies	324.78	376.43	446.46	598.88	567.88	510.24
Central	185.00	227.54	153.10	227.45	209.76	236.44
Local	139.78	148.89	293.36	371.43	369.12	273.80
Price Subsidies	257.48	294.60	316.82	373.55	380.80	373.77
Central	15.91	34.89	36.10	38.29	40.04	50.22
Local	241.57	259.71	280.72	335.26	340.76	323.55

Source: Ministry of Finance.

have been diverted to functional or sectoral departments and hidden under other budgetary categories.

The largest component is "administration," which includes civil servants in government agencies (excluding school teachers). These costs rose from Y6 billion in 1979 to Y38 billion in 1991, growing at an average annual rate of 16.6 per cent in nominal terms, much faster than the 9.4 per cent annual growth in total budgetary expenditures. As a result, "administration" grew in expenditure shares from 3.9 per cent in 1979 to 8.7 per cent in 1991 (Table 2.2, page 62). Other administrative costs are borne by sectoral departments such as agriculture, forestry, fisheries, industry, transport, and commerce.

Because the division of expenditures between central and local governments is mainly by subordination relations, administrative costs are overwhelmingly borne at the local level, which accounts for about 80 per cent of the total, and the combined costs under "administration" and the sectoral departments absorb nearly 20 per cent of total local expenditures (Table 3.12).

Administrative costs have risen rapidly for three reasons. First and by far the most important is the rapid rise of urban wages, which has increased labor costs in government agencies. During 1978 to 1990, average wages in the state sector rose from Y644 to Y2140, growing at an average annual rate of 10.5 per cent. While the average wage for civil servants is slightly lower than that for workers in SOEs, government salaries tend to follow the trend set by SOEs – in 1990 the average annual wage in SOEs was Y2347 compared to Y2113 for government employees and Y2180 for workers in social institutions. If civil service wages grew at the same rate as the state sector, wage increases alone would have accounted for 10.5 per cent of the 13 per cent annual growth in local expenditures on administration.

In government administration, rising wages could have been offset by a reduction in the size of the work force, which would have seemed logical given the government's announced intent to reduce its role in economic management. However, contrary to expectation, the number of administrative personnel has risen by 45 per cent during 1978-1990, from 20 million to 29 million, an annual growth of 3.1 per cent (Lee 1990). In more recent years, the number of administrative personnel has reportedly grown at an even faster rate – 5 per cent a year. Both are higher than the overall rate of growth in state sector employment, of 2.8 per cent a year during 1978-1990 (State Statistical Bureau 1991).

In the government's defense, it can be said that reforms have imposed some new demands for administrative services: one example is the creation of a new layer of financial management and tax collection at the township level to handle the greatly expanded work load created by decollectivization and the diversification of the rural economy. With decollectivization in agriculture, instead of collecting taxes from 6 million production teams that were tightly controlled by the 50,000 communes, the government now collects from nearly 200 million farm households. Moreover, the rapid growth of rural enterprises and trade means that taxes have grown more varied and complicated, as well as more lucrative, justifying the creation of 47,000 new finance offices at the township level. However, this apparently added only approximately 200,000 staff members (Zhang Hongbing 1990).

Another cause of the increase in the number of administrative personnel is the inclusion of retirees in statistical reporting: because there is no social security program for government employees, the cost of pensions is carried by current budgetary outlays, so that payroll reports include both active and retired members of government employees. For example, the State Statistical Bureau gives the number of employees in government,

Party and social organization as 10.79 million at the end of 1990, while others report the figure as 9 million. The difference is probably due to the inclusion of pensioners in the larger number.

However, the government has also been slow to cut or even transfer personnel from departments that are obviated by the reform process. A prime example is the hierarchy of price bureaus that extends from the central level down to the counties. With the reduction of state price control and the progressive freeing of prices to market determination, the bureaus' functions have been largely eliminated. Yet the bureaus have expanded since the mid-1980s. In one medium-sized city in Jiangsu, the city level bureau had, in mid-1991, a staff of 49 to supervise 38 locally controlled prices and to oversee the work of ten price bureaus in the subordinate counties and cities, each with an average staff of ten people. These staffing levels had grown several fold since 1983, when there had been 12 in the city bureau, and 3-4 at each of the county level offices.[21] The government's inability or unwillingness to lay off unneeded workers is attributable to the resistance to the expectation that pervades the whole state sector of lifelong employment. But this attitude often goes further, to seeing the government as the employer of last resort. For example, the civil service has absorbed many military personnel who were cut in the process of trimming defense expenditure. In addition to taking on demobilized soldiers, in some areas government departments have even been asked to take on technical school graduates unable to find placement in the productive sectors (*Xinjiang Caizheng Nianjian* 1986).

Culture, Education, Science, and Health

"Culture, education, science, and health" (CESH) is the second largest component of local expenditures in the budget (after price subsidies). Overall expenditures on this component have grown rapidly in the reform period, from Y11.3 billion in 1978 to Y77 billion planned in the 1992 draft budget, an average growth of 14.7 per cent a year in nominal expenditures. The local share was budgeted at Y68.2 billion, absorbing nearly one quarter of total local outlays. Education absorbs close to 60 per cent of CESH.

---

[21] Christine Wong's interview with city officials in June 1991.

Health care is a distant second, with another 20-24 per cent of the total (Table 3.14).

Budgetary expenditures on education grew from Y6.56 billion in 1978 to Y18.4 billion in 1985 and Y27.87 in 1988. In the 1992 draft budget, it received Y45.2 billion. This represents an average annual growth of 14.8 per cent in nominal terms during 1978-1992 (14.7 per cent since 1985).

The rapid growth has been partly a response to educational reforms implemented in 1985, and the Law on Compulsory Education, which was implemented in 1986. In these measures, the government called for promoting a universal, compulsory nine years of basic education throughout the PRC. To finance it, they called on all levels of government to allocate an increasing share of budgetary expenditures to compulsory education, and to provide it free of charge. Even before 1986, provincial budget reports had emphasized increasing resource allocation to education as part of the reform and modernization program. For example, Sichuan Province had raised its education and health expenditures from 25 per cent of the budget during the Fifth Five-Year Plan to 34 per cent in the Sixth Five-Year Plan (*Sichuan Jingji Nianjian* 1986). In Guangdong, Liaoning, and Sichuan Provinces education and CESH expenditures have grown faster than overall budgetary expenditures throughout the 1980s.

Table 3.14:   Breakdown of Expenditures on
Culture, Education, Science, and Health
(Y100 million)

Item	1978	1985	1986	1987	1988	1989	1990
Culture	4.1	11.3	13.5	13.5	15.4	16.4	17.9
Education	65.6	184.2	214.3	226.7	278.7	316.2	352.6
Health	27.3	70.3	83.1	86.2	101.0	74.4	81.2
Physical Education	2.5	7.5	9.9	10.0	11.7	13.8	16.0
Science	5.4	13.7	21.4	29.5	35.7	38.4	44.4
Communications and Broadcasting	3.8	11.2	14.2	14.2	16.1	17.9	19.7
Family Planning	2.0	7.5	8.0	8.5	10.0	11.7	13.5
Others	2.0	11.1	15.4	14.2	17.6	64.5	72.0
Total	112.7	316.7	379.9	402.8	486.1	553.3	617.3
Share of: Education (%)	58.2	58.2	56.4	56.3	57.3	57.1	57.1
Health (%)	24.2	22.2	21.9	21.4	20.8	13.4	13.2

Source: Ministry of Finance, *Zhongguo Caizheng Tongji* 1950-1988, p. 82.

Unfortunately, much of the increased spending has been swallowed by rising wage costs: from 1978 to 1990, CESH expenditures per capita rose from Y10.4 to Y46.3, a growth of 13.3 per cent a year. Netting out wage increases, however, the real improvement is closer to only 3-4 per cent a year. (If we use the GNP deflator, the real growth is 8 per cent a year. However, since state sector wages rose 10.5 per cent a year during the period, and since CESH is heavily weighted toward wages, the GNP deflator [of 4.9 per cent annual change] is far too small.) This typifies a central problem in local finance: with wage increases absorbing about two thirds of increased expenditures on CESH, relatively little is left for improving the scope and quality of services despite strenuous efforts to increase spending. The problem is especially acute in poor provinces, where expenditures on CESH can barely cover personnel costs.

Capital Construction

Prior to the beginning of reform, capital construction was the largest component of expenditure at both the central and local levels. In 1978, local governments spent a total of Y20 billion on capital construction, equal to 30 per cent of total local expenditures and 5.6 per cent of GNP. In 1991, local expenditures on capital construction had fallen to Y19.2 billion. As a share of local expenditures, this had fallen to 7.5 per cent (Table 3.11). The decline has been even steeper in real terms and as a share of GNP (to 1.0 per cent).

Assessing Expenditure Patterns

Two conclusions regarding the pattern of local spending can be drawn from this examination of the trends in local expenditure.

First, a large portion—nearly half of the total—is tied up in price subsidies and government administration, which absorbed 47 per cent of total local expenditures in 1990. Large parts of those expenditures may be considered nondiscretionary from the local perspective because they are largely determined by central policy and by forces unleashed by reform. Until May 1991, price subsidies grew rapidly as grain procurement and handling costs rose, and there was little local governments could do because the urban retail price of grain was determined by central policy. The cost of government administration was likewise inflated relentlessly by a reform program that allowed state sector wages to rise rapidly.

The second conclusion is that local governments have done little to adjust their operations to the decentralizing environment. Despite the significant cutback in planning and the use of direct control levers, the government bureaucracy continues to grow, with an organizational structure that has remained largely unchanged. This behavior permeates all levels of government, and has been an important cause of fiscal problems. For local governments, complaints of revenue inadequacy have to be partly considered against this expenditure behavior.

Given the behavioral inertia, spending on CESH and capital construction is highly constrained. Moreover, the trade-off between current consumption in CESH and investment in infrastructure poses for local governments difficulties that are compounded by fiscal incentives, where the surest path to revenue growth is local industrial development. Moreover, "success" for local governments is still largely measured by economic performance, and short-term job growth in the local economy depends on industrial growth. The overall effect of the competing needs is chronic underinvestment in infrastructure, and slow improvements in the provision of social services.

The regional effects of the expenditure pattern are more pernicious. This can be seen in the data on CESH expenditures, which shows a trend of growing regional disparities between 1978 and 1990. Table 3.15 presents per capita expenditures on CESH by province for 1978 and 1990. The 1978 average expenditure for the country was Y10.4 per capita. Excluding Tibet, the range was from Y7.8 in Sichuan, to Y28.7 in Beijing. At the bottom, Sichuan, Henan, Anhui, Hunan, Guizhou, Jiangsu, and Shandong were clustered together, with per capita expenditures of Y7.8 to Y8.6. By 1990, the ranking of the provinces by per capita CESH expenditure had changed only slightly, but the range had widened, with the ratio of top to bottom expenditures having grown from 3.94 to 5.38. At the top, Beijing spent Y148 per capita, compared to Y27.5 in Henan. Even among the top five spenders, the gap had widened: between first-placed Beijing and fourth and fifth-placed Qinghai and Xinjiang there was a difference of nearly Y70.

Table 3.15: Provincial Culture, Education, Science, and Health and Capital Construction Expenditures

	1978				1990			
	CESH Per Capita (Y)	CESH %E	CC %E	CESH+CC %E	CESH Per Capita (Y)	CESH %E	CC %E	CESH+CC %E
Top Five								
Beijing	28.7	11.9	53.4	65.3	147.9	23.4	17.3	40.7
Shanghai	27.8	11.7	40.6	52.7	128.4	22.7	10.7	33.4
Qinghai	24.9	13.4	34.4	47.8	106.9	23.5	18.5	42
Tianjin	24.3	12.1	41.4	53.5	80.4	21	8.5	39.5
Ningxia	22.2	13.7	39.6	53.3	79.3	25.4	9.8	35.2
Bottom Seven								
Sichuan	7.8	21.3	31.2	52.5	27.5	25.9	5.9	31.8
Henan	8.2	20.9	29	49.9	29.4	27.1	5.6	32.7
Anhui	8.3	21.5	23.1	44.6	33.7	25.5	7	32.5
Hunan	8.4	17.7	31.2	48.9	34.3	23.1	9.3	32.4
Guizhou	8.5	18.5	27.7	46.2	35.5	26.6	6.6	33.2
Jiangsu	8.5	17.5	-	-	-	-	-	-
Shandong	8.6	19.3	-	-	-	-	-	-
National Average	10.4	17	33.9	50.9	46.3	26.3	8.9	35.2

E = Budgetary Expenditures
CC = Capital Construction
CESH = Culture, Education,Science, and Health

Source: World Bank, 1992a, p. 85.

Across provinces, there is an inverse relationship between per capita CESH expenditure and the share of budgetary expenditures devoted to it, with poor provinces spending more of their budget on CESH but achieving per capita expenditure levels that are below the national average. In 1978, the top five provinces spent 11.9-13.7 per cent of their total expenditures on CESH, less than the national average of 17.0 per cent, and had per capita expenditures that were more than twice the national average. In contrast, the bottom seven all spent more than 17 per cent of their budgets, but had per capita expenditure levels that were 17-25 per cent below the national average. The same pattern held for 1990, but the poor provinces had slipped further behind, with per capita CESH expenditures 23-41 per cent below the national average. These patterns were found in all three provinces studied (Guangdong, Liaoning and Sichuan).

More significantly, there is an inverse relationship between CESH and capital construction (CC) as shares of total expenditures—compared to national averages, the top provinces in CESH expenditure devoted a smaller share of their budgets to CESH and more to CC, while the bottom provinces spent more on CESH and had less for CC. Moreover, the sum of CC and CESH is on average higher in the rich provinces than in poor, indicating that on the whole the costs of price subsidies and government administration were less burdensome for the former group, so that they were able to devote a greater portion of their budgets to spending on development and social services. These observed trends in CESH and CC expenditures across provinces have three important implications: first, given their relatively poorer initial endowment of infrastructure, the lower levels of spending on capital construction are likely to doom the poor provinces to a lower growth path. Second, since economic growth is necessary to generate revenue growth, these provinces will continue to lag in financing capability, starving their social and economic programs unless central subsidies are available to offset their deficiencies. Finally, because CESH spending represents investment in human capital, inadequate investment in this area will cause the poor provinces to fall further behind and be locked into a vicious circle of poverty.

The Crisis in Intergovernmental Relations and Dysfunctional Incentives

Intergovernmental fiscal relations in the PRC can be characterized as reaching a state of crisis, with a high level of dissatisfaction and distrust on all sides. This is a crisis because the system remains dependent on local collection and vertical revenue sharing, and the deterioration in intergovernmental relations has had a devastating effect on attempts to mobilize revenues and stem the continuing decline in the revenue-GNP ratio. In the recent past, every effort by the central government to raise the revenue-GNP ratio and the ratio of central/local shares in the budget has been met by strategic responses by local governments, who anticipate that increased collections will invite imposition of a greater remittance quota in the next round. The outcome is a vicious circle, with repeated central attempts to increase its revenues being evaded by local governments, resulting in growing intergovernmental tensions and continuing fiscal decline that the government seems powerless to stem.

The present system of revenue sharing is no longer workable because of its growing incompatibility with a decentralized economy, where the conflict between efficiency and equity concerns hamper revenue collection. In Shanghai, for example, under the prereform central planning regime, the city earned extremely high revenues per capita, partly because of its preponderance of profitable light industries and high-value processing industries that enjoyed the benefits of high administered prices. Under the old system, Shanghai was obligated to turn over most of its revenues to the central government, the proceeds of which financed redistributions to poorer regions, partially as compensation for having supplied Shanghai with low cost raw materials. In the reform period, Shanghai has been increasingly unwilling to bear what it saw as extractive remittance rates. Ultimately, the central government was forced to reduce Shanghai's remittance obligations because the high rates were acting as a major deterrent to the city's tax efforts.

The dwindling ability of the central budget to play a redistributive role means that the PRC fiscal system has moved toward self-financing, with local governments almost entirely dependent on their own tax bases to finance government and investment. Aside from the problems of growing regional disparities in service provision (see Central-Local Expenditure Divisions, p. 110), self-financing has reinforced the dysfunctional incentives created by two features of the fiscal system: decentralized tax administration and the dependence of budgetary revenues on industry and commerce. The perverse outcomes often serve to undermine reform objectives and the fiscal system itself, and they explain the liberal granting of tax exemptions to local enterprises that was identified in Chapter 2 as a major cause of fiscal decline.

Local government responses can be grouped roughly into three types: The first is the relatively benign and passive negotiation with higher levels for a more favorable division of revenues and responsibilities. Both of the others are more problematic: (1) the attempt to expand the local tax base, and (2) reaching outside the budget to tap the extrabudgetary funds of enterprises, to push expenditures off budget onto the enterprises and the private sector, or to divert budgetary funds into extrabudgetary channels.

Of all the responses, the one most favored by government officials and the Ministry of Finance is that of promoting local economic growth to expand the tax base. The Ministry of Finance has repeatedly called on local governments to promote growth by providing investment funds and other forms of support to lower levels. Given the tax structure, where industry continues to account for most of the revenues, much energy is focused on promoting and supporting local industrial development.

The strategy of reaching outside the budget to tap extrabudgetary funds is problematic because nearly three quarters of the huge and growing extrabudgetary funds are retained profits and depreciation funds controlled by enterprises and their supervisory departments. Under severe fiscal pressure, many local governments have succumbed to tapping enterprise funds by imposing a variety of legal and illegal levies (including educational surcharges, utility surcharges, environmental protection fees, etc.), or by shifting costs to enterprises for responsibilities ranging from road building and environmental protection to hosting banquets for governmental functions. Lacking a strong legal framework to protect enterprises from fiscal predation, such practices have proliferated despite promulgation of myriad regulations to prohibit them (Clarke 1989).

A variation of "reaching outside the budget" is that of pushing governmental expenditures off budget. This is so pervasive that local governments routinely refer to the budget as *chifan caizheng*— (a "meal ticket," for subsistence only), which pays salaries of government employees; all other expenditures have to be financed outside the budget, through extrabudgetary funds or off-budget funds of local governments. For example, in Baoan County, Shenzhen, the budget allocates only Y12,000 per kilometer for road building, while the real cost is over Y300,000. To build roads needed to support further development, the county is forced to find resources from its off-budget funds. In other instances, to finance basic education, provinces are increasingly seeking nonbudgetary funds to supplement budgetary appropriations, including running factories to earn incomes for schools and collecting contributions from local enterprises and residents. In the poor provinces, and especially in the rural sector, many costs are passed along to parents, by charging tuition and fees and by obligating parents to help subsidize the paltry wages of rural teachers (World Bank 1992b). Even government employees are sometimes paid from extrabudgetary funds or off-budget funds of local governments. For example, in Xuzhou City, Jiangsu, only 160 of the 660 personnel in the city's finance departments (with offices in 180 townships, 6 counties, and 1 district) were on the government budgetary payroll. All the rest were paid from the mostly industry-generated, off-budget funds of the township governments (Zhao and Zhang 1985).

Many of these actions run counter to the reform program's objectives and have negative effects on the distribution of income. Government predation over enterprise funds clearly violates the spirit of enterprise reform, which aims to increase enterprise autonomy and to insulate enterprises from government interference. Even the "positive" response of promoting local industrial growth has had adverse effects on allocative efficiency in the presence of distorted prices and an unreformed tax structure.

First, the need to generate revenue growth at the local level has contributed to macroeconomic imbalance by encouraging too much growth. The distorted price and tax structures cause resources to be channeled to the wrong sectors, creating excess capacity in processing industries where rates of returns were initially high. Because these price and tax structures are uniform nationwide, the regional compositions of industry have tended to be duplicative, since resources are channeled to the same high-profit, high-tax industries everywhere. To maximize revenue growth, provinces have even subsidized high-cost producers in high-tax industries. For example, Guangxi paid out subsidies totaling Y29.85 million in 1986 to support production of high-tax products in the tobacco-drying and cigarette industries (*Guangxi Nianjian* 1987). The convergence of the composition of industry across regions exacerbates the tendency toward protectionism and hinders the development of a national market. Through the reform decade, the dependence of local revenues on the financial health of local enterprises has induced local officials to take an active interest in enterprise operations. Their tendency to intervene whenever possible to protect their resources and markets has caused intermittent outbreaks of "wool wars" and "silk cocoon wars" and has created other regional barriers to resource flows.

Another set of problems is tax evasion and avoidance. By offering tax relief to enterprises, local governments effectively divert funds from the budgetary sector, where funds have to be shared with higher levels, to the extrabudgetary in the form of enterprises' retained profits where they are not shared. In several cities visited, enterprises reported receiving exemptions from income tax and VAT with the clear understanding that the exemptions were intended to help them finance capital investments that would expand the local tax base.

Aside from the deleterious effect on revenue buoyancy under revenue-sharing arrangements where retention rates vary a great deal across provinces, allowing lower level governments to make tax expenditures creates a highly regressive tax structure. The structure makes revenue-rich provinces more generous in offering tax expenditures than poor ones because they can share the costs of tax expenditures with the central government, while poor provinces have to bear more of the costs themselves. Moreover, because of the intense pressures on their budgets, poor provinces can scarcely afford to forego present revenues for future revenues. The increasing use of tax expenditures therefore ultimately results in lower effective tax rates in rich areas than in poor ones, with very adverse implications for regional income growth.

Issues in Intergovernmental Fiscal Relations

The PRC government recently expressed its desire to raise the central share of total revenues from the present 40 per cent to about 60 per cent. This is consistent with the conventional view among Western public finance experts, who hold that a high degree of fiscal centralization is often desirable in developing countries because stabilization—international as well as domestic—is often an important concern. Stabilization is especially important for transitional economies, where macroeconomic control is weak during the shift from the use of direct controls (such as material allocation, credit allocation, and administrative pricing) to indirect economic levers. The shift requires central government control of fiscal and monetary policy including external borrowing.

Box 3.5: The 1992 Tax-Sharing System (*Fenshuizhi*)

A new system of "tax sharing" (*fenshuizhi*) was introduced on 1 January 1992 in six cities and three provinces: Chongqing, Dalian, Qingdao, Shenyang, Tianjin, Wuhan, Liaoning, Xinjiang, and Zhejiang. This represented a new attempt at dividing revenues between the central and provincial governments.

Under this system, revenues were still divided into three types: central-fixed, local-fixed, and shared. Two significant changes include: (1) returning turnover taxes on enterprises under the petroleum, power, petrochemical, and nonferrous metals ministries to the general pool of revenues, eliminating the special central claim on these sectors (in Chongqing, it was reported that this change alone will give the city an additional Y30 million a year); and (2) moving most shared taxes to local fixed revenues, including direct taxes on local state-owned enterprises, so that only five tax types were left as shared taxes – the product tax, VAT, business tax, consolidated industrial and commercial tax, and residence tax.

The sharing was done in two steps. In step one, the central government took 50 per cent of the shared revenues (20 per cent was taken in minority regions). In step two, the remittance quota (from the remaining revenues) was set as follows:

$Y_f + Y_s - E^* = R$
where: Y_f = local fixed revenue in the base year 1989,
         Y_s = retained shared revenues in the base year 1989,
         E^* = approved expenditures in the base year 1989, and
         R = remittance quota in the base year 1989.
If $R \geq 0$, the remittance was set to grow by 5 per cent per year.
If $R \leq 0$, it was the province's quota subsidy from the center, with zero growth adjustment provision.

Moreover, a strong central role is necessary if income redistribution is a desired objective.

The sweeping program adopted by the 14th Party Congress (November 1993) represents a bold step toward reform and strengthening central control over aggregate demand. A central component of the announced package of fiscal reform is the introduction of the tax-sharing system to all provinces (and line item cities) in 1994. While many details remain to be worked out, the introduction of the tax-sharing system will be a big step in the right direction toward putting central-provincial fiscal relations on a more objective basis, by specifying a system of tax

These remittance contracts were set for four years (through the Eighth Five-Year Plan).

The objectives of the new tax-sharing were twofold. First, they were to reduce the negotiability of revenue shares by applying uniform rates to the sharing of taxes – 50 per cent on turnover taxes in most provinces, and 80 per cent retention in minority regions. In the second step of remittance, the contractual form was also uniform, with all provinces remitting their entire surplus based on 1989 figures, with a uniform incremental growth of 5 per cent a year in their remittance obligation. Nevertheless, while there was much greater uniformity in tax assignments and revenue-sharing contracts, some alterations were permitted. For example, Tianjin was permitted to exclude resource tax revenues from sharing with the central government. The second objective was to increase the central government's share of revenues by taking a bigger share of the most buoyant tax type – the turnover taxes.

The Ministry of Finance had planned to extend this system to more provinces and cities each year, so that by the end of the Eighth Five-Year Plan, all 39 budgetary units would be under the scheme. This pace was sharply accelerated in 1993, when the Third Plenary Session of the 14th Central Committee of the Chinese Communist Party adopted the plan to implement the tax sharing system nationwide beginning in January 1994 (see Issues in Intergovernmental Fiscal Relations, the last section of Chapter 3).

One extremely contentious issue surrounding the tax-sharing system is that it will sharply reduce the number of revenue-surplus provinces after nationwide implementation. Under the 1992 program, it was projected that only two provinces, Jiangsu and Zhejiang, would still have revenue surpluses. The remaining 25 would be receiving quota subsidies from the center. In the 1994 version, tax sharing will turn all provinces into net recipients of central transfers, a shift likely to be resisted by provincial officials.

assignments and making revenue sharing more uniform across provinces. Under the tax-sharing system, which has been modified from the 1992 version (Box 3.5), only three taxes will be shared: VAT, the resource tax, and the stock market trading tax. It will raise the central share of total revenues by claiming a larger share (75 per cent) of VAT, the most buoyant tax type. To eliminate the recent problem of local tax expenditures eroding revenue buoyancy, tax administration will also be reformed: the State Tax Bureau will be split into two, with separate agencies for collecting central and local taxes.

This reform program will, when fully implemented, introduce a far higher degree of transparency to revenue-sharing arrangements. It will simplify the tax structure by replacing product taxes with VAT, merging VAT rates to 1-2 steps, and offering equal tax treatment of domestic enterprises—be they state-owned, collective or private—by unifying all profit tax rates at 33 per cent. These steps should make it far easier to assess tax capacity and tax effort across regions and thus should improve monitoring and tax administration.

However, to win local acceptance of this reform program, it is necessary to rebuild trust. This requires the central government to (1) cease its recent practices of revenue-grabbing outside the (revenue-sharing) system by changing the scope of central fixed revenues, "borrowing" etc. and unilaterally resetting contract terms in mid-course; and (2) make strong and credible guarantees of local government rights and responsibilities. The PRC may even have to move toward some form of quasi-fiscal federalism, with legal guarantees of provincial autonomy over their financial resources, in order to help reduce the degree of uncertainty and improve incentives for local governments.

The role of government must be rethought and the division of labor among administrative levels clarified. The discussion in Central-Local Expenditure Divisions (p. 110) had emphasized that problems of revenue adequacy at all levels of government can be attributed partly to the conservativism regarding cutting government bureaucracy in a decentralizing economy—the behavioral inertia at all governmental levels has allowed administrative costs to rise throughout the reform decade despite diminishing management responsibilities in many sectors. The central government must take the lead by setting an example by implementing cuts in the bureaucracy.

Because of the alarming growth in regional disparities in expenditure on basic services, a program of equalization grants is urgently needed to ensure adequate financing in poor provinces and to stem the erosion in such basic provisions as rural education. Some of these grants may have to be earmarked and funneled directly to the appropriate level of administration to ensure that they reach their targeted recipients.

Chapter 4

The Economic, Financial and Budgetary Consequences of Enterprise Reform

CHRONOLOGY AND STRUCTURAL CHANGES

The three stages in the decentralization of the PRC's state industrial sector occurred from 1979 to 1983, 1984 to 1988, and 1989 to the present.

Three key changes occurred during the first stage (1979-1983).

1. Enterprises were allowed to retain part of their profits. By mid-1980, the 6600 SOEs that participated in the profit retention scheme produced 60 per cent of the output and 70 per cent of the profits under the state plan (Tidrick and Chen 1987).
2. The bonus system was introduced to provide incentives for workers in SOEs to improve labor productivity. The bonus was generally required to be less than 25 per cent of the centrally set basic wage.
3. In 1983, the government transferred the financing of working capital from budgetary grants to bank loans, and the system of profit remittance was replaced by an income tax in order to separate the role of the state as tax collector from its role as enterprise owner.

In the 1979-1983 period, there was little change to the system of price controls, and most production was still determined by the central plan. Only a limited number of enterprises were allowed to sell their above quota production freely.

The second stage of SOE reforms began with the 1984 unveiling of the "Provisional Regulations on Expansion of Self-

Management Powers in State-Run Enterprises," which gave the SOEs much greater autonomy in production mix, production level, labor compensation, investment, and use of retained profits. There was also an increase in the power of the SOE manager. The party secretary at the factory had less say in the production aspects of the factory.

The scope of activities directed by the central plan was significantly reduced during the 1984-1988 period. The number of products under price controls was also steadily reduced.

Another important change in 1984 was the introduction of a progressive bonus tax to control the generous dispensation of bonuses. An annual bonus of up to four months of basic wages was exempted from the bonus tax, but a fifth-month bonus would require the SOE to pay a 100 per cent bonus tax (i.e., a full month's salary), a sixth-month bonus would be subject to a 200 per cent bonus tax, a seventh-month bonus would be subject to a 300 per cent bonus tax, and so forth.

Different forms of ownership were allowed in 1984 and accorded legal status in 1988 with a constitutional amendment. The monopoly status of the state sector was reduced by allowing collective and private enterprises to enter many industries, especially small-scale service industries (e.g., restaurants) and commercial activities (e.g., retailing). Restrictions on the size of TVEs and their freedom to set the prices of their output were removed.

The income tax was largely replaced by the contract responsibility system in 1987. An SOE would enter into a contract with the state (the owner) that would specify the amounts (instead of rates) of taxes and profits that it would pay each period. This change was partly the result of the government's desire to stop the decline in revenue from the SOEs and partly the result of the government's belief that a low marginal tax rate was conducive to growth.

In 1988-1990, microeconomic reforms were slowed as a macroeconomic adjustment program was implemented. With macroeconomic stability restored, the State Council issued Decree No. 103 ("Regulations on Shift of Management Mechanism for the State-Owned Industrial Enterprises") in June 1992 to further expand managerial authority and control the growth of labor compensation. The decree made clear that the increased enterprise autonomy meant that SOEs cannot count on subsidies in the case of losses.

The ownership structure of production has changed immensely during reforms. SOEs now produce only slightly more than half of industrial output, compared with the 78 per cent in 1978. The PRC is still predominantly a public-ownership economy, the SOEs and collectives presently produce over 80 per cent of industrial output.

The PRC has made impressive reforms in its enterprise sector. Most price controls on industrial products have been removed, the bonus scheme appears to have sharpened work efforts, SOEs now enjoy autonomy in their output and investment decisions, and there are now a variety of ownership forms. The result has been an accelerated growth rate in the 1980s.

However, enterprise reforms need to be deepened in order to remove the fiscal difficulties that the enterprise sector is causing. As noted earlier, the enterprise tax revenue/profits and profits/GNP ratios have fallen since 1980.

TAX TREATMENT OF ENTERPRISES

Because the key features of the main direct and indirect taxes are described in Chapter 2, this section will concentrate on the effects that these taxes have on the process of enterprise reform.

Indirect Taxes

Since 1984, domestic enterprises have paid product tax, VAT, or business tax on their output, depending on the nature of their product. In contrast, foreign enterprises and joint ventures continue to pay the consolidated industrial and commercial tax, which had been applied to all enterprises from 1958 to 1983. This situation leads to unequal tax treatment of foreign and domestic enterprises, and therefore to a misallocation of resources between them. The plan to extend VAT and business tax to foreign enterprises and joint ventures should contribute to enterprise reform by eliminating this distortion.[22]

---

[22]   SOEs that are subject to VAT can claim a refund for the consolidated industrial and commercial tax paid on purchases from foreign ventures. However, they may not claim exactly the right amount, because some tax offices apply a composite rate for VAT input credits to avoid the complications of dealing with many different tax rates.

Product tax and business tax are both cascading taxes because they do not provide any relief for taxes already paid on inputs into production. This produces an unwanted incentive for vertical integration, and represents an obstacle to breaking up inefficiently large enterprises. The gradual replacement of product tax by VAT is reducing this problem and should therefore contribute to enterprise reform. The complete elimination of the problem requires the full introduction of VAT to replace business and product taxes, except in cases where product tax acts as a supplementary excise tax.

A more serious problem with the current indirect tax system, and one that is getting worse rather than better, is the widespread use of tax exemptions. The revenue effects of these exemptions are discussed in Chapter 2 but are raised again here because, although the exemptions are often defended as encouragement for new enterprises and technological improvement, their discretionary nature subverts the fundamental aims of enterprise reform - the distancing of the enterprises from the state and the promotion of fair competition. The granting of exemptions was widespread. Even more worrying, these exemptions are planned to increase in the future: in Chongqing, the limit to turnover tax exemptions that can be granted by districts and counties was increased from Y5,000 to Y30,000 a year in 1992.

Many countries use tax exemptions as an instrument of industrial policy, or to further more general economic and social aims. The revenue costs of such exemptions are often referred to as tax expenditures. In recent years, the size of these tax expenditures has been seen as an obstacle to the reduction of tax rates, and there has been a move to reduce the scope of such exemptions. Clearly, the PRC government must take account of the fact that high levels of tax expenditure are very costly. However, it is equally important to understand that the way in which these exemptions are administered in developed market economies is different in several respects from that observed in the PRC.

In developed market economies, exemptions from VAT or other indirect taxes are never granted on an enterprise-by-enterprise basis: they are applied on a nationwide basis according to clear criteria that are specified by law. Thus, particular goods might be exempted for social reasons. Or all firms with a gross output value below a certain level might be exempted in order to reduce administrative and compliance costs. This approach means that there is no scope for negotiation between individual enterprises and their local tax offices.

Exemptions that are determined on an enterprise-by-enterprise basis are designed to encourage particular activities, such as investment or technical improvement. These are always applied to the enterprise income tax, never to indirect taxes. The rules are laid down at a national level, and are specified in detail by law, thus reducing the scope for negotiation. Also, the amount of tax exempted bears a strict relationship to the cost that the enterprise has incurred in making the investment or technical improvement. However, in the PRC, an enterprise might receive a tax holiday as a result of technological improvement, with no provision to ensure that the value of the tax exemption is limited to the cost of the improvement. Outside the PRC, tax holidays are widely practiced only to encourage direct foreign investment, although there is considerable doubt as to their effectiveness.

Finally, enterprise losses are never used as a reason for granting tax exemptions in developed market economies. Indeed it is often the enforcement of tax collection that pushes enterprises into bankruptcy. If a government wishes to save a particular unprofitable enterprise, it must provide an explicit subsidy rather than a tax rebate. This has the advantage of bringing the costs of saving the enterprise to the attention of policymakers.

Enterprise Income Taxation and Profit Remittance

As explained in Chapter 2, income taxation (the *"ligaishui"* system) gradually replaced the system of profit remittance for SOEs in the early 1980s, and the process was virtually complete by 1984. This allowed the enterprises to keep a higher proportion of their profits, but it was accompanied by a reduction in the amount of investment that was funded by the state budget. The overall reform was intended to make enterprises take greater managerial responsibility, and to remove the element of negotiation in the relationship between the enterprise and the state, which had existed during the period of profit remittance.

Enterprise income tax is levied on progressive scale of eight rates for small SOEs, but large and medium-sized SOEs pay a flat rate of 55 per cent. In addition, large and medium-sized SOEs are liable to pay the enterprise income adjustment tax, which is aimed at capturing the excess profits that some enterprises earn. The rate of this tax varies from enterprise to enterprise, depending on the enterprise's profit margin in 1983 (the year before the tax was introduced). The use of a base year figure allowed payments to the state to be tailored to the enterprise's individual financial circumstances in much the same way as the profit remittance system, but avoided the element of negotiation and so contributed to the goals of enterprise reform.

This switch from profit remittance to taxation was seen as a success, mainly because it allowed enterprises to predict the effect of their actions on their retained earnings. Specifically, expansion was encouraged because it was clear that the state would not claim all of the additional profits. However, the system still has some problems.

First, many SOEs run at a loss and have to negotiate subsidies from the government. They have clearly not achieved the independence that is one of the aims of enterprise reform. The same is true of enterprises that are nominally profitable, but do not earn enough profit to pay the same level of employee bonus paid by other SOEs. Such low-profit enterprises often receive subsidies or a negotiated reduction in taxation. This process of negotiation is facilitated because the enterprise income tax and the enterprise income adjustment tax continue to be paid to the unit of government that owns the enterprise, just as under the profit remittance system.

Second, the taxation of enterprises follows different rules, depending on whether they are SOEs, collectives, joint ventures, foreign enterprises, household enterprises, or private enterprises. The various tax rules include different tax rates as well as differences in accounting rules, such as depreciation rates and the ability to deduct the repayment of loan principal. Thus, foreign enterprises pay a lower rate of tax but are not allowed to deduct loan principal repayments.

These differences in tax treatment are increased by the Energy and Transport Key Construction Fund, to which SOEs must contribute 15 per cent of the sum of their after tax profits and their depreciation allowance. In 1989, this was increased by the introduction of the Budget Adjustment Fund, levied at a rate of

10 per cent on the same base as the Energy and Transport Key Construction Fund.

Such differences form a major obstacle to enterprise reform by preventing equal competition. Therefore, the plans to reduce and eventually eliminate these differences will be essential for reform.

The Contract Responsibility System

The tax system for SOEs was the dominant mode only from 1984 to 1986. Although it still survives, the current dominant mode for revenue collection from SOEs is the contract responsibility system (CRS). Under the CRS, enterprises contract to pay income taxes on a specific level of profit. If they do not achieve that level of profit, they are supposed to make up the taxes from their own resources. If they exceed that level of profit, they pay taxes at a lower rate (often zero) on their additional profit.

The CRS clearly provides a considerable incentive for SOEs to make more profits. However, it has two major disadvantages: loss of government revenue and the reintroduction of negotiation between enterprises and the state. The loss of government revenue has been discussed in Chapter 2 and so the reintroduction of negotiation is considered here.

Because these contracts are negotiated on an enterprise-by-enterprise basis, the CRS could be viewed as simply a return to the old profit remittance system. Indeed, the extent of negotiation is just as great: there is negotiation over the terms of the contract and then over what to do when the enterprise does not reach its profit target, especially if it can blame government policies such as price control. The CRS therefore fundamentally undermines the goals of enterprise reform.

However, there are differences from the profit remittance system. First, the enterprise's share of additional profits is now much larger than it was under profit remittance. From this point of view, the CRS continues a trend of increasing incentives that was started by the introduction of the enterprise income tax system. Second, because the contracts last a number of years, the enterprise is in a better position to predict the effect of its actions on retained earnings than it was under the profit remittance system.

These two points imply that the CRS is not just a return to the past. However, its effect on revenue buoyancy and its subversion of enterprise reform show that the CRS represents a barrier to the successful development of a socialist market economy.

The Separation of Profits and Taxes
(The *Shuili Fenliu* Reform)

Despite its difficulties, the CRS cannot simply be abandoned in favor of the *ligaishui* system that dominated from 1984 to 1986. To do that would be to ignore the problems with the previous system, including:

1.   A 55 per cent rate of income tax on SOEs, increased by a possible adjustment tax and the contributions to the two funds, Energy and Transport Key Construction Fund and the Budgetary Adjustment Fund. This high rate is generally seen as a discouragement to profit seeking.
2.   Different tax rates and accounting rules apply to different types of enterprise.
3.   If investments are financed by loans, then the allowance of principal repayments as an expense for SOEs produces an excessive incentive for investment.

All of these problems could in principle be dealt with by taxing all enterprises, including SOEs, in the same way as joint ventures. In addition to unifying the taxation of all enterprises, this would lower the tax rate to 33 per cent (30 per cent plus a 3 per cent local surcharge) and require SOEs to repay loan principal out of after-tax income.[23]

The 33 per cent rate is about the same as current estimates of the average enterprise income tax burden of SOEs (32.8 per cent of gross profits before loan repayments in 1991, according to the Department of Industry and Communication, Ministry of Finance). Thus, the cut in rate is partly offset by the abolition of the allowance for principal repayment and has partly been anticipated by the reduced rates of the CRS.

However, the calculation leaves out the enterprise income adjustment tax, direct profit remittances that some SOEs make

---

[23]   Loans from the People's Construction Bank of China and loans for capital construction that are approved by the enterprise's supervisory bureau can enjoy repayments (including principal) before tax.

in addition to their enterprise income tax liability, and the contributions to the two funds. The inclusion of adjustment taxes and profit remittances raises the average SOE tax burden to 36.9 per cent, and the payments to the two funds raise it to over 40 per cent.

Thus, revenue would be lost from the switch to a 33 per cent rate, unless additional payments were made to the government. However, a case for such payments can be made on the grounds that many SOEs have received investment funds from the level of government that owns them. Thus, governments should receive a return on their capital, in addition to the tax revenue. They could be regarded as shareholders of their SOEs and receive a dividend out of after-tax profits. This idea has been referred to as the separation of profit and tax and has been the subject of experiments in a number of cities over the past few years.

The Separating Profits and Taxes Reform (SPTR) experiments started in 1987 and have involved more than 2000 SOEs of all sizes. In the experiments, a distinction is made between the taxes paid by the enterprises (at 33 per cent) and the profit remittance that is paid out of after-tax profit, accruing to the owner of the enterprise. No contracting is allowed on the tax component, but contracting is used to determine the profit remittance. In addition, loan principal repayment is supposed to be made from after-tax profit.

The results from the SPTR experiments appear to be sufficiently positive for the State Tax Bureau to propose introducing the system nationwide in 1994. The system has three clear advantages: it reduces the differences between the tax treatment of different types of enterprise, it distinguishes between the role of the state as tax collector and its role as owner, and it reduces the excessive incentive to invest by improving the treatment of loan principal repayment. However, there are some difficulties with the experimental system.

First, it has not eliminated the differences in tax treatment, because SOEs still have to contribute to the two funds. As the Energy and Transportation Key Construction Fund alone raised over Y18 billion in 1991, the abolition of this difference would clearly have major budgetary implications.

Second, the distinction between the two roles of the state is still obscured because the taxes and the profit remittance are paid to the same level of government. It would be more appropriate for the destination of the tax revenue to be independent of the ownership of the enterprise.

Third, not all loans are being repaid out of after-tax income, because many enterprises are so heavily burdened by debt that they are unable to afford the repayments out of after-tax profits. They have therefore been allowed to repay some proportion of their debt before tax. The average proportion is about 50 per cent, but varies between enterprises and appears to be subject to negotiation. In principle, all "new loans" (those taken out since 1990) are supposed to be repaid out of after-tax income but it is not clear whether this is being enforced, especially as there is a difficulty knowing how to treat "new loans" that are taken out to pay "old loans." This situation has three serious disadvantages:

1. The individual negotiation of the proportion of old loans that must be repaid from after-tax income subverts enterprise reform,
2. Permitting repayment before tax loses some of the revenue gain that was supposed to balance the rate reduction, and
3. To the extent that new loans are also being repaid before tax, investment is still being excessively encouraged.

Fourth, this system can do nothing to disengage the state from negotiation with the two thirds of SOEs that are unprofitable or only barely profitable.

The data from one of the experimental cities, Chongqing, which experienced a large economic contraction during 1988-1990 shows the stabilizing property of the SPTR. As shown in Table 4.1, the proportion of retained profits would have fallen under the CRS because of the contract-specified payment of a fixed amount of taxes cum profits regardless of the economic downturn, whereas under the SPTR, the proportion of retained profits in 1990 was almost the same as in 1988.

The evidence is mixed on whether the new SPTR system can be introduced without substantial losses of revenue, even if the two funds are not abolished. The average proportion of profits paid in tax and profit remittance in the ten experimental cities increased to 37 per cent in 1990, about equal to the national average SOE burden under the present system calculated for 1991. Thus,

**Table 4.1: Distribution of Profits under Separating Profits
and Taxes Reform**
(per cent of total)

Location and Profits	1988	1989	1990
Chongqing Municipality			
Income Tax and Remitted Profits	27	29	32
Retained Profits	40	45	39
Principal Repayment	33	26	29
All Ten Cities			
Income Tax and Remitted Profits		29	37
Retained Profits		48	35
Principal Repayments		23	28

Source: Ministry of Finance.

the introduction of the new system would be approximately
revenue neutral. However, in Chongqing, the proportion had only
increased to 32 per cent by 1990, suggesting that different cities
could well have very different experiences from the introduction
of the new system. It would therefore be prudent to consider
whether the ten experimental cities are really representative of
the country as a whole before concluding that there would be
no revenue loss in extending the experiment to the whole country.

THE CONSEQUENCES OF INCOMPLETE
ENTERPRISE REFORMS

The main reason for the declining profits/GNP ratio in the last
six years is that the tax base is too narrowly focused on the industrial SOEs. The industrial SOEs have been generating less
profits vis-à-vis value added, and the value added of industrial
SOEs has fallen as a share of GNP.

Two reasons account for the fall in the profits of industrial
SOEs vis-à-vis their value added:[24] (1) new firms entered the traditional SOE strongholds, and (2) the wage bill continued to rise.

---

[24] A rise in input prices will lower the amount of profit and the amount of value
added, but it does not necessarily lower the ratio of profit to value added.

The essence of PRC economic reforms is to encourage market allocation of resources. Nonstate industrial enterprises have appeared to compete with industrial SOEs in many sectors. State revenue has fallen because the nonstate industrial enterprises have been more successful at evading taxes, and competition has lowered product prices.

The competition-induced decline in SOE profit rates cannot be the whole story, however. The decline in SOE profitability has occurred across the board, even in industries where there has not been substantial entry by nonstate industrial enterprises. One may be tempted to blame the broad decline in SOE profitability on the economic slowdown in 1990 and 1991. However, the decline in SOE profitability can be seen at least from 1986 onward, and it is unusually large for a cyclical downturn. At least one third of PRC enterprises in 1990 and 1991 were operating at a loss. No market economy has experienced such a high proportion of failing enterprises since the 1930s.

The proportion of unprofitable SOEs remained unchanged in 1992, a boom year where real GDP grew 12.8 per cent. Thus, the continued losses in SOEs in 1992 can not be attributed to competition from nonstate industrial enterprises, and are probably structural in nature.

SOEs in Shenyang and Chongqing gave wage increases to their workers even though half of them were running losses. This peculiar wage practice also occurred in the urban collective enterprises in Jiangbei County, outside of Chongqing. (These enterprises are owned and supervised by the county government.) Even though the value of output fell from Y29 million in 1989 to Y28 million in 1990 and Y27 million in 1991 in these enterprises, the average wage increased from Y1205 in 1989 to Y1233 in 1990 and Y1356 in 1991.

The most surprising statistic that the authors encountered in the six weeks of interviews for this study is that at the peak of every economic boom in the 1980s, at least 20 per cent of SOEs were running open losses. Since 20 per cent greatly exceeds the number of SOEs that face binding price ceilings, this statistic (if true) suggests widespread serious mismanagement in the SOEs.

Observations such as these suggest that unfavorable wage trends and imprudent investments have decreased the profitability of SOEs, and hence helped to reduce the profits/GNP ratio.[25] The three reasons for the unfavorable wage trends and imprudent investments are the absence of incentives for workers to moderate their wage demands, the absence of incentives for managers to resist wage demands, and the unhealthy relationship linking SOEs, local governments, and local banks.

No Incentives to Moderate Wage Demands

It is rational for workers to aggressively seek income increases. First, an enterprise can fire workers only with great difficulty. Second, an enterprise that would be bankrupted by high wage cost will, if past experience holds, be bailed out by the state through tax exemptions, bank loans for working capital, bank loans for technical upgrading to improve efficiency, and (sometimes) direct subsidies. Thus, workers feel secure in demanding ever-rising compensation.

SOEs can grant increases in labor income: (1) as direct income, which is the sum of the (centrally-set) basic wage and different types of bonuses and cash subsidies; and (2) as indirect income that is noncash payment in kind.

Increases in payments to SOE employees are not necessarily undesirable. The issue is whether the increases in total employee income (direct and indirect) have reduced profits (i.e., the state's) share of the output.

When bonuses were reintroduced in 1978, the government prevented excessive increases in direct income by limiting the bonus to a maximum of three months of basic wage. Because of the difficulty of maintaining the bonus cap and complaints about the negative effect of its inflexibility on work effort, the bonus cap was replaced by a progressive bonus tax in 1984.

The bonus tax failed to hold down increases in direct income in SOEs. During the 1989-1991 austerity period, the government imposed a link between the rate of wage increase and the rate of efficiency improvement. The most commonly used measure of efficiency is the amount of profits.

---

[25] This hypothesis is supported by other research. See, for example, Fan and Woo; and Reynolds, 1987.

Given the many government attempts to control undue increases in labor cost, many SOEs have sought to evade these controls by increasing the indirect (noncash) component of labor compensation, e.g., better housing.

Direct Income to Employees

Table 4.2 shows how the composition of direct income to SOE employees has changed over time. The basic wage accounted for 85 per cent of direct income in 1978, 57 per cent in 1985, and only 49 per cent in 1991. Bonuses and subsidies went from 9 per cent of direct income in 1978 to 31 per cent in 1985 and then to 40 per cent in 1991. The biggest increases in bonuses and subsidies occurred at the beginning of the reforms (because of the low base they were starting from) and during the boom periods of 1984-1985 and 1987-1988.

Table 4.3 shows that employees direct income has gone up in industrial SOEs, but so has labor productivity. For industrial SOEs, the average annual rate of growth of productivity was 4.4 per cent in the 1978-1990 period, and the average real wage growth was 4.1 per cent—see Table 4.4. The difference between the two averages was statistically insignificant, suggesting that direct employee income and labor productivity in industrial SOEs increased at the same rate during 1978-1990 period.

However, it is well known that measurement of labor productivity in PRC industries is biased upward because of inadequate deflation[26] and that direct employee income is an understatement of total employee income. Thus, total employee income growth probably exceeded productivity growth and hence reduced profit's share of output.

The increase in direct labor compensation to SOE employees is greater than that in collectively owned industrial enterprises. For collectively owned industrial enterprises in the 1978-1990 period, the average growth rate is 8.3 per cent for labor

---

[26] The deflation is particularly inadequate when a firm introduces a new product. The first problem is the imputation of the price of the new product to the base year level using quantity characteristics, e.g., determining the 1987 price of a 486 computer (which was not commercially available in 1987) from the 1987 price of the 286 computer by comparing some arbitrary quantity characteristics of the two computers. The second problem in deflation is that the initial price of a new product usually overstates its relative price in equilibrium.

Table 4.2: Composition of Direct Labor Compensation

Year	Basic Wage	Piece Wage	Bonuses	Subsidies	Overtime	Others
A. Composition of Direct Income to SOE Employees, % of total						
1978	85.00	0.80	2.30	6.50	2.00	3.40
1979	75.50	2.50	7.50	8.80	2.00	3.70
1980	69.80	3.20	9.10	14.10	1.60	2.20
1981	67.20	5.50	10.20	14.00	1.60	1.50
1982	64.40	7.60	10.90	14.10	1.50	1.50
1983	63.50	8.50	11.10	14.10	1.30	1.50
1984	58.50	9.50	14.40	14.50	1.50	1.60
1985	57.20	9.50	12.40	18.50	1.60	0.80
1986	56.30	8.70	12.80	18.80	1.80	1.60
1987	54.30	9.20	14.70	18.90	1.90	1.00
1988	49.00	9.40	17.20	21.40	1.90	1.10
1989	47.40	9.20	17.60	23.10	1.70	1.00
1990	48.90	8.90	17.00	21.80	1.60	1.80
1991	48.60	9.00	17.80	22.10	1.70	0.80
B. Level of Each Component, Yuan per year						
1978	547.40	5.15	14.81	41.86	12.88	21.90
1979	532.28	17.63	52.88	62.04	14.10	26.09
1980	560.49	25.70	73.07	113.22	12.85	17.67
1981	545.66	44.66	82.82	113.68	12.99	12.18
1982	538.38	63.54	91.12	117.88	12.54	12.54
1983	549.28	73.53	96.02	121.97	11.25	12.98
1984	604.89	98.23	148.90	149.93	15.51	16.54
1985	693.84	115.24	150.41	224.41	19.41	9.70
1986	796.08	123.02	180.99	265.83	25.45	22.62
1987	839.48	142.23	227.26	292.19	29.37	15.46
1988	907.97	174.18	318.72	396.54	35.21	20.38
1989	974.07	189.06	361.68	474.71	34.94	20.55
1990	1,116.88	203.28	388.28	497.91	36.54	41.11
1991	1,203.82	222.93	440.91	547.42	42.11	19.82
C. Rate of Increase, %						
1979	-2.76	242.10	256.97	48.21	9.47	19.13
1980	5.30	45.79	38.20	82.50	-8.88	-32.28
1981	-2.65	73.80	13.34	0.40	1.12	-31.05
1982	-1.33	42.27	10.02	3.69	-3.48	2.96
1983	2.02	15.72	5.37	3.47	-10.33	3.47
1984	10.13	33.60	55.08	22.93	37.93	27.51
1985	14.70	17.31	1.02	49.67	25.13	-41.34
1986	14.74	6.75	20.33	18.46	31.14	133.14
1987	5.45	15.62	25.56	9.92	15.41	-31.67
1988	8.16	22.46	40.24	35.71	19.86	31.84
1989	7.28	8.54	13.48	19.71	-0.77	0.82
1990	14.66	7.52	7.35	4.89	4.61	100.06
1991	7.78	9.67	13.55	9.94	15.23	-51.80

Source: State Statistical Bureau, *China Statistical Yearbook*, various issues.

Table 4.3: Labor Productivity and Wages in Industrial SOEs

Year	Labor Productivity (Y/person, 1980 prices)	Nominal Wage (Yuan)	Real Wage (Yuan, 1980 prices)
1978	11,131	681	746
1990	18,639	2,409	1,187

Source: State Statistical Bureau 1991.

productivity and 3.6 per cent for real wage. Labor productivity growth in SOEs was less than labor productivity growth in industrial collectives, but real wage growth in SOEs exceeded real wage growth in industrial collectives.

Table 4.4: Labor Productivity and Real Wages
(annual growth, per cent)

Year	Industrial SOEs		Collectively-owned Industrial Enterprises	
	Labor Productivity	Real Wages	Labor Productivity	Real Wages
1979	6.35	8.84	2.35	4.46
1980	2.05	4.94	11.61	8.93
1981	-1.80	-2.58	2.26	0.99
1982	2.28	-0.61	4.06	0.29
1983	7.55	-0.36	9.21	1.77
1984	7.82	18.78	21.23	14.43
1985	7.18	3.46	-11.07	7.69
1986	2.46	9.23	4.80	4.07
1987	7.90	1.63	16.03	1.79
1988	8.31	-0.06	22.21	-1.60
1989	1.46	-3.06	8.00	-5.71
1990	1.74	9.25	8.26	5.96
1991	4.75	3.76	13.72	-18.52
Average 1979-1991	4.47	4.09	8.67	1.89

Source: State Statistical Bureau 1992, Tables 4.35, 4.36, 7.2, and 10.16.

Indirect Income to Employees

In reaction to the government's increasingly stringent regulations on the growth of direct income, SOEs have been using indirect income to raise labor compensation. The three components to the indirect income received by SOE personnel are collective consumption, distribution of private consumer goods, and housing. SOEs typically hide the first two components as production costs and the third as investment expenditure.

Collective consumption comes from the myriad services SOEs supply to their employees. The range of services provided is so broad that an SOE resembles a self-contained social community. SOE welfare funds pay for kindergartens, hospitals, transportation, recreational facilities, dining facilities, funeral facilities, and relief work. The size of the welfare fund allowed by state regulations is proportional to the amount of cash income (wages plus bonuses) and retained profits.

The result of the higher labor costs is that less profits have been remitted to the state. In a sample of 300 SOEs, Fan and Woo (1992) found a 240 per cent increase in the size of the welfare fund over the 1984-1988 period.

SOE distribution of consumer goods occurs at two levels: the common and the elite. Consumer goods are distributed at the common level so that workers avoid the bonus tax. Many SOEs buy grain, fruits, meat, eggs, fish, clothes, furniture, and housewares and distribute them to their employees. The costs of these items are charged mostly to "material costs" and "nonproduction expenditure". Two studies have suggested that the distribution of consumer goods accounted for 25-33 per cent of the total personal income of SOE employees (Zhang Shuguang 1990; and Zhao 1989).

The distribution of consumer goods at the elite level occurs mainly in the management office and the sales department. Consumption takes the form of lavish banquets, tourist travel, high-class hotels, luxurious official cars, and expensive office furniture.

The third component of the indirect income paid by SOEs is physical facilities. SOEs use a significant portion of their retained profits to build low-rent apartments, kindergartens, club houses, and dance halls.

An undesirable outcome of the proliferation of methods to dispense indirect income to the SOE employees is that some of the methods (for example, good housing) impede labor mobility.

Controlling Labor Cost

The attempt to control wage costs by linking their rate of increase to the rate of increase in efficiency has failed. Wage changes are asymmetrical. Wages go up when efficiency goes up, but they seldom reverse direction with efficiency decreases.

The regulation that the elasticity of wage to efficiency should be within 0.3 to 0.7 is often breached whenever economic conditions are good.[27] One profitable state enterprise informed the authors that the local supervisory body had always set the elasticity at 0.8. (When reminded of the regulation, the enterprise amended its reply to fluctuations between 0.7 and 0.8.)

One important flaw of limiting wage increases to some portion of the rise in efficiency is that it can hold down only the cash component of labor income and not total labor income. The common practice of noncash labor compensation (e.g., distribution of goods, greater subsidies to the enterprise canteen, sales meetings at holiday resorts) increases labor income at the expense of profits. Until the SOEs are truly independent financial entities, they are motivated to use indirect income to evade the rules that control direct income.

The wage-efficiency link has been used for other purposes beside controlling wage growth. By using different definitions of efficiency in different industries, these other goals are pursued. For example, for some export-oriented SOEs, increase in efficiency is defined as increase in foreign exchange earnings; and for some loss-making coal mines, efficiency growth is equated with output growth. These other uses of the wage-efficiency link are unfortunate because there are less distortionary ways to achieve these other objectives, e.g., promoting exports by unifying the exchange rate at the swap market rate, and promoting coal production by direct subsidies.

---

[27]   Elasticity refers to the percentage increase in wage to each percentage increase in efficiency.

The Nature of the Incentives Facing Managers

A major flaw of the present SOE system is the absence of incentives for the managers and workers to produce a high rate of return to the invested capital. Managers are practically "married" to their work forces. Dismissing unsuitable workers is procedurally difficult, and, worse, can be misinterpreted as a lack of ability to motivate by alternative means.

Since managers also have to take responsibility for the housing, medical and education needs of their work forces, and managers' promotions depend on fulfilling these social welfare obligations, there is always the temptation to use profits that should be passed on to the government for increasing the living standard of the work force. A reputation of being popular with workers is invaluable when a manager is being considered for promotion (Walder 1989).

Since the decentralization began in earnest in early 1980, a new term, "hunger for investment", appeared in discussions on the economy. The term refers to the surge in demand for investment funds in every economic sector in every province. The generalized "hunger for investment" is a major flaw of the system.

The flaw is the product of four factors.

1. The first factor is that SOEs view investment as the best vehicle by which they can increase their levels of future consumption. Higher investment today means higher output (hence higher income and consumption) tomorrow.
2. The second factor is that managers realize that SOEs will not be closed even if an imprudent investment were to result in bankruptcy. Since SOEs count on being bailed out during adversity, they are biased toward investment activities.[28]
3. The third factor behind the "hunger for investment" is the career considerations of the SOE managers. Managers realize that their promotion to a larger SOE would be helped if they have a record of engineering large expansions in output, and adding production capacity is one sure way of doing so.
4. The fourth factor is that, when investments are financed by loans, principal repayments are deducted before taxes are

---

[28] This is the "soft budget constraint" popularized in Kornai 1980.

applied. As the depreciation allowance already compensates for the reduction in capital stock from wear and tear, principal repayments are a form of SOE saving. They represent the amount of equity that the SOE is taking in the value of the capital stock. The deduction of principal repayments before taxation of SOE income is analogous to granting tax exemption to the portion of personal income that is saved. The resulting desire to generate higher principal repayments should cause higher investments.

What allows the "hunger for investment" to be realized is the triangular relationship among managers, the local banks and the local governments. Since the promotion of managers depends strongly on both the expansion of the enterprises under their stewardship and the increase in their workers' welfare (consumption), managers should face a trade-off between increasing workers' consumption and increasing investment. But thanks to the desire of the local government to promote local development and the duty of state-owned banks (SBs) to meet the financial needs of SOEs, this trade-off is reduced by tax exemptions and bank loans. That the local government has some supervisory authority over the local banks increases pressure on the banks to accommodate rollover of nonperforming loans and applications for new loans.

From the manager's perspective, it would be optimal to get a loan larger than the investment. The extra funds could be used for employee (and self) consumption to solidify the manager's popularity. The wage demands of the workers and the career considerations of the manager bias a SOE toward overinvestment and overconsumption, and the symbiotic relationship between the local governments and the banks allows these tendencies to be fulfilled.

INVESTMENT FINANCE

The enterprise reforms have drastically changed the structure of investment finance. Prior to 1978, practically all fixed capital investment was financed by budgetary grants because SOEs had to remit all of their profits and most of the depreciation funds to the government. When the profit retention system was instituted in 1980, small investments in certain industries could be undertaken without approval. In general, up to 1983, the cost of capital was zero but its use was controlled by the state.

It was clear to the government that if investment autonomy were given to SOEs, there had to be a nonzero cost of capital in order to ensure rational use of it. In 1983, the state reduced the amount of investment grants in the budget and channeled the investment funds through SBs. But SBs did not have much discretion in dispensing the credit. The government would designate the breakdown of funds between circulating and fixed capital, the sectoral distribution of funds, the interest rates for the different types of loans depending on the industry, and the maturity structure of the loans. Key enterprises would also be singled out for special credit allocation at preferential rates. Thus, SBs became fiscal agents of the state.

At the same time, the state sought to encourage the SBs' intermediation function by giving them greater discretion in lending funds that they raised independently, mainly through deposits. The SBs were instructed to be financially more self-reliant, and pay more attention to profitability. In 1985, SBs were allowed to issue financial bonds to raise funds.

The People's Construction Bank of China (PCBC) is a good, if extreme, example of a bank operating under directives over most of its lending and with instruction to be profitable. PCBC was established in 1954 to be responsible for the financial supervision of the state's construction projects. PCBC's functions have diversified since the introduction of economic reforms in 1978. PCBC was allowed to finance urban real estate development (houses for SOEs and individuals) in 1980, to participate in international banking in 1986, and in 1988, to extend loans to enterprises in industry and communications.

The first priority of PCBC is to finance the projects allocated to it by the state. PCBC is obliged to appraise each project before financing it. If a project is deemed to be financially too risky, PCBC refers it to the government for reconsideration. If the government decides to proceed with the project, then PCBC handles it if all of its financing is provided by the state.

If the government can provide only partial funding for that project (which is nearly always the case), then PCBC can in principle refuse to handle it as it cannot knowingly risk the saving of its depositors. In most cases, PCBC will finally agree to handle the project after getting additional funds from the People's Bank of China, or after a reappraisal of a modified version of the project.

In 1991, PCBC extended Y159 billion in fixed asset loans, Y58 billion in working capital loans and Y43 billion in other loans. (Only 50 per cent of the fixed asset loans were financed by budget allocations.) In addition, on behalf of the government, it made Y159 billion in directed investment loans and Y96 billion in entrusted loans.

The retained funds (retained profits and depreciation funds) of the SOEs are correctly considered funds of the state. To emphasize that the government (central and local) has yielded the right to use these funds to the enterprises, retained funds are reported as extrabudgetary revenue. (Of the Y271 billion in 1991, Y207 billion was held by SOEs and their supervising agencies.)

Correspondingly, the use of these retained funds is reported as extrabudgetary expenditure. In 1989, total extrabudgetary expenditure was Y250 billion. The three biggest items were investment in fixed assets (Y86 billion), major repair (Y28 billion), and workers' welfare (Y21 billion).

The central and local governments have not completely given up their rights to the extrabudgetary revenue, especially with their tight budget situations at the present. In 1989, SOEs contributed Y31 billion from extrabudgetary revenue to the government funds for energy, industry, transportation, and key construction projects, paid Y41 billion in nonbusiness fees and Y12 billion in road use fees, and spent Y5 billion on city maintenance.[29] The extent of government influence over an enterprise's extrabudgetary revenue appears to be particularistic (depending on the region, the industry, and the personnel involved) and variable over time.

With the decline in investment financing from the state budget, fixed capital investment is now less under central plan directive than ever before. Only 9 per cent of fixed asset investment in 1990 was financed through the state budget compared to 28 per cent in 1981, whereas the proportion of investment by extrabudgetary revenue increased from 55 per cent in 1981 to 65

---

[29]   State Statistical Bureau 1992, Table 6-15, p. 229.

Table 4.5: Sources of Fixed Asset Investment Financing
(per cent of total financing)

Source	1981	1985	1990
State Budget	28	16	9
Domestic Loans	13	20	20
Foreign Investment	4	4	6
Extrabudgetary Revenue	55	60	65

Source: State Statistical Bureau 1991.

per cent in 1990 (see Table 4.5). However, not all of the extra-budgetary investments have benefited the economy. This is because market signals have been distorted by continued price controls on key inputs and essential products.

At the same time, national industrial policy is still very important in determining the overall structure of production. It continues to be implemented through grants and preferential loans to key SOEs.

Table 4.6 shows that SOEs receive a disproportionate share of investment funds. Almost 80 per cent of domestic loans for fixed asset investment in 1990 went to SOEs even though they produced less than 40 per cent of output. Only the allocation of extrabudgetary revenue corresponded to the division of output by ownership.

The importance of extrabudgetary financing of investment is well captured by the financing sources of the Y5 billion spent on capital construction in Chongqing in 1991.

1. Y0.5 billion (10 per cent) was from the finance bureau—Y0.2 billion was from budgetary and extrabudgetary revenue and Y0.3 billion from earmarked funds.
2. Y2.5 billion (50 per cent) was from bank loans—of which Y0.3 billion was from foreign banks.
3. Y1 billion (20 per cent) was from retained profits.
4. Y1 billion (20 per cent) was from financial markets—of which Y0.5 billion was from long-term bonds, Y0.2 billion from

short-term bonds, Y0.1 billion from bonds issued by investment trust corporations, and Y0.07 billion from equities.

The Y1 billion raised in the local financial markets is a pow-
erful testimony to the markets' ability to mobilize resources. The
Y0.07 billion raised from equities is an insignificant amount but
reveals of a potentially big financing source. The shares were
openly sold in Chongqing to the general public even though no
formal stock market has been approved.

The Stock Markets

An improvement in the financial performance of SOEs is vital
for easing the state's fiscal difficulties. The SOEs must be motivated to maximize profits (which the government will tax). One
method of doing so would be to subject them to constant monitoring by the participants in a stock market. Changes in the prices
of the equities would be good indicators of how well a manager
was resisting wage demands, selecting investments and running
the firm. The development of stock markets could increase tax
revenue from the SOE sector, and provide a noninflationary way
of financing investments.

**Table 4.6: Destination of Funds for Fixed Asset Investment
by Ownership Type in 1990**
(per cent from each source)

Destination	SOEs	Collectives		Individuals
		Urban	Rural	
State Budget	99	1	0	0
Domestic Loans	79	7	10	4
Foreign Investment	96	4	0	0
Extrabudgetary Revenue	53	4	7	36
Others	60	0	18	23

Source: State Statistical Bureau 1991.

As stock markets are a recent and limited phenomenon in the PRC, the amount of investment funds raised from them has been small. The experience so far indicates that stock markets will be extremely effective in mobilizing funds if they are allowed to do so. Economic theory and foreign experience suggest that stock markets also promote better management of enterprises.

The PRC has approved two stock markets, one in Shanghai and the other in Shenzhen—with the latter being bigger and more active. Only spot trading is allowed. There are two kinds of shares. A shares can be held only by PRC citizens, and B shares only by foreigners. The trading of A shares started in December 1990, and B shares in November 1991. The B shares are denominated in renminbi, and the exchange rate used for transactions is the rate determined in the foreign exchange swap centers. Trade in A shares has to be settled by the next business day, and trade in B shares has to be settled within three business days.

Both stock exchanges are regulated by the People's Bank of China. It was announced in September 1992 that an independent supervisory body will be established to take over the regulating and running of the two exchanges. The withdrawal of the central bank from direct regulation of the stock markets is desirable. First, it preserves the specialized focus of the central bank on overall economic conditions. Second, by distancing itself from the stock market, the chief financial body can better withstand the temptation and pressures to guarantee the face value of shares.

In July 1992, 18 companies were listed on the Shenzhen stock exchange, and 8 of them issued B shares. The total issued capital was Y1.6 billion for A shares, Y0.4 billion for B shares and Y0.3 billion for bonds. The total market capitalization was Y44.6 billion for A shares, Y5.4 billion for B shares, and Y0.3 billion for bonds. The daily average value traded was Y0.3 billion. In September 1992, the price-earnings ratio was 86 for A shares and 37 for B shares, producing an average of 70.

Before it can be considered for listing on the Shenzhen exchange, a company must (1) have more than 1000 shareholders, (2) have main products that do not contravene the goals of Shenzhen's industrial policy, and (3) have tangible net assets that are greater than 25 per cent of total net assets.

Forty companies are waiting for approval to float shares on the Shenzhen stock market. The announcement that domestic agents could buy application forms to purchase Y1 billion of new equities to be issued by companies that were to be listed soon sparked a chaotic rush for these forms in August 1992, and the first public demonstration for the right to buy stocks.

Enterprises that are either not situated in one of these two cities or not approved to list their shares can apply for permission to sell a minority portion of their shares to their workers. Workers who leave these companies will have to sell their shares to the other workers. For example, 99 companies in Shenzhen have such internal stock markets and are allowed to sell up to 30 per cent of their shares to workers.

In practice, workers have been known to sell their shares to outsiders. Active informal stock exchanges are reported to exist in large cities such as Shenyang, Chengdu, and Chongqing. In 1991, several SOEs in Chongqing actually raised Y72 million from open sales of equities to the general public.

Taken together, the high price-earnings ratio for the A shares, the large demand for share applications in Shenzhen and the existence of informal stock markets indicate that the supply of equities is greatly exceeded by the demand for them. The authors strongly recommend that the number of stock exchanges and listings be increased rapidly to solve this shortage of equities.

Expansion of the stock market would be beneficial in four ways:

1. Enterprises could tap into a vast pool of savings to finance their investment,
2. Participants would be attracted away from informal markets and put under government supervision (thus, realized capital gains could be taxed),
3. The market mechanism would direct savings to investments with the highest rate of return, and
4. The SOEs would contribute more to the state budget because constant scrutiny would force managers to focus more on profitability and not only on production efficiency. SOE managers would have to be more responsive to changes in demand shifts and technological innovations, and be more resistant to demands for higher compensation by the work force.

For the stock market to function smoothly, high priority should be assigned to standardizing SOE accounting practices and strengthening the auditing capabilities of the stock market regulatory agency. A more determined enforcement of the bankruptcy laws would promote more prudent participation in the stock markets.

Other Sources of Investment Financing

During periods of tight credit, non-SOEs have more difficulty getting bank loans than do SOEs. In 1989, ceilings were imposed on loans to rural collectives (township, village, and production team enterprises); and working capital credit from banks to private enterprises was severely curtailed. (Banks gave virtually no fixed capital credit to private enterprises before then.) Consequently, the number of private enterprises dropped from 225,000 in mid-1988 to 98,000 in early 1991.

For private and small collective enterprises, working capital credit from the banks was hard to get even before the credit crunch started in 1988. A fast-growing private electronics company in Bao An County paid an interest rate of 2.5 per cent each month on its working capital, and its original start-up capital came from the savings of the partners and informal loans from friends. The reliance of nonstate industrial enterprises on self-financing is reflected in aggregate data on fixed asset investment financing in Table 4.7.

Table 4.7: **Source of Investment Financing in Enterprises by Ownership Type in 1990**
(per cent of each unit's total)

| | | Collectives | | |
Source	SOEs	Urban	Rural	Individuals
State Budget	13	1	0	0
Domestic Loans	24	35	24	4
Foreign Investment	9	8	0	0
Extrabudgetary Funds	42	56	47	83
Others	12	0	29	13

Source: State Statistical Bureau 1991.

Given the heavy reliance by rural collectives and individual enterprises on nonformal investment financing, a new financial instrument called employee bond has emerged as a significant source of funds. An employee bond is purchased by an employee, often a new one, upon joining the enterprise. Typically it carries an interest rate at least equal to that of a time deposit with the same maturity. For example, a factory in Chongqing reportedly raised Y3 million from employee bonds to acquire its Y14 million of fixed assets, while one in Chengdu raised Y1.5 million.

Many nonstate industrial enterprises also issue a hybrid equity-bond instrument that, in addition to paying a fixed base rate, also pays a bonus rate, the size of which is contingent on the profitability of the enterprise.[30]

In many cases, especially with collectives, tax exemption is an important source of investment financing. Since many counties, towns, and villages are on tax contracts with upper level governments that specify a fixed contribution, they typically start exempting taxes once their tax quotas are reached and provided that the extra retained funds will be invested. A big Chengdu factory[31] was given tax concessions worth Y3.5 million a year to allow it to accumulate funds to double its present output.

ASSESSMENT OF PERFORMANCE

The Effects on Microeconomic Efficiency

It is useful to distinguish between two aspects of efficiency: static and dynamic. Static efficiency is concerned with the allocation of a given quantity of resources in a particular time period, such as a year. Dynamic efficiency has to do with the accumulation of resources, particularly capital goods, over time.

In both cases, it is not possible to assess performance by simply looking at figures on the level of output, the rate of growth or the rate of capital accumulation. It is clear that the output of the PRC's manufacturing sector has grown very rapidly over the last ten years, and that a high proportion of the national income was invested in buildings and machinery. However, this infor-

---

[30] For a survey of informal financial instruments, see Tam 1991.
[31] From an interview at a Chengdu factory, 5 October 1992.

mation does not preclude the possibility that an even higher level of output could have been achieved, or that the investment could have been directed more efficiently.

In a market economy, efficiency is frequently analyzed by looking at the price and tax systems to see whether incentives are being distorted. It is possible to do this for the PRC, but such an analysis must always be qualified by the observation that government regulations may either offset or reinforce particular adverse incentives.

In terms of static efficiency, the key market features are the flexibility of prices and the neutrality of taxes on resource allocation. There can be no doubt that the prices of manufactured goods in the PRC have become more flexible in recent years as more goods are being sold in the free markets. This trend is continuing, with many moves towards market liberalization in 1992. However, some key goods are still subject to strict price controls, and this is probably causing inefficient allocation of resources.

On the tax side, indirect taxes inevitably cause market distortions. In the PRC, these distortions are compounded by the inequalities in tax treatment, cascading, and exemptions. Also, the large number of different tax rates (e.g., 12 VAT rates) has a distortionary effect. It is therefore good to see that many of these distortions will be eliminated by the rationalization and the simplification of the indirect tax system that is planned. The major qualification to this optimistic view is the widespread use of administrative exemptions, which must be controlled if resources are to be allocated on objective economic criteria.

While indirect taxes can distort static allocation, the enterprise income tax can influence investment by its effect on the after-tax return that an enterprise receives. The major distortion is the practice of allowing loan principal repayments to be made before tax, which can make investment projects with a negative rate of return profitable for an enterprise. Thus some of the investments made over the past few years may well have reduced the national income, even though they were attractive to the enterprises that made them. The moves to reduce, and hopefully eliminate, pretax loan repayments are therefore very important in promoting efficiency.

While the current enterprise income tax does too much to encourage investment, other taxes reduce it, e.g., the fixed assets investment orientation tax. Because of insufficient data, the overall effects of these taxes were not calculated but it is clear that, at the very least, the different income tax treatment of different types of enterprises must lead to distortions in the incentives to invest.

However, taxes are not the only forces that affect investment. A large part of investment in the PRC is still influenced by the planning system, either through direct controls or the provision of subsidized credit. It is hard to know whether these controls offset or reinforce the distortions caused by the tax system, but they almost certainly introduce additional distortions of their own.

The Effects on Macroeconomic Stability

The individual optimizing behavior of the SOEs has led to expansion of the money supply through two routes.

The first route went from the increases in labor compensation to the widening of the budget deficit, a large proportion of which was immediately monetized. In fact, total real government revenue fell through 1986-1989 because prices rose faster than revenue.

After 1986, the budget deficit widened because total expenditure growth did not slow in proportion to slower revenue growth. The proportion of expenditure covered by revenue fell from 94 per cent in 1984 to 90 per cent in 1989. One major reason that expenditure growth could not be reduced was that large increases in subsidies went to cover enterprises' mounting losses after the decentralization reforms. Enterprise subsidies soared from Y20 billion in 1984 to Y60 billion in 1989, raising subsidies as a share of total expenditure from 10 per cent to 17 per cent.

In a nutshell, the large income increases of SOE personnel enlarged the budget deficit by denying the state (owner) of its revenue, and, in some cases, bankrupting the firms, which then required the state to disburse subsidies in order to maintain employment. The first route through which SOEs destabilized the economy can be described as the "overconsumption/money creation" mechanism.

The second route is the "overinvestment/money creation" mechanism. The discussion on investment finance pointed out that the great "hunger for investment" was being satisfied by externally-raised funds. The easy availability of credit is confirmed by the balance sheet of the central bank (the People's Bank of China), see Table 1.3, p. 36.[32] Part C shows that "loans to state-owned banks" was the biggest factor behind the expansion of reserve money, and that this was the item reined in whenever the state needed to cool the economy. In the expansionary phase (1986 and 1989), "loans to state-owned banks" was responsible for over 80 per cent of the increase in reserve money. In the contractionary phases (1987, 1990 and 1991), the growth of "loans to state-owned banks" would be reduced, and, given its large share in the composition of high-power money, this would lower reserve money growth.

The primary importance of "loans to state-owned banks" to overall credit availability supports the hypothesis that macroeconomic instability originated from local firms being helped in their quest for capital formation by local banks. The incentives for overinvestment at the firm level are clear, and what Table 1.3, confirms is that local banks have been able to squeeze the central bank for more reserves.

The decomposition of GDP growth in the 1981-1989 period confirms this analysis in Table 4.8. Consumption leapt forward 11 per cent and investment spending 21 per cent with the decentralization reforms in 1984. However, with a given output capacity at any point in time, overconsumption and overinvestment cannot both be realized on a prolonged basis unless massive external borrowing occurs. Monetary policy determines which type of overexpenditure will dominate.

The 1984 change in the incentives faced by the financial system is the reason why investment exceeded consumption as the leading expenditure category during 1985-1987. The burst of bank credits in 1985 allowed domestic investment spending to contribute 11 percentage points to the overall growth rate. The credit expansion allowed investment to crowd out consumption in the competition for the use of resources. This is why consumption grew only 3 per cent in 1986.

However, with the reining in of credit in late 1988, the overconsumption tendency asserted itself. Consumption grew 9 per cent in 1989 despite the slowdown in GDP growth to 3 per cent.

---

[32] Data are available only from June 1985 because the People's Bank of China assumed the traditional bank functions in 1984.

Table 4.8: National Account Analysis, 1980-1989

	1980	1981	1982	1983	1984	1985	1986	1987	1988	1989
A. In Constant 1987 Prices (Y billion)										
Private Consumption	391.3	412.8	429.9	470.5	522.2	570.4	585.0	621.9	685.4	746.2
Government Consumption	34.0	45.4	48.1	52.5	58.1	61.2	64.3	70.0	78.4	85.6
Domestic Investment	191.4	182.1	200.5	225.6	272.4	368.5	404.2	445.0	491.1	477.3
Net Exports	-14.8	-9.0	5.3	2.1	-2.0	-43.7	-21.5	-1.1	-7.0	-21.8
Gross Domestic Product	601.9	631.3	683.8	750.7	850.7	956.4	1032	1135.8	1247.9	1287.3
B. Rate of Growth (%)										
Private Consumption		5.5	4.1	9.4	11.0	9.2	2.6	6.3	10.2	8.9
Government Consumption		33.5	5.9	9.1	10.7	5.3	5.1	8.9	12.0	9.2
Domestic Investment		-4.9	10.1	12.5	20.7	35.3	9.7	10.1	10.4	-2.8
Net Exports		-39.2	-158.9	-60.4	-195.2	2085.0	-50.8	-94.9	536.4	211.4
Gross Domestic Product		4.9	8.3	9.8	13.3	12.4	7.9	10.1	9.9	3.2
C. Contribution to Growth (percentage points)										
Private Consumption		3.6	2.7	6.0	6.9	5.6	1.6	3.6	5.8	4.9
Government Consumption		1.9	0.4	0.6	0.7	0.4	0.3	0.5	0.6	0.6
Domestic Investment		-1.6	2.9	3.7	6.2	11.3	3.7	4.0	4.0	-1.1
Net Exports		1.0	2.3	-0.5	-0.5	-4.9	2.2	1.9	-0.5	-1.2
Gross Domestic Product		4.9	8.3	9.8	13.3	12.4	7.8	10.0	9.9	3.2

Source: Part A from World Bank 1991.

The overcompensation of workers and the overinvestment by SOEs are results of incomplete enterprise reforms and not of decentralization. Decentralization might have increased the technical efficiency of SOEs, but by itself is incapable of improving the SOEs' financial performance. The cure for the financial misbehavior is to change the mechanism that supervises SOEs: the stock market is the appropriate supervision mechanism for SOEs in the PRC.

ISSUES IN ENTERPRISE REFORM

Enterprise reforms are fundamental to stopping the decline in the tax revenue/GNP ratio. As noted, both the tax revenue/profits and profits/GNP ratios have fallen since 1980. To stop the decline in the tax revenue/GNP ratio, the system of enterprise taxation must be changed. To stop the decline in the profits/GNP ratio, a broad range of reforms that encompass changes outside of the SOE sector need to be implemented in order to induce enterprise behavior that is compatible with the working of a market economy.

Reforming Enterprise Taxation

Even though the GDP share of value added generated in the industrial SOE sector has declined significantly since 1978, the decline is not reflected in the share of tax revenue from this sector. It is therefore necessary and equitable that tax collection be widened to cover nonstate industrial enterprises, which should bear the same tax burden as the SOEs, and be audited more frequently to reduce tax evasion.

Taxes on consumers should be raised to retrieve part of the SOE profits transferred to consumers via the lower prices caused by the entry of nonstate industrial enterprises.

It is also important that more attention be given to the collection of taxes in the nonindustrial sectors. The service sector is now unnaturally small in the PRC, but the acceleration to a market economy will make it a significant contributor to state revenue if collection procedures are in place.

From the macroeconomic perspective, the recommended tax increases should be done through income taxes and not turnover taxes (product tax, VAT, and business tax). An increase in income taxes will reduce aggregate demand and exert downward pressure on prices. An increase in turnover taxes will directly cause price increases, and the subsequent drop in aggregate demand may not be enough to offset the initial price jump. However, since only about 1 per cent of the population currently pay personal income tax, raising the VAT rate may be the most efficient of the solutions feasible in the medium term.

From the macroeconomic perspective, the present enterprise profit contracting system is destabilizing. During an economic downturn, the fixed amount of tax and profit remittance means that the proportion of profits that is retained as discretionary income is decreased. The reverse happens during an economic upturn. The result is amplification of the cyclical fluctuations. The macroeconomic view would favor a tax system that makes the proportion of profits retained either counter-cyclical or cyclically neutral.

Arguing against this macroeconomic consideration is the suggestive evidence that the zero marginal tax rate on profits of the profit contracting system has been more successful in encouraging growth than the proportional tax system of 1983-1985.

Results from the experimental SPTR system are encouraging. The system combines proportional taxation of profits with a fixed remittance quota on after-tax profits. It will tax profits at only 33 per cent, compared with the present 55 per cent tax rate. Furthermore, the proportional tax aspect will ensure that the elasticity of revenue with respect to profits will be roughly one, hence not allowing the revenue/profits ratio to decline as under the present profit contracting system.

The SPTR system is generally a good plan but it has at least two major problems. (1) It will be revenue neutral only if the Energy and Transport Key Construction Fund contributions continue to be levied. (2) The proposal that an enterprise pays tax to the level of government that owns it runs contrary to the spirit of separating profit and tax, and perpetuates the lack of incentives for local governments to be vigilant in collecting income taxes from central enterprises and in overseeing their operations.

All enterprise income taxes should therefore be shared by the central and local governments.

Improving the Financial Performance of the SOE Sector

From both the competition induced and excessive wage explanations of the drop in the profitability of industrial SOEs, it should be clear that the drop in profitability cannot be equated with a drop in productivity. Financial performance and technical productivity are two different things. Technical productivity may indeed have improved while financial performance has worsened.

The recovery of the profits/GNP ratio requires first, that the incentive system and institutional constraints be changed to curb the present overconsumption and overinvestment by SOEs. Increases in managerial reward and employees' consumption should be in line with profit growth, and the relationships between the enterprise and outside agents (e.g., local government and bank) should be changed to a mode compatible with the functioning of a market economy. Second, that new citywide (and, eventually, nationwide) social security and housing arrangements be established to ease the restructuring of SOEs.

One efficient method of increasing the pressure for management improvement is to convert SOEs into joint-stock companies with the state as a stockholder in each one. The people's degree of satisfaction with a SOE's financial performance and assessment of its economic future will be reflected in the prices of its stocks. Such transparent "voting" by the people on different enterprises in the same industry will (1) constrain the supervising ministry from introducing too many noneconomic considerations into its appraisal of management performance, and (2) generate a natural indicator for the supervising ministry to use in approving managers' and workers' compensation.

A necessary prerequisite for the rational working of the stock market is the universal adoption of a common accounting framework that matches the analytical categories of modern economics. The present industry-specific accounting practices are, in any case, unsuitable for conducting policy analysis. Changes in accounting practices are clearly a first priority regardless of whether and when a stock market is introduced nationwide.

Another possible way of elevating profit maximization to be the primary goal of SOE managers is to set up state asset management corporations (SAMCs) to take over enterprise supervision from the various ministries. Shenzhen City established the Shenzhen Investment Management Company in 1987 to oversee its SOEs. The Shenzhen Investment Management Company has set up profit-sharing arrangements with SOEs and made managers personally responsible for part of any losses and profits, has the power to sell and merge SOEs, and approves the dividend and bonus practices of each SOE.[33] There are now over 30 such asset management corporations in the PRC, with four of them at the provincial level.[34]

The authors recommend a combination of the stock market approach and the asset management approach to be the new supervision mechanism of SOEs. The following two sets of measures should be simultaneously implemented.

First, regional SAMCs will be established. SAMCs will be charged with reorganizing the SOEs, into corporations, selling a specified proportion of their portfolios every year, approving all forms of labor and managerial compensation, and (when necessary) reorganizing the enterprises. SOEs can be shut down with the approval of the Ministry of Finance. SAMCs will be required to link the incomes of SOE managers to the success of investments initiated by them. In turn, the income of a SAMC manager will be determined by comparing the rate of return on the manager's portfolio with the rates of return achieved by nonstate investment institutions and other SAMCs. Furthermore, collusion among SAMCs will be severely punished.

Second, the external environment that the SAMCs operate under will be modified. Nationally linked stock exchanges should be set up, a commercial code and bankruptcy laws introduced, and the formation of nonstate investment firms encouraged. A labor market should be established by starting the social insurance and housing reforms (see Chapter 5). The financial sector should be restructured to eliminate the "soft" loan constraint, and the fiscal system reformed to remove the "soft" tax subsidy constraint. Furthermore, the financial sector and the fiscal sys-

---

[33] A fuller discussion of the working of the Shenzhen Investment Management Company is included as Appendix IV.

[34] *China Daily*, 5 December 1992.

tem should not favor any particular type of enterprise in their operations.

With the establishment of a social safety net, SAMCs will be allowed to close SOEs without approval from the Ministry of Finance. Over time, with the greater sophistication of the stock markets and the smaller portfolios of SAMCs, the power of SAMCs over the running of SOEs will be reduced to that of an ordinary shareholder.

Another complementary step that should be implemented to force SOEs to focus on economic efficiency is to increase the level of competition they face in the goods market. The legal barriers to setting up collective, cooperative, and private enterprises, and the local restrictions on regional trade should be reduced.

Much has been made of the unemployment costs associated with closing inefficient and outmoded enterprises, but perhaps not enough of the benefits associated with the transformation to a socialist market economy. Temporary unemployment is unfortunately unavoidable if the structure of production has to be reoriented. There is no better way to shorten the unemployment period and to guarantee a higher living standard than to have a fast growing economy, and the best way to accelerate growth is to quickly eliminate the inefficient enterprises. The government's present efforts to establish a comprehensive unemployment insurance scheme (See Chapter 5) is the right approach to attenuate the sacrifice during the adjustment to the socialist market economy.

Chapter 5

Social Insurance and Housing Reforms

THE SOCIAL INSURANCE SYSTEM

Social insurance in the PRC consists of three components.

1. *Disaster relief* is provided in times of natural calamities such as earthquakes, floods, fires, and drought. Its provision is the responsibility of the Ministry of Civil Affairs.

2. *Welfare support* is provided to economically or physically disadvantaged individuals. Welfare support takes the forms of cash disbursement and the provision of social facilities (e.g., orphanages, mental institutions), training programs and jobs (through "welfare enterprises" where half of the workers have physical handicaps). Because of such training schemes and job opportunities, the employment rate for the disabled is 70 per cent in the countryside and 90 per cent in the big cities. The Ministry of Civil Affairs is also in charge of these welfare programs.

3. *Labor insurance* was originally established for the employees of SOEs, big collectives, and government departments. Labor insurance encompasses pensions, medical insurance (including maternity leave) and unemployment insurance. The Ministry of Labor supervises labor insurance in SOEs, big collective enterprises, joint venture enterprises, and foreign enterprises. The Ministry of Personnel supervises labor insurance for employees in the government, the Party and nonprofit institutions. The People's Insurance Company of China supervises labor insurance in small collective enterprises and private enterprises.

Total expenditure on social insurance has increased mark-edly from Y114 billion during 1981-1985 to Y316 billion during 1986-1990. The growth in social insurance expenditure has risen more than the growth of the total wage bill for every type of industrial enterprise (see Table 5.1).

Table 5.1:   Trends in the Cost of Labor Insurance and Welfare Benefits

Item	1978	1987
State Units		
Total (Y billion)	6.9	41.6
As share of total wage bill (%)	14.7	28.5
Collective Units		
Total (Y billion)	0.9	9.0
As share of total wage bill (%)	9.0	22.0
Joint Units		
Total (Y billion)	–	0.3
As share of total wage bill (%)	–	23.8
Total of all Units		
Total (Y billion)	7.8	50.9
As share of total wage bill (%)	13.7	27.0
As share of GDP (%)	2.2	4.6
Retirement and disability component		
(Y billion)	1.7	23.8
– As share of total wage bill (%)	3.0	12.7
– As share of GDP (%)	0.5	2.2

Source: Adapted from World Bank 1990b, Table 2.2.

Given this mushrooming of social insurance expenditure, it is important to consider what reforms are needed in the social insurance programs to improve their effectiveness and to con-trol the upward cost trend. Of particular importance is the re-tirement and disability component, which has grown twice as fast as total social insurance expenditure vis-a-vis GDP.

Social insurance reforms are a necessary complement to enterprise reforms. To achieve the goal of a market economy, the enterprise budget must be separated from the government budget to make the enterprises responsible for their own profits and losses. With financial independence, each enterprise has an incentive to economize on the use of inputs, develop and adopt cost-saving innovations, improve the quality of its output, introduce new product lines, and seek new markets for its products. However, for financial performance to accurately reflect economic efficiency, the enterprise must be shorn of its noneconomic responsibilities. The difference in financial situations between any two firms in the same industry should reflect the difference in managerial competence and employees' diligence rather than the difference in the number of retired workers that each firm is obliged to support.

Social insurance reforms consist of creating new arrangements to take over the social welfare functions that are now performed by enterprises. The aim of social insurance reforms is to enable enterprises to focus mainly on economic activities while protecting employees from the effects of restructuring.

Permanent (guaranteed lifetime) employment is undesirable when an economy is making the transition to a market economy. As economic restructuring will necessarily involve reallocation of labor across industries, temporary unemployment will appear because it takes time for the mismatch between the rise in labor demand in one economic sector and the fall in labor demand in another sector to be eliminated. The provision of unemployment insurance will reduce the costs of moving to a market economy.

Social insurance reforms are needed not only to provide a social safety net but also to improve the mobility of workers between enterprises (and between regions, eventually). If switching jobs entails the forfeiture of retirement contributions, even workers in shrinking industries are understandably reluctant to move to new enterprises in growing industries. The existing enterprise-specific pension schemes must be reformed in order to rationalize the financial positions of SOEs and to ease labor reallocation. The discussion of social insurance reforms will concentrate on pension reforms and unemployment insurance reforms.

The Pension System

Retirement Insurance Schemes

A retirement insurance scheme was established for workers in SOEs and big collectives with the promulgation of the "Labor Insurance Regulations of the People's Republic of China" in March 1951 (amended in 1953). A separate retirement insurance scheme was established for workers in government departments, the Party and nonprofit organizations in 1954. The Ministry of Labor provided the operational guidelines to the provincial and local labor bureaus which, after taking local conditions into account, issued to the enterprises instructions on how to implement the retirement insurance scheme.

In some areas such as Chongqing during the 1950s, each enterprise contributed 2 per cent of the total wage bill to a local pension fund. But in most places, each enterprise administered its own pension scheme, a practice that became universal after the Cultural Revolution. Since most enterprises administered their retirement schemes with little supervision, there was great variety in the total retirement package (pension plus in-kind benefits such as housing and occasional distribution of consumer goods) across enterprises.

The pension was funded as a pay-as-you-go scheme that was deducted as operating expenses of the enterprise with no contributions from the active workers. If there was a shortfall, the government subsidized the loss—a logical consequence of no separation between the enterprise budget and the government budget.

With the efforts (starting in 1984) to make SOEs financially independent, the unequal retirement burden across enterprises made retirement insurance reforms inevitable. Some long established enterprises in Chongqing even had a 1 to 1 ratio between active and retired workers. Three major changes have been made to the 1951 scheme.

1. In 1979, enterprises were instructed to adjust their pensions periodically to compensate for the erosion of purchasing power by inflation. These instructions were advisory in nature because they did not include explicit guidelines on the

amount of price indexation or the frequency of the adjustment. The result was that inflation adjustment depended on
the financial position of the enterprise concerned.

2.   In 1986, all SOEs under the control of city and county gov-
     ernments were directed to pool their pensions, except SOEs
     under the control of central ministries and provincial gov-
     ernments. By 1992, 2270 cities and counties (i.e., 96 per cent
     of cities and counties) were under this new system, which
     covered 52 million permanent workers and 12 million con-
     tract workers in SOEs, and supported 10 million retirees.[35]
     A separate pension pool covers big collective enterprises.
     In 1992, 1548 cities and counties had pension pools for col-
     lective enterprises.

3.   Also in 1986, a new category of workers was created and had
     to contribute to the pension scheme. A labor contract system
     was introduced to replace the lifetime employment system
     for new employees. (The new labor contract system was not
     strictly enforced for a number of years.) The basic wage of a
     contract worker is 10 per cent higher than that of a perma-
     nent worker. In 1991, SOEs had 14 million contract workers
     (14 per cent of the SOE labor force), and collectives had 3
     million contract workers (10 per cent of their labor force).

Permanent workers continue to make no contributions to SOE
pension funds, and the average contribution by an SOE is 18 per
cent of total wages and bonuses. (Shanghai, which has one of
the highest proportions of retirees, requires its SOEs to pay pension contributions that come to 22.5 per cent of total wages and
bonuses.) Contract workers, on the other hand, have to contribute 3 per cent of their basic wage to the pension fund while the
enterprise has to contribute 15 per cent of total wages.

The pension pool and benefits of the permanent and contract workers are kept separate. The permanent workers' pension scheme continues to be pay-as-you-go. The contract workers' pension scheme is a funded scheme because the employees
hired since 1986 are young. In 1991, 82 per cent of the SOE labor
force participated in one of these pension pools.

---

[35]   Information from State Commission on Economic Restructuring, 23 September
       1992. Author's interview at the Ministry of Finance, 14 October 1992, put the number
       of retirees at 15 million.

The present entitlement criteria and benefit levels of the pension plan are summarized in Table 5.2. The normal retirement age for men is 60, and for women, 50. For workers with hazardous jobs, the retirement age is 55 for men and 45 for women. The typical new retiree (who started work after 1949 and has 20 years of continuous work) is entitled to a retirement income that equals 75 per cent of the standard wage received in the last period of employment.

Pensions paid by SOEs are double the amount paid by collective enterprises and are well above the income received by the average urban household. The data for 1987 are shown in Table 5.3.

Table 5.2: Entitlement Criteria and Benefit Levels for Workers in State Enterprises, Government and Party Organizations

Entitlement Criteria

| | Eligible Retirement Age | | Length of Continuous Service | Other Factors |
	Men	Women		
A.	60	50	10	
B.	55	45	10	Hazardous jobs.
C.	50	45	10	Loss of ability to work due to illness.
D.	-	-	-	Loss of ability to work due to injury on the job.

Benefit Levels

Recipient	Percentage of Standard Wage
Category A, B or C	
1. Started work during World War II (1937-1945)	90%
2. Started work during 1945-1949	80%
3. Started work after 1949 and for 20 years continuously	75%
4. Worked between 15 and 20 years continuously	70%
5. Worked between 10 and 15 years continuously	60%
6. If pension is less than Y30	Y30
Category D	
7. Dependent on care	90% plus some care expenses
8. Not dependent on care	80%
9. Pension less than Y40	Y40

Source: World Bank, 1990b.

This generous payment of retirement benefits explains why 48 per cent of total labor insurance and welfare benefits paid by state units in 1987 went to retired workers even though there were more than six active workers for every retired worker. In 1987, retired SOE workers received Y14 billion in pensions, Y2 billion in medical care, and Y4 billion in welfare benefits. State units paid Y41 billion in labor insurance and welfare benefits.

The State Reform Commission is studying the desirability of (1) requiring permanent workers in SOEs to contribute to the pension schemes, (2) including a supplementary pension scheme

Table 5.3: Pensions in State and Collective Enterprises, 1987

Item	Average	SOEs	Collective Enterprises
Pension per Retiree (Y)	1,263	1,470	718
Ratio of Average Pension to Average Wage	87%	95%	60%
Ratio of Average Pension to Urban Household Income per Capita	125%	145%	71%
Ratio of Average Pension to Urban Household Living Expenditure per Capita	143%	166%	81%

Source: World Bank 1990b, Table 2.8

where workers and enterprises can buy additional coverage, and (3) having independent pension companies provide pension coverage to town and village enterprises, private enterprises, joint-venture enterprises, self-employed individuals, and elected village cadres.

In May 1992, Shenzhen adopted a new pension system ("The Temporary Provisions on Social Insurance of Shenzhen City.")[36]

---

[36] The pension reforms were part of a social security package that reorganized the pension system, medicare insurance, and housing accumulation funds. Work injury insurance and unemployment insurance were not changed.

Every PRC citizen working in Shenzhen is eligible for coverage under this citywide pension pool. A worker's contribution rate varies with the total monthly wage (see Table 5.4).

Table 5.4: Shenzhen Workers' Pension Contribution Rates
(per cent)

Workers' Total Monthly Wage	Contribution Rate
Less than Y600	5
Y600-700	6
Y700 - 800	7
Y800-900	8
Y900-1000	9
Greater than 1000	10

Source: Shenzhen Municipal Government, Article 10.

If a worker's total wage is less than 60 per cent of the average wage in Shenzhen in the preceding year, then the employer will pay the 5 per cent contribution on the worker's behalf.

The firm contributes 16 per cent of its workers' total wages to their individual accounts in the pension plan. The firm reduces its contribution by the same percentage points that the worker's contribution rate is above 5 per cent. Five percentage points of the firm's contribution is put into a common (coinsurance) pool, and the rest into the worker's individual account where the 5 per cent contribution was deposited.

At retirement, the worker receives a monthly amount proportional to the principal and interest accumulated in the account. The common (coinsurance) pool will continue pension payments if the worker is still alive after his or her individual account has been used up.

Shenzhen set up the Social Insurance Commission to manage this citywide pension system.[37] As of 9 November 1992, 288,000 workers in 3,527 enterprises and institutions have joined this new pension system.[38]

---

[37]   The Social Insurance Commission also manages the housing accumulation fund, and a new Medical Insurance Administration Bureau manages the reorganized medicare insurance scheme.

[38]   *China Daily*, 28 December 1992.

The Ministry of Civil Affairs is testing an experimental pension program for farmers. More than 7 million farmers from 800 counties in 29 provinces, autonomous regions, and municipalities are participating in the experiment. The pension pool now amounts to Y400 million. To encourage participation, the monthly premiums vary across areas, from Y2 to Y20. It is estimated that a person who starts contributing in his or her 20s will draw Y800 a year upon turning 60. This pension program for farmers is expected to be nationwide by 1995.[39]

Problems with the Pension System

The pension system has weakened the fiscal position of the government in two ways.

1. Since the permanent SOE workers who are most of the participants do not make contributions, enterprise profits and hence state revenue are lowered.
2. SOEs with few retirees have been granted tax exemptions to induce them to join the pension pool.

The pension system is being undermined by the growing population of retirees, especially by the "pay-as-you-go" system for the permanent workers. The ratio of active workers to retired workers was 30:1 in 1978 but had fallen to 5.9:1 in 1990. The World Bank has projected that the ratio will drop to 5.4:1 in 2000 and 2.5:1 in 2030 (World Bank 1990b, p. 27).

The pension system provides narrow and fragmented coverage. It covers only workers in SOEs and big collectives, and even then in separate pools; and these pools are specific to each city and county. Thus, the pension scheme inhibits labor mobility across enterprises with different types of ownership, or across regions.

The pension pools have encouraged enterprises to use early retirements as substitutes for raising the wages of skilled workers. The World Bank (1990b, p.26) reported that

---

[39] *China Daily*, 23 September 1992.

"an enterprise in Shanghai with a standard wage of Y100
per month . . . rehires its skilled retirees at Y120 per month
... [Retiring] and rehiring such workers rather than simply
raising their wages represents an effort to shift the cost of
retaining skilled labor to the newly formed pension pools.
Enterprises and workers feel they can use these pools to
increase their income at everyone else's expense".[40]

Pension pools are being drained to be used as income supplements by the older workers. With the vigorous expansion of
the nonstate sector since 1984, many older workers retired with
full pension benefits and took new jobs with nonstate firms. SOEs
are ready to approve retirement with full benefits to older workers who claim to be in bad health because the SOEs can then get
younger (hence, more productive and better educated) workers.
The result is a high incidence of men retiring at 50 and women at
45 on account of illness (this is the minimum age to be eligible
for full benefits without being disabled by work-related injuries).
The cost of this collusion between the older workers and the SOEs
can be substantial, as in the case of Yinkou City in Liaoning. When
the retirement approval process was transferred from the enterprises to the city government, the annual number of disability
retirements dropped from 1000 to 100 (World Bank 1990b, p.50).
Cities and counties control pension funds without any supervision. Management fees amounting to Y330 million were
charged to the pension funds in 1991, an average of Y19,000 for
each employee administering the pension scheme. In one extreme
case, the management fee came to Y92,000 per administrator.

Issues in Pension Reforms

Pension contributions have to be made more portable, otherwise
labor flows will not occur with the ease demanded by a rapidly-
changing economy. Four steps need to be undertaken to increase
portability.

1.   Relieve enterprises of their administration of the pension
      schemes and centralize the administration to the city and

---

[40]   World Bank, op. cit, p. 26.

county level (then, after a number of years, to the provincial level; and eventually to the national level) so that job changes do not make record-keeping a burdensome task.
2.   Create a city pension pool by combining the separate pension pools of permanent workers at SOEs, contract workers at SOEs, and workers at big collectives.
3.   Standardize the contribution and benefit levels across enterprises and workers. Permanent workers at SOEs should pay 3 per cent of their standard wages into the pension plan, as the workers at collective enterprises do. Participating enterprises must pay the same rate regardless of the number of retirees they have.
4.   Widen the pension pool over time by eliminating the widespread exemptions of SOEs from participation in the pension pool; and (eventually) extend coverage to town and village enterprises, private enterprises, and individuals.

The administration of the pension pool must be tightened. There should be rigorous examination of applications for early retirements on the basis of bad health, and frequent independent auditing of management fees.

The practice of investing the entire pension funds in time deposits at banks should be discontinued. The pension funds should also be invested in the domestic security markets, subject to a ceiling on the proportion of investment in any one asset. Managers of the pension funds should receive salaries tied to the performance of the investments to encourage the right mix of risk-taking and prudence.

The existing retirement ages are low by international standards. Retirement ages should be raised by five years to deal with the demographic problem of an aging population. Furthermore, since women live longer than men by about three years, their retirement ages should equal those of men.

As the standard (basic) wage is a shrinking proportion of the total wage, the base for contributions and benefits should be changed to the total wage (which includes bonuses). In this way, pension benefits will be made proportional to work effort. The greater the work effort, the larger the bonus, and hence the larger the size of future pension income.

To dilute a firm's effort to give large wage increases in an employee's last period before retirement, the base for pension calculation should be changed from total wage in the last year to the average of total wages over the last three years. A lengthening of the base period will also reduce the incentive of workers to boost pension payments by striving to receive a big bonus during the final few months of work.

UNEMPLOYMENT INSURANCE

The Unemployment Insurance System

Eradicating the assumption of assured lifelong employment and easing labor flows among enterprises are vital to the success of enterprise reforms. Guaranteed lifelong employment was ended with the July 1986 regulation that most new employees (unless exempted) of SOEs from October 1986 onward would be contract workers. Terminating the tenureship of permanent workers was made easier with the July 1986 regulation, "Dismissal of Discipline – Violating Workers of State-Owned Enterprises".

To cope with resulting temporary unemployment, an unemployment insurance scheme for SOE workers ("Interim Regulations for State-Owned Enterprise Workers' Waiting-for-Employment Insurance") was launched at the same time. Workers who lose their jobs after five or more years of service receive 60 to 75 per cent of the basic wage in the first year of unemployment and 50 per cent in the second year. (The basic wage is set by the government and is a declining share of labor compensation because of the growing importance of bonuses and subsidies.) Workers who have less than five years of service receive 60 to 75 per cent of the basic wage for a maximum of one year. Workers who twice turn down job offers recommended by the labor department are taken off unemployment insurance. The unemployment insurance scheme is funded by enterprises, which contribute 1 per cent of their basic wage bill. See Box 5.1 for additional details of the scheme.

The Chinese benefit rates (60 to 75 per cent of standard wage) are comparable to those in Europe. In 1985, an unemployed worker received 63 per cent of previous after-tax income in West Ger-

---

**Box 5.1: Main Features of Unemployment Insurance
Introduced in 1986**

Eligibility:
1. workers of bankrupt enterprises,
2. workers made redundant by near-bankrupt enterprises during reorganization,
3. contract workers after expiration or cancellation of their contracts, and
4. workers dismissed for disciplinary reasons.

Relief allowance:
1. workers with 5 or more years of service receive up to 24 months' support, during the first 12 months they receive 60-75 per cent of standard wage; during the next 12 months they receive 50 per cent (the standard wage is calculated as the worker's average monthly standard wage over two years before leaving the enterprise); and
2. workers with less than 5 years of service receive up to 12 months' support at 60-75 per cent of standard wage

Other benefits:
1. for those in categories 1 and 2, medical expenses, funeral and burial subsidies for workers and immediate families, retirement pensions (where there is no centralized retirement pension plan), and early retirement pensions for those less than five years from retirement age); and

2. for those in categories 3 and 4, medical subsidies.

Ineligibility: People who have twice refused for no legitimate reason to accept a job recommended by relevant agencies will be excluded.

Funding: Enterprises contribute 1 per cent of their basic wage bill; in addition financed by interest paid by banks on unemployment insurance funds and local government subsidies.

Administration: by local labor service companies.

Retraining: Funds may be used to pay for retraining of job-awaiting workers, or to construct training facilities.

Source: World Bank 1990b.

many, and 57 to 75 per cent in France. But the two-year benefit period in the PRC is more generous than the one-year period in Canada, Germany, and the United States.

With this social safety net in place, the government adopted an enterprise bankruptcy law in November 1988.[41] The existence of a social safety net in the PRC is unusual for a country at its level of development. The Social Security Administration of the United States conducted an international survey in 1987, and found that of the 32 countries in the "low-income" category only one (Ghana) had an unemployment insurance scheme and that, of the 32 countries in the "lower middle-income" category, only four (Chile, Ecuador, Egypt, and Tunisia) had unemployment insurance schemes.[42]

In 1991, 88 per cent (70 million) of the SOE labor force was covered by unemployment insurance. Qingdao and Hangzhou have now extended unemployment insurance coverage to the whole formal urban area.

The draw on unemployment insurance funds has been small, resulting in an annual surplus that is added to the large reserves held at the local banks. For example, the contribution of SOEs to the unemployment insurance fund in 1991 was Y837 million, but only Y24 million was paid out in benefits that year—a minuscule amount compared to the Y72 million for management fees in 1991.

The reason for the low draw on unemployment insurance benefit is simple. SOEs are under great pressure to hold on to their surplus workers and, when necessary, the SOEs receive tax exemptions and bank loans to do so. So, despite two economic slowdowns between the last quarter of 1986 and the second quarter of 1992, only 400,000 people have received unemployment insurance: 200,000 people from the fourth quarter of 1986 through 1990; 100,000 through 1991; and 100,000 through the first half of 1992.

In Chongqing in 1992, about half of the SOEs were running losses, but there were only 1963 unemployed workers receiving unemployment insurance benefits. The unemployment insurance

---

[41]   The first bankruptcy since 1949 had occurred two years earlier, when Shenyang City government shut down the Shenyang Anti-Explosion Device Plant in August 1986.

[42]   U.S. Department of Health and Human Services 1987.

office in Ningbo requires the employer to contribute for each laid-off worker money amounting to the 24 months of benefits that the worker is eligible for. The result is that enterprises lay off only quarrelsome workers whose presence affected the performance of the other workers.

Given the large reserve of unemployment insurance funds, some regions have used the reserves to extend loans to SOEs to enable them to hold on to their surplus labor, e.g., Xinxiang in Henan. In one case (Anyang in Henan), loans were given to a bankrupt firm on the condition that the manager would be replaced. The manager was replaced and the firm turned a profit six months later. It is not clear how typical the Anyang case is.

Information on the working of the unemployment insurance scheme raises troubling questions on whether the funds are well managed. The management fee in 1991 was three times the amount of unemployment insurance benefits paid out. A coal mine in the northwest went bankrupt, and, because the local office had deposited the funds in a five-year bank account, the workers did not receive benefits for a substantial period until the local office had worked out alternative financing. It might be less costly to pay unemployment insurance benefits to the surplus workers directly than to pay enterprises to let the surplus workers continue producing goods that are not improving the financial situation of the enterprise.

Issues in Unemployment Insurance Reforms

It is important to increase supervision over the management of the unemployment insurance funds. Regular audits of management costs and regular assessments of investment performance should be institutionalized immediately.

The coverage should be increased in phases: first, extend coverage to the temporary and seasonal workers at SOEs; then, to nonstate urban enterprises; and, finally, to town and village enterprises.

The establishment of retraining programs for the unemployed would be desirable, especially after the economy has entered into a more knowledge-intensive mode of production.

HOUSING REFORM

In the reform period, the provision of housing in urban areas has become one of the largest, but mostly hidden, items of government expenditure. With decentralization of economic management, beginning in 1979 the pace of housing construction has quickened. Each year the number of housing units and amount of floor space completed have risen (see Table 5.5). Through the 1980s, up to 8 per cent of GNP and 30 per cent of gross fixed asset formation were devoted to investment in housing construction (Table 5.6). These levels of expenditure on housing investment seem excessive in the international context, where such expenditures (in terms of housing investment to GNP ratio and housing investment's share in total capital formation) are more commonly associated with per capita GNP of $7500 or more, far in excess of PRC income levels (World Bank 1992c). Moreover, since rents remained at extremely low levels throughout the 1980s, the rapid additions to public housing stock brought with them rapidly growing recurrent costs in subsidizing the maintenance and management of public housing.

Table 5.5: Rate of Housing Construction

Year	Dwelling Units Completed (million)	Floor Area Completed (million m²)
1949-78 Average	1.67	100.0
1978	2.12	134.5
1979	6.61	462.6
1980	7.98	582.3
1981	9.26	694.4
1982	9.53	714.6
1983	11.54	865.4
1984	10.11	758.2
1985	12.13	909.7
1986	15.69	1,176.6
1987	14.36	1,076.9
1988	13.97	1,048.0
1989	11.09	831.9

Source: Center for Policy Research, Ministry of Construction, cited in World Bank 1992c.

**Table 5.6: Housing Investment as a Proportion
of GNP and GFAF[a]**
(per cent)

Year	GNP	GFAF
1949-78 average	1.50	n.a.
1978	2.01	7.44
1979	3.70	14.80
1980	5.07	21.14
1981	6.39	31.95
1982	7.09	29.57
1983	7.39	29.56
1984	6.89	26.53
1985	7.70	25.64
1986	7.71	24.90
1987	7.89	24.70
1988	7.61	23.82
1989	6.79	25.84

a   GFAF = Gross Fixed Asset Formation

Source: Center for Policy Research, Ministry of Construction, cited in World Bank 1992c.

From the fiscal perspective, reform is urgently needed to curb the insatiable appetite for housing, which is fueled on the consumers' side by low rents that absorb less than 1 per cent of total consumption expenditures. On the supply side, rapid housing construction is partly fueled by soft budget constraints at SOEs, but is also encouraged by government agencies wishing to improve living conditions for the populace. Reform that reduces the huge expenditures on housing subsidy will help balance the budget and free resources for better targeted government programs. At the same time, housing reform is an essential part of the overall program of transition toward a market economy, by correcting the single most distorted price for a key consumer good. As noted in Chapter 4, housing reform will also help SOEs shed a large social welfare burden and reduce distortions in their cost structure. Reform that severs housing provision from work units is also needed to eliminate a significant obstacle to interenterprise labor mobility in the PRC, by reducing worker dependence on the work units.

This section examines reforms under way in the provision of urban housing. Rural housing is not examined because it is virtually all privately owned and enjoys a few subsidies from the government. The system of urban housing provision is first examined. The current reform agenda and a few local programs are then described. The concluding subsection presents issues to consider for the future.

Current Status of Housing Provision

Housing is mostly publicly owned in Chinese cities. From the late 1950s through 1970s, private ownership was restricted. Estimates vary somewhat on the share of urban housing that is publicly owned, from two thirds to about three quarters (Cai 1991 and World Bank 1992c). The share of private ownership is up to 50 per cent in small towns.

Public housing is allocated administratively, largely on a per capita basis. Rents are set at extremely low levels. Indeed, from an average of Y0.3 per square meter in 1952, rents were lowered gradually through the 1960s and 1970s to an average of Y0.13, which remained in effect through most of the 1980s. As household incomes rose rapidly in the 1980s, rent payments fell to 0.6-0.7 per cent of household expenditures.

Housing "reform" began early. In April 1980, Deng Xiaoping suggested four changes in the provision of housing: (1) letting consumers buy or build their own housing, (2) allowing some public housing to be sold to consumers, (3) raising rents to encourage private home ownership, and (4) providing subsidies to low income households to offset rent increases.

The most important effect of these early reforms was to decentralize housing construction decisions by clearing the way to letting availability of financing dictate the pace and location of housing construction. As reforms also decentralized the management of resources, this quickly led to a boom in housing construction. During 1979-1990, a total of 1.5 billion square meters of urban housing were added, costing Y280 billion in investment, compared with a total of 0.5 billion square meters built during 1950-1978, at a cost of Y37 billion. As a result, per capita urban housing availability rose from 3.6 square meters in 1978 to 7.1 square meters in 1990 (Wang Yukun 1992).

The share of housing investment financed by the state budget fell sharply, from over 90 per cent before reforms. For the 1978-1989 period, the government accounted for only 23 per cent of total investment in housing, while enterprises accounted for 60 per cent and private sources 17 per cent. For 1988, the shares were: central government 16 per cent, local governments 6 per cent, private sources 20 per cent, SOEs 52 per cent, and collective enterprises 6 per cent (World Bank 1992c).

Corresponding to these investment shares, ownership has become more diversified. Given their dominant share in recent investment in housing construction, enterprises now own more than half of the stock of public housing. "Public housing" is presently owned and managed by three types of agencies: municipal housing bureaus, administrative organizations, and enterprises. Their respective portions vary across cities. Overall, the share owned by municipal housing bureaus is about 20 per cent, but ranges from a high of 71 per cent in Shanghai to 43 per cent in Tianjin, 30 per cent in Changzhou, and 24 per cent in Beijing. Administrative units own another 20 per cent. This leaves about 60 per cent owned by enterprises, almost all of them SOEs (Yun, Bai, and Tan 1991; World Bank 1992c).

While the "reform" has alleviated the extreme shortage of housing that characterized the 1970s and improved the average quality of available housing, it has done little to move the urban housing supply system toward market allocation. In fact, because rent levels remain far below even the variable costs for maintaining and servicing the housing stock, the housing boom imposed huge and growing recurrent costs on the providers (i.e., local governments and work units) to subsidize the shortfall.

Estimating the size of housing subsidies is difficult in the PRC's semireformed economy. In the absence of a market for housing, asset values of the housing stock are difficult to ascertain, because (1) little information is available on differential land values across cities and neighborhoods, and (2) the vintage and quality of the housing stock differs as do the true opportunity costs of investment capital, and the real costs of maintenance and management. Few studies have attempted to derive accurate or comprehensive estimates for the costs of housing provision.

The Ministry of Finance estimates the direct budgetary cost of maintaining public housing at Y2.2 billion per year, and total housing subsidies cost to the economy as Y7.7 billion (World Bank 1992c, p.8). However, these numbers refer most likely only to out-of-pocket costs. When the opportunity costs of investment and taxes are included, cost estimates for total subsidies are much higher. For example, using an extremely low asset value of Y200 per square meter of construction, which is estimated to be the construction cost for structure (excluding land acquisition and infrastructural costs) in 1987, the Ministry of Construction estimated that a "standard rent" of Y1.84 per square meter was needed to cover the costs of depreciation, maintenance, management, and real estate taxes, and to provide a 3 per cent return on investment. Using an asset value of Y400 per square meter and allowing a 10 per cent rate of return on investment raised the "standard rent" to Y7.55, or 58 times the average per square meter rent of Y0.13. These two alternative scenarios are detailed in Table 5.7.

Wang Yukun (1991) estimated total subsidies for urban housing as the gap between "rational rents" that cover the opportunity costs of providing housing and actual rental payments. His estimates for 1978-1988 are presented in Table 5.8. For 1988, he estimated total housing subsidy cost at Y58.4 billion, based on asset values of Y241 per square meter of constructed space and opportunity cost of capital at commercial lending rates. The total subsidy was equal to 4.2 per cent of GNP and 16 per cent of total worker compensation. This amount was larger than budgetary outlays for either price subsidies or SOE loss subsidies for the year, which were Y31.7 billion and Y44.6 billion, respectively (Table 3.12). Since the costs of the subsidies are borne by the providers of housing, i.e., SOEs and administrative units, as well as local governments, only a portion of the costs fall directly on the budget. However, most of these costs are eventually passed through to the budget as a result of increased costs, reduced profits, increased subsidies, or reduced growth because productive investment is squeezed out by expenditures on housing.

Not only is the current urban housing supply system fiscally costly, it is also inefficient and inequitable. The process of sequential allocation within the work unit as housing becomes available produces many poor matches between supply and demand in terms of dwelling size, location, and quality. These allocative inefficiencies tend to persist since matching cannot be improved

Table 5.7: Illustrative Standard Rents for New Housing Units under Alternative Assumptions

Item	Standard Rent Scenario	
	Low	High
Asset Value Assumed	Y200/m^2 of construction	Y400/m^2 of construction
Rentable Space as % of Construction Space	0.75	0.75
Depreciation[a]	Y0.44	Y0.89
Maintenance[b]	Y0.36	Y0.71
Return on Investment[c]	Y0.67	Y4.44
Management Fee[d]	Y0.15	Y0.60
Real Estate Taxes[e]	Y0.22	Y0.91
Total Rent	Y1.84	Y7.55

a   2 per cent of usable assets value/12.
b   80 per cent of depreciation charge. Some analysts use lower absolute levels rather than a formula.
c   Computed at 3 per cent in low case and 10 per cent in high case.
d   10 per cent of the sum of depreciation, maintenance, return on investment, management fees, and taxes.
e   12 per cent of the sum of depreciation, maintenance, return on investment, management fees, and taxes.

Source: Ministry of Construction; cited in World Bank 1992c.

by secondary swaps. The system is inequitable since the quantity and quality of housing supply vary across work units, depending on the unit's profitability and access to credit. The system also creates a huge gulf of inequality between the state and nonstate sectors, because the latter can rarely provide housing to workers and employees.[43] Even within work units, complaints

---

43   In joint venture enterprises, this inequality is offset by the much higher wages paid, but workers in collective and individual enterprises do not enjoy any offsetting compensation. Rural residents do not receive any housing subsidies, which is also a major source of urban-rural income inequalities.

Table 5.8: Size of Urban Housing Subsidies, 1978-1988

Year	Living Space		Rational Rent (Y/m²)	Current Rent (Y/m²)	Housing Subsidy (Y/m²)	Subsidy per Worker (Y)	Total Workers ('000)	Total Subsidies (million)
	Per Capita (m²)	Per Worker (m²)						
1978	4.20	6.36	0.78	0.13	0.65	49.64	94,990	4,715
1979	-	-	0.90	0.13	0.77	-	99,670	-
1980	-	-	1.03	0.13	0.90	-	104,440	-
1981	5.27	6.99	1.19	0.13	1.06	88.60	109,400	9,701
1982	5.61	7.28	1.36	0.13	1.23	107.01	112,810	12,162
1983	5.90	7.57	1.57	0.13	1.44	130.69	115,150	15,044
1984	6.32	8.11	1.04	0.13	1.67	162.84	118,900	19,362
1985	7.46	10.13	2.08	0.13	1.95	236.34	123,500	29,207
1986	8.04	10.85	2.39	0.13	2.26	293.78	128,090	37,579
1987	8.47	11.37	2.74	0.13	2.61	356.60	132,140	47,132
1988	8.80	11.81	3.16	0.13	3.03	428.93	136,080	58,368

Notes:

(1) Living space per capita is from State Statistical Bureau, 1986-1989. From 1978-1984, living space per capita is based on a worker household survey in cities. From 1985, it includes private business workers, residents in small towns, and nonworker households. Including residents in small towns might give an upward bias to housing space estimates (for example, the 1985 National Housing Census reveals that usable floor space per capita is 10.04 m² nationwide, 9.22 m² in cities, and 11.56 m² in towns). But including nonworker households might cut down the estimate of housing space. The two factors probably offset each other. Considering the lower values used in calculating the land cost and interest rate, there is probably no overestimation in calculating the housing subsidy.

(2) Living space per worker = (living space per capita) x (the coefficient of persons/workers) x 0.75. The factor 0.75 is used because 75 per cent of the total workers lived in public housing stock.

(3) Housing subsidy = rational rent - current rent. Annual housing subsidy per worker = (housing space per worker) x (housing subsidy per month) x (12) x (0.75).

Source: Wang Yukun 1992b, Table 4.

of favoritism and unequal distribution are common. Finally, and most egregiously, even as housing availability has nearly doubled in the 1980s, about 15 per cent of urban households remain on government rolls as dire need of housing relief, attesting to the poor targeting of this costly subsidy. Moreover, the housing supply system ties workers to their jobs and severely hinders labor mobility, which in turn impedes the development of labor markets and slows down economic reform.

Reform Implementation and Proposals

Since 1979, housing reform has gone through five stages of implementation (Ministry of Finance 1992 and Yun, Bai, and Tan 1991). Beginning in 1979, some money was allocated from the budget to build urban housing for sale to consumers. These units were offered at full construction cost, then averaging Y120-150 per square meter. However, because these prices far exceeded affordable levels at current wages, and because rents remained extremely low, the program was unpopular, and less than 100,000 square meters was sold over the three-year period 1979-1981 (Yun Bai, and Tan 1991).

In the second stage (1982-1985), experimental programs were adopted for selling public housing to individuals on a subsidized basis, with the state, work units, and individuals each paying one third of the costs and sharing property rights to the housing units. After experimentation in four cities (Changzhou, Shashi, Siping, and Zhengzhou), the program spread to 160 cities and over 300 county towns in 1984-1985. At the same time, some cities began to apply "new rents" to some new housing, rents that covered depreciation, maintenance, and management costs. Apartment sizes were decreased in cities such as Shanghai, where some substandard units were built to provide quicker housing "relief" to newlyweds and other young couples on the waiting list for housing allocation. In Shanghai, these are two-room apartments of 25-40 square meters, with shared kitchen and bathroom facilities. They are often located in undeveloped neighborhoods with minimal infrastructural support.

Through the first two stages, the focus of reform was primarily on increasing the supply of housing by inviting new sources of finance, including private investment. It was not until the third stage (1986-1987) when attention was turned to the much more complicated problem of adjusting rents on the huge stock of public housing. In 1986, three cities, Yantai, Bengbu, and Tangshan, were chosen as experimental cities in implementing comprehensive housing reform, the primary focus of which was to be raising rents and providing partially off-setting wage subsidies to workers. In Yantai, standard rents were raised in one step from the prevailing average of Y0.06 per square meter to Y1.28, the amount estimated to be required for covering the "five cost factors" in rational rent calculations: depreciation, maintenance, management, returns to investment, and real estate taxes. To offset the higher rents, workers received certificates worth 23.5 per cent of basic wages as "housing coupons," with which they could make rent payments. In Tangshan a more gradual approach was proposed to raise rents in several steps, with commensurate wage supplements at each step. At the same time, the reform program also encouraged private home ownership through selling off public housing.

These reforms were to be implemented nationwide during the fourth stage (1988-1990), as outlined in the Plan for Housing Reform, issued by the State Council in February 1988. The plan marked the first attempt at adjusting rents to shift some of the costs to individuals. By giving wage supplements to cushion the effect of rent increases, these reforms would have the effect of gradually monetizing the housing benefit now enjoyed by the urban work force. Unfortunately, it appears that little progress was made in rent reform before the program was put on hold, although a wave of privatization occurred. During the second half of 1988 and through 1989, some public housing was sold to individuals at heavy discounts. Most was sold at prices that were less than 15 per cent of replacement costs, some for as little as 5 per cent (Wang Yukun 1992).

The year 1991 marked the start of the fifth stage, when the State Council reiterated the call for housing reform to be implemented under the guidelines established in the 1988 Plan for Housing Reform. For implementing the dual provisions of rent adjustment and privatization, provinces and cities were asked to formulate specific proposals that set a pace of reform appropriate for local conditions and financial capabilities. The three municipalities of Beijing, Shanghai, and Tianjin were expected to lead the way, along with coastal cities. All other cities were expected to follow by the end of 1992.

Housing Reform in Liaoning Province[44]

The Liaoning provincial guidelines appear to be typical, and they follow closely the State Council Plan outline. The main stipulations are:

1. *Rent Adjustments*. Rents are to be raised gradually to market levels over a 15-year period. During the Eighth Five-Year Plan period, they will be raised to cover three cost factors: maintenance, management fees, and depreciation. By the end of the Ninth Five-Year Plan, they will be raised to cover the five cost factors, including real estate taxes and return to investment. During the Tenth Five-Year Plan, they will be further raised to approach market levels. As a first step, in 1992 rents were raised to an average of Y0.35-0.4 per square meter of usable space.

   During each period, wage supplements will be issued to help offset the higher rents, under the principle that subsidies should cover less than the full cost of rent increases. The suggested amount in 1992 is 2 per cent of standard wages in 1990, although work units with more resources are permitted to issue larger supplements.

   The cost of the wage supplements is to be covered from the housing fund of enterprises and administrative units. When the housing fund is insufficient, work units can apply for approval from financial departments to include a portion under production costs in the case of enterprises, or as part of annual budget for administrative units. The Ministry of Civil Affairs will bear the cost of subsidies for cadres who joined Party work before Liberation and for poor families on social relief.

   To ensure equity, people who have more public housing than permitted under allocation quotas set by the state and the province will be assessed rents equal to the full costs for the amount of excess housing.

---

[44] This section is based on the State Council document, Housing Reform Document No. 3, 1992.

2.   *Selling Public Housing.* Simultaneous with rent adjustments, individuals are encouraged to buy their own homes. The standard price for new units should cover construction costs, land acquisition costs, and compensation payments to displaced residents. For older housing, the price is to cover the depreciated value of replacement cost, plus land acquisition costs. Once housing is privatized, owners will be required to pay fees to the housing bureau to cover maintenance costs. However, given the current low wages, during the initial period of privatization, the enterprises or administrative units will absorb the land acquisition and relocation compensations, so that private buyers pay only construction costs. Real estate taxes are exempted for owner-occupied housing.

Property Rights of Home Ownership. People who purchase homes at these concessional prices acquire partial ownership rights that include inheritance and resale rights. If they resell their home within five years of the purchase, they the must resell the unit to the original seller at the original price. After five years, the original seller has only the first right of purchase. After-tax capital gains are to be divided among the state, enterprise, and individual according to ownership shares as specified in the house title.

3.   *Introducing a New Rental System for New Housing.* People who are allocated housing beginning on 1 January 1992 will come under new rules. Rents for newly allocated housing must cover three cost factors: maintenance, management and depreciation. If rents cannot reach this level all at once, residents must pay a housing deposit of Y30-50 per square meter, or buy housing bonds worth Y60-80 per square meter. Housing deposits will be returned either when the unit is vacated, or when rents reach the level of the three cost factors. Housing bonds are redeemable in 5-10 years. Interest for both the housing deposit and housing bonds are pegged at the rate for bank demand deposits, and enterprise managers are charged with enforcing payments of deposits or purchase of housing bonds.

4.   *Providing Encouragement for Constructing Cooperative Housing.* The province will encourage housing financed by pool-

ing funds under cooperative arrangements. These arrangements call for private contributions to cover most of the construction costs, while work units contribute the land, the city district provides infrastructural support, and the government aids with tax concessions. Property rights for individuals who contribute 70 per cent or more to construction costs of the main structure are the same as those for home ownership at concessional prices. Those contributing 50-70 per cent pay no rent, but property rights to the housing unit remain with the work unit.

5. *Building a System of Housing Finance* through the following:

   a. *Setting up a Housing Fund.* Municipal housing funds consist of locally retained investment orientation tax revenues, real estate taxes, budgetary funds for housing construction and maintenance, and revenues from selling public housing. Enterprise housing funds include retained profits that are set aside for housing construction, revenues from housing sales, and depreciation and major repairs funds for enterprise-owned housing.

   b. *Setting up a Public Accumulation Fund for Housing Purchase, Construction, and Renovation.* Workers and work units must each contribute 5 per cent of the standard wage per month to a public accumulation fund. Workers will recoup their contributions, with interest (at demand deposit rates) upon retirement. The contribution of a worker who transfers to another unit is also transferred to the new unit. For work units, these contributions are also to be drawn from the housing fund, along with wage supplements for offsetting rent increases. Work units facing difficulty in making these contributions can negotiate to have the amount reduced, with the shortfall to be made up in the future.

   c. *Selling Housing Bonds.* Workers living in public housing are required to buy bonds at the rate of Y3 per year for each square meter of living space. These purchases are on a monthly basis and are mandatory for three years.

A reduction of 1 per cent is applied to the bond quota for each year of the occupant's age. The bonds are redeemable after five years, with interest at demand deposit rates. Funds raised through housing bonds are to provide funds for mortgages and for financing housing construction loans.

6. *Housing Reform in County Towns.* To emphasize privatization, rents should be raised during the Eighth Five-Year Plan to cover three cost factors.

Housing Reform in Chongqing[45]

As approved by the Sichuan Provincial Government, the housing reform proposal in Chongqing Municipality is very similar to that in Liaoning. A few key differences with the Liaoning proposal are noted.

1. *Rent adjustment.* Chongqing plans first to unify rents at Y0.25 per square meter for all public housing, then gradually raise them to Y1.40 to cover the five cost factors by the year 2000. For old housing, cost-covering rents will be held to Y0.70.

2. *Sales.* The Municipality will encourage the privatization of public housing by allowing enterprises and administrative units to sell to workers at concessional prices. These prices will be announced each year by the Municipal Real Estate Management Bureau. For 1992, prices were set at Y200-300 per square meter for housing within city districts, and Y180-260 in the two suburban districts and suburban counties. The prices will vary somewhat depending on the quality of the neighborhood, facilities, location, etc. Prices for older housing will be set at replacement cost minus depreciation, and will be supervised by the real estate office and the price bureau. Prices for older self-contained apartments will be set at no less than Y120 per square meter.

---

[45] This is based on housing reform documents issued by the Sichuan Provincial People's Government (1991, Number 628), and the Chongqing Municipal People's Government (1992, Numbers 13, 14, 46, and 119).

To encourage housing finance, revenues from sales of enterprise housing stock are exempted from the levy of the Energy and Transport Key Construction Fund and Budget Adjustment Fund if reinvested in housing construction.

Housing Reform in Shenzhen[46]

The Scheme for Reforming the Housing System in Shenzhen Special Economic Zone was approved in June 1988 and implemented in October. Under the scheme, Shenzhen aggressively pursued privatization as the main focus of reform. By the end of 1991, 38,400 apartments had been sold as "welfare housing" (*fulifang*), which accounted for 88.7 per cent of all public housing. The volume of sales and average prices are shown in Table 5.9. Unit prices rose rapidly from 1988 to 1991, from an average of Y179 per square meter to Y376; they also varied by seller, sometimes by large amounts.

Table 5.10 shows that during 1988-1990, rents were progressively raised on the remaining units, to about Y6 per square meter per month in 1990, or Y450 per apartment. However, rent levels were rolled back to an average of Y2.30 per square meter in 1991 for reasons that are unclear. One hypothesis may be that rents were rolled back to accommodate lower income families (who are the only ones that do not own their homes). Another is that units that were unsold in 1991 were the least desirable. However, the second hypothesis is not borne out by the large average size of units rented.

According to the Shenzhen Housing Bureau, the selling of housing has reduced state outlays on housing and accomplished the objective of cost sharing: in the past, the government spent an average of Y43,000 in one-time construction costs per apartment, which was borne entirely by the government and enterprises. With revenues of Y815 million, these sales of housing units have recouped about 53 per cent of construction costs, a big step toward cost sharing between the government and consumers. In addition, presale monthly subsidies for maintenance had averaged 24.9 per cent of basic wages per worker. With privatization, all maintenance costs are now borne by home owners, who must

---

46 Adapted from *Shenzhen Statistical Yearbook 1992*, pp. 127-129.

Table 5.9: Sales of Public Housing in Shenzhen

Item	Total	Type of Owner			
		City Housing Bureau	Party and Administrative Units	City-owned Enterprises	Outside Units Stationed in Shenzhen
Cumulative Total Sold					
Number of Apartments	38,424.0	11,351.0	8,419.0	15,120.0	3,534.0
Floor Space (thousand m²)	3,207.2	957.3	716.2	1,222.2	311.5
Revenues (Y million)	815.3	221.4	178.6	311.7	103.6
Average Price (Y/m²)	254.0	231.0	249.0	255.0	232.0
October 1988-December 1989					
Number of Apartments	22,713.0	8,020.0	6,271.0	7,772.0	650.0
Floor Space (thousand m²)	1,776.6	681.7	478.8	559.9	56.2
Revenues (Y million)	317.8	128.7	96.6	81.5	10.9
Average Price (Y/m²)	179.0	189.0	202.0	146.0	194.0
Average Size of Apartments (m²)	78.2	85.0	76.4	72.0	86.5
Average Price per Apartment (Y)	13,991.0	16,045.0	15,411.0	10,492.0	16,815.0
1990					
Number of Apartments	4,089.0	300.0	478.0	2,678.0	633.0
Floor Space (thousand m²)	344.5	24.0	42.8	221.1	56.6
Revenues (Y million)	89.0	9.0	5.7	57.2	17.1
Average Price (Y/m²)	258.0	375.0	133.0	259.0	303.0
Average Size of Apartments (m²)	84.3	80.0	90.0	82.6	89.4
Average Price per Apartment (Y)	21,768.0	30,000.0	11,883.0	21,356.0	27,077.0
1991					
Number of Apartments	11,622.0	3,031.0	1,670.0	4,670.0	2,251.0
Floor Space (thousand m²)	1,086.1	251.6	194.6	441.2	198.7
Revenues (Y million)	408.5	83.7	76.3	173.0	75.5
Average Price (Y/m²)	376.0	333.0	392.0	392.0	380.0
Average Size of Apartments (m²)	93.5	83.0	116.5	94.5	88.3
Average Price per Apartment (Y)	35,152.0	27,628.0	45,090.0	37,045.0	33,541.0

Source: *Shenzhen Statistical Yearbook 1992.*

Table 5.10: Rental of Public Housing in Shenzhen

Item	Total	Type of Owner			
		City Housing Bureau	Party and Administrative Units	City-owned Enterprises	Outside Units Stationed in Shenzhen
October 1988-December 1989					
Number of Apartments	1,926.0	224.0	531.0	951.0	220.0
Floor Space (thousand m²)	123.6	14.6	33.3	67.1	8.6
Total Rental Income (Y '000)	6,038.4	717.6	1,792.8	3,112.8	415.2
Average Rent/m² (Y/month)	4.1	4.1	4.5	3.9	4.0
Average Rent/Apartment (Y/month)	261.3	267.0	281.0	273.0	157.0
1990					
Number of Apartments	982.0	50.0	135.0	608.0	189.0
Floor Space (thousand m²)	73.7	4.0	10.1	48.6	11.0
Total Rental Income (Y '000)	5,302.8	296.8	748.9	3,604.2	652.9
Average Rent/m² (Y/month)	6.0	6.2	6.2	6.2	5.0
Average Rent/Apartment (Y/month)	450.0	495.0	462.0	494.0	288.0
1991					
Number of Apartments	512.0	140.0	109.0	153.0	110.0
Floor Space (thousand m²)	38.7	4.9	7.7	12.2	13.9
Total Rental Income (Y '000)	1,069.1	152.4	208.8	330.9	377.0
Average Rent/m² (Y/month)	2.3	2.6	2.3	2.3	2.3
Average Rent/Apartment (Y/month)	174.0	90.7	160.0	180.0	286.0

Source: *Shenzhen Statistical Yearbook 1992.*

also pay monthly fees to cover the costs of maintenance of exterior and public spaces and facilities.

According to the stipulations of the Shenzhen Housing Reform Scheme, revenues from housing sales are to be deposited with the City Construction Bank's Residential Mortgage Department, as earmarked funds dedicated to financing further housing investment. This is intended to activate a beneficent cycle of construction and selling of housing.

Table 5.11 shows that in 1991 wage supplements averaging Y58.81 per month were issued to employees in administrative units, which were far below the increased costs of rents and mortgage payments. As a result, housing reform has greatly increased the cost of housing to consumers in Shenzhen and reduced the degree of distortion in consumer spending—housing now absorbs 20-25 per cent of consumer expenditures in Shenzhen, compared with only 1 per cent before housing reform.

Table 5.11: Housing Subsidies for Administrative Personnel in Shenzhen, 1991

Administrative Unit	Number of Administrative Units	Number of Employees	Subsidy per Employee (Y/month)
Total	824	68,111	58.81
Special Economic Zone	510	58,411	57.78
Baoan County	313	9,700	65.26
Central Government Units	29	9,026	45.77
Provincial Government Units			
Subtotal	7	1,430	63.19
in Special Economic Zone	6	908	70.1
in Baoan County	1	522	51.54
Shenzhen Municipality	475	48,477	59.72
Baoan County	313	9,178	66.06

Source: *Shenzhen Statistical Yearbook 1992.*

Assessment of Reform Plan

Under the present system, housing is considered part of the wage package offered to urban (especially state sector) workers. Even by the very conservative estimates of Table 5.6, it is by far the biggest in-kind payment, and its share has risen from 7 per cent to 16 per cent of the total compensation package. Through the 1980s, housing clearly led the growth of in-kind wage benefits; housing's annual growth of 28.6 per cent during the 1978-1988 period was symptomatic of the government's inability to control wage payments.

The importance of housing as a wage good makes housing reform a politically sensitive issue, and the government has been understandably cautious in its design and implementation. However, the authors believe that excessive conservatism has caused the present housing reform plan to be fundamentally flawed, and thus unlikely to achieve its primary objectives.

The amount of rent reform achieved under this program will be extremely limited. First, the pace of rent increases called for in the Liaoning and Chongqing plans is extremely modest: it aims to cover the costs of maintenance, depreciation, and management by 1995, real estate taxes and returns to investments by year 2000, and to approach market levels by 2005 (see pp. 197 and 200). Moreover, as rent targets are stipulated in nominal terms, at the level of 1987 costs, these rent increases will be quickly eroded by inflation, leaving the real pace of rent reform even slower. For example, in Chongqing, the target for full cost recovery is assumed to be a unit rent of Y1.40. By the time this level is reached, in year 2000, it will likely only cover a small portion of the actual costs.

Second, the rent increases are to be accompanied by increases in wage supplements to offset partially the higher rents. Guidelines stipulate that these should be limited to no more than 25 per cent of standard wages in total. As a start, Liaoning suggested 2 per cent of the 1990 standard wage be issued in 1992, although work units with more resources are permitted to issue larger supplements—i.e., as long as it is not paid directly by government funds. In practice, these ceilings appear to limit the amount of rent increases. For example, this accounts for the modest step taken in Liaoning to raise rents to only Y0.35-0.4. At the same time, the stipulation that these supplements be paid out of housing funds opens the door to repeated and contentious bargaining over the amount of wage supplements, and how their costs will be divided between work units and government, given the competing uses of housing funds for both new construction and subsidizing the existing stock.

Together, these two aspects make rent reform extremely unattractive to local governments. As it is presently designed, the rent reform program commits local governments to a protracted process that involves contentious negotiations and complicated bookkeeping maneuvers while providing little budgetary relief. Moreover, its slow pace ensures that it will produce no clearcut victories for market reform that enable the cities to launch new initiatives.

The program of privatization is more popular because, in contrast to rent reform, it provides significant revenue incentives for both local governments and work units, both to shed large cost burdens and to raise funds for further housing development. As envisioned in the 1988 Plan, revenues from sales will be a major source of finance for wage supplements as well. Indeed, one danger is that the present reform plan has created incentives that are lopsided in favor of privatization, where local governments and SOEs operating under severe financial pressures will find it difficult to resist the temptation to sell off their housing stock to produce revenues.

However, the authors believe that large-scale privatization of urban housing is premature under the present circumstances, and it is unlikely that the goal of selling off half or more of the public housing stock can be achieved without heavy discounts. First, the combination of very low rents and restricted property rights makes the purchase option unattractive. Even for those who see home ownership as a speculative investment akin to stock market purchases, demand will be restrained by the lack of housing finance. At present, local sell-off schemes require down payments of 30-40 per cent, accompanied by relatively short payment periods of 10-15 years. While buyers may obtain a bank mortgage, given the underdeveloped state of mortgage financing, most of the carrying costs will have to be borne by the sellers. Finally, and most egregiously, the housing units that are being produced are beyond affordability for average PRC consumers. Using a cost-recovering rent of Y7 per square meter, a 40 square meter apartment costs Y280 per month, equal to 73 per cent of average household income in Tianjin (World Bank 1992c, p. 14). These translate into equally unaffordable purchase prices.

In Shenzhen, sale prices averaged Y179 in 1989, Y258 in 1990, and Y376 in 1991. In Chongqing, prices were set in 1992 at Y200-300 per square meter for new housing within city limits and Y180-260 in suburban areas. All of these are far below replacement costs for structure, in clear contravention of guidelines in the 1988 Plan (and included in the Liaoning Plan), which called for concessional prices to cover construction costs of structure. One reason local plans containing these prices are approved at the State Council is that everyone is still using cost calculations from 1987, when planning was carried out for housing reform to be implemented in 1988. At the time, Y200 was the average cost derived for structure, not including land and infrastructure. By 1988-1989, these construction costs had increased to Y300-400 per square meter, with on-site infrastructure adding another Y100 per square meter of floor space. Total costs were then estimated at over Y600 (World Bank 1992c). It seems likely that cost levels in 1992 were at least as high.

More importantly, prevailing concern about affordability is clearly influencing price-setting. In Chongqing, while "commodity" housing was being sold in mid-1992 to work units at Y1700 per square meter, workers' housing was priced at Y200-300 on the assumption that families with two workers can afford about Y12,000–15,000 for an apartment. Similar reasoning led Chongqing University to set a price of Y200 per square meter for its apartments, which were being sold for Y14,000, for 70 square meters of floor space and 30 years use-right. The Municipal Public Security Bureau was selling apartments for only Y8,000, though the use-right period is shorter, 20 years.

While affordability is obviously an important concern for a key wage good such as housing, allowing it to dictate the price defeats a central objective of housing reform, that of rationalizing relative prices. From the fiscal perspective, the slow pace of rent reform means that the government will derive little fiscal relief, either through shedding subsidy costs or from restraining demand for housing. Selling at prices below cost perpetuates the subsidy relationship between consumers and providers and maintains the undesirable dependency of workers to work units, since the latter remain the source of low cost housing. These prices also create ambiguous and complicated property rights, since units selling housing below cost will retain partial ownership rights. Restricted property rights will hinder the development of the housing market in the future.

Issues

Motivation for housing reform stems from concern in a number of areas. From the fiscal perspective, the government hopes to rein in this component of unrestrained wage growth that has contributed to fiscal decline in the reform period. The government is also concerned that the extremely robust investment in housing is squeezing out investments in the productive sectors. The government's desire to shift housing costs toward consumers is consistent with requirements of market-oriented reform: getting the prices right (both for housing and for labor) and moving the housing system toward market allocation. It is hoped that the market will eliminate many of the inefficiencies and some of the inequities of the present system of distribution (the lack of choice, the unresponsiveness to consumer demand, and the rigidities of administrative allocation) and will improve the "flow" of housing units. Equally important, housing reform is seen as an essential part of enterprise reforms and creating a labor market in the PRC.

This reform should produce a system where

1. housing provision should be separated from work units;
2. rents should cover the total cost of providing housing (it is necessary to eliminate subsidies in order to sever the dependency relations between provider and consumer, to allow free exchange of housing, and to allow the higher costs to curb demand for housing);
3. fiscal subsidies to housing should be sharply targeted, to provide a safety net for indigent families, but not to subsidize all or most urban residents; and
4. government involvement in housing development should be confined to planning urban space use and providing supporting infrastructure for well-planned, well-organized neighborhoods.

Steps necessary to achieve these goals include

1. reducing fiscal subsidies to shift more costs to consumers (given the rapid growth in income and standards of living in recent years, the government can and should take bolder steps in this direction);
2. severing the link between housing provision and work place (in the short term this may require "recentralization" of public housing under city housing bureaus to remove enterprise involvement in housing, and to centralize the provision of subsidies);
3. allowing more competition in housing production to improve efficiency and output mix (to end housing subsidies, housing supply must become more affordable, through downsizing and production of a more diverse range of housing); and
4. building a financial system to support private housing purchase.

Chapter 6

Recommendations for Reform

Previous chapters have looked in turn at important features of the PRC fiscal system and identified areas that require reform. There is a need for substantial reforms to (1) the tax system, to reduce distortions and improve revenue buoyancy; (2) the banking system, to control credit creation; (3) central-local fiscal relations, to improve resource mobilization and prevent unnecessary conflict; (4) SOEs, to improve financial performance; and (5) social security and housing provision, to improve labor mobility and relieve enterprises of costs that are unrelated to current production. This chapter brings these separate recommendations together, and combines them with the findings of the country visits to produce an overall view of the direction that reforms should take.

One of the difficulties in designing a package of reforms is that different aspects of reform are interrelated. In the PRC context, the control of both the budget deficit and monetary growth require imposing financial discipline on SOEs, but that requires accepting redundancies and bankruptcy, which in turn depends on a social security and housing system that permits labor mobility.

Even the apparently straightforward idea of improving tax collections is related to the reform of central-local fiscal relations, because many of the tax exemptions are encouraged by the conflict of interest between central and local government: the local official who grants the exemption can see that this might well benefit the locality, while the central government will bear a large share of the cost.

These interrelationships imply that the order in which reforms are carried out can be of considerable importance, and this will be a major concern of this chapter. However, it is also important to have a clear idea of the final system to which the reforms will lead. It is here that the international comparisons are particularly useful because they illustrate the advantages and disadvantages of alternative systems. They are of less use in deciding the order of reforms because other countries have started from the same position as the PRC.

The discussion in this chapter therefore starts by looking at what international experience and this study of the PRC can tell us about the final system to which the reforms are directed. Attention is then turned towards to the sequencing of these reforms.

INTERNATIONAL EXPERIENCE AND THE CHOICE OF FISCAL SYSTEM

The three study countries—Canada, India, and the United Kingdom (UK)—provide useful comparisons with the PRC in terms of the interrelated areas of central-local fiscal relations and the structure of tax administration. They also provide useful comparisons for the system of macroeconomic management. Canada and the UK provide a basis of comparison of social security systems, while India is the only one that can provide a proper comparison for the management of SOEs.

Another area in which international comparisons are useful is the design of a tax structure for a decentralized economy with changing sectoral balance and different forms of ownership. Although this was not a particular focus of the study visits, the design will be included because of its importance.

Central-Local Fiscal Relations

The three countries differ markedly in their management of central-local fiscal relations. In Canada, the responsibilities of federal and provincial governments are defined in the constitution and each levies its own taxes to finance its expenditures. There are income taxes belonging to each level, which share the same base. The federal government uses some of its revenue to transfer resources to provinces with low tax capacities.

The Indian system is similar to Canada's in that the responsibilities of federal and state governments are defined in the constitution. However, it is similar to the PRC in that there are central fixed incomes, local fixed incomes, and shared incomes. However, the shared incomes (personal income tax and commodity tax) are divided among the states in a completely different way. The PRC uses a "base number" method, in which any change to the revenue sharing system is designed so that each local government would receive the same amount of revenue as it did in the "base year" (usually the year immediately before the change). However, in India, a distribution formula is devised on the basis of objective measures such as level of economic development and population density in each state.

In contrast to the federal systems in Canada and India, the UK is a unitary state. This is shown in the far greater control that the central government has over the activities of local governments, determining their expenditure responsibilities and setting limits on the amount of local taxes that they can raise. This level of formal control by the center is similar to that in the PRC, but there are important differences. First, the proportion of revenue that comes to the central government is much larger in the UK. This means that local governments finance a large part of their expenditures from central government grants. Second, in the UK the distribution of central government grants is determined by a combination of fiscal capacity (as in Canada) and objective measures of need (as in India). Indeed the grants are calculated as the difference between the level of expenditure that the local government is judged to need and the amount that it can raise from a given rate of local taxation.

The three examples illustrate the fact that most countries, whether unitary or federal, have systems where revenues are clearly divided among levels of government, either by tax assignment or by tax sharing with fixed formulas. In addition, all three devote a considerable amount of central government revenues to equalization programs that attempt to compensate local governments for differences in fiscal capacities and, in some cases, differences in need. These equalization programs can only be afforded because the central government receives most of the revenues—over 70 per cent in Canada and India, and over 90 per cent in the UK.

Only by adopting some system of this sort can the PRC move towards providing equal access to basic services such as health care and education for all PRC citizens. In addition, a move away from the "base numbers" approach towards a formula-based system of redistribution would reduce the amount of negotiation and renegotiation that creates such mistrust between levels of government in the PRC.

Given the large regional disparities in income and tax capacity, the low degree of population (and capital) mobility across provinces, and the need for macroeconomic stabilization, the study concludes that a larger share of revenues should be controlled by the central government. However, recentralization of revenues should not be accompanied by recentralization of control over expenditures. Given the PRC's large size, where provinces have populations that are far larger than those of most countries in the world, the provision of public goods should be decentralized to maximize efficiency. The extent of expenditure decentralization in the PRC appears to be correct, except for some duplication, and needs only to be established in law so that each level of government has a clear picture of its responsibilities.

Thus, in conformance with practices in the three countries visited (and elsewhere in the world), the recentralization of revenues should be accompanied by the introduction of equalization programs that redistribute to the provinces a substantial portion of central revenues. Some urgent attention may also be needed to the division of expenditures and revenues at the subprovincial levels to ensure that appropriate assignments are passed from the provinces to the lower levels.

The required substantial increase in central revenue should be obtained by assigning all revenues from product tax, business tax, and VAT to the center. This transfer of taxes would eliminate the misallocation of resources produced by each province wanting to establish industries that are heavily taxed, so that they can collect a share of the high tax payments.

The central and local fixed incomes could stay as they are, with the exception of enterprise income taxation. As explained in Chapters 2, 3, and 4, the idea of each level of government receiving enterprise income tax from the enterprises it owns runs against the whole idea of enterprise reform. Enterprise income taxes from enterprises of all ownerships should be seen as one revenue source. The enterprise income tax from transport, communications, banking, and insurance would be difficult to allocate between provinces. It is therefore neater for all enterprise income taxes to become central fixed revenue. Alternatively, enterprise income tax could become a fixed local revenue, with the profit tax on the transport, communications, banking, and insurance enterprises apportioned between provinces on the basis of population (not all of the profits would be apportioned: the after tax profits will still accrue to the owner).

In addition to the tax revenue redistributed from the center, one potentially rich source of revenues for local governments is property taxes on land and buildings, over which local governments should be given autonomy in setting tax rates and defining the tax base. In other countries, property taxes are a major source of local revenues—in Canada, they account for 98 per cent of local revenues below the provincial level, in the UK, for 100 per cent. In the PRC, property taxes could develop into a large source of revenues with the increasing marketing of land and real estate, although its development may take some time.

The rest of this section is devoted to discussing an example that demonstrates the feasibility of the radical reforms proposed in this study. The section shows the effects of centralizing the revenue from the three main indirect taxes (VAT, product tax, and business tax) and redistributing the revenue between provinces according to a formula.

One of the advantages of centralizing revenue and using a formula for redistribution is that it eliminates the need for the other channels through which revenue is passed between the central government and the provinces. This study therefore assumes that the total funding for expenditure by each province consists of its reduced revenue (current revenue minus the three indirect taxes it currently collects) plus the new formula grant from the central government.

For each province, the difference between its current expenditure and its reduced revenue can be regarded as a "fiscal gap" that must be filled by the formula grant if current expenditure levels are to be maintained.

In order to limit the number of provinces that would lose from such a funding change, a grant formula was chosen to come as close as possible to meeting the provinces' fiscal gaps. The variables in the formula are: population, nonagricultural population, minority population and, national income. The inclusion of more variables in the formula would have made it fit the fiscal gaps more closely.

Table 6.1 shows the results of this exercise. The first column shows the fiscal gap per capita for each province or city, which is a simple measure of the difference between reduced revenue and current expenditure. The second column shows the total fiscal gap: the first column multiplied by the population of the province or city. The third column shows the amount each province or city would receive from the formula grant. Finally, the fourth column shows the change in expenditure that would result from adopting the formula grant, as expenditures would have to adjust to the new incomes.

The fourth column shows that the changes in expenditure for some provinces and cities are large. If the central government decided to fully compensate all the provinces that lose, it would cost Y12.7 billion. However, the combination of centralizing revenues and replacing all other central-local transfers by the formula grants leads to a saving of Y2.2 billion. Thus, the introduction of this system together with compensating the provinces that lose will have a net cost of only Y10.5 billion, less than 7 per cent of the total revenue from the three taxes. Given the very poor recent collection record of these three taxes, whose share of GNP has fallen by a quarter in five years, such a cost could easily be covered by the increased collections that would be obtained by setting up an efficient national tax service.

In addition, an improvement in the formula could substantially reduce the extent of provincial losses, and thus the cost of compensating the losers. The table shows that the main gainers include the three independent cities (Beijing, Shanghai, and Tianjin), while the main losers are provinces with particularly large minority populations. It should be possible to alter the formula to improve the grant for the minority provinces at the expense of the cities.

The formula used in this example is for illustrative purposes only, to show that it is possible to replace the current complex system of central-local financial flows with a simple system based on revenue recentralization and formula-based grants. In fact, the formula in the example is not sufficiently redistributive. The provinces that were identified in Chapter 3 as requiring additional resources to finance expenditures on culture, education, science, and health are not the main gainers from the introduction of the formula. Also, the formula is not as redistributive as those used in other countries, including the three study countries.

Table 6.1: Revenue-Sharing Example

Province/City	Per Capita Fiscal Gap (Y/person)	Total Fiscal Gap (million)	Grant (million)	Difference (% of expenditure)
Beijing	99.9	1,093	2,022	11.5%
Shanghai	5.4	73	2,636	25.2%
Tianjin	112.5	1,023	1,580	11.7%
Anhui	104.1	5,997	5,012	-11.6%
Fujian	123.6	3,806	2,825	-12.6%
Gansu	156.8	3,583	2,379	-23.5%
Guangdong	130.1	8,377	6,625	9.6%
Guangxi	111.2	4,809	6,662	24.4%
Guizhou	123.8	4,105	4,110	0.0%
Hainan	214.5	1,446	833	-30.7%
Hebei	74.4	4,626	5,611	10.1%
Heilongjiang	144.4	5,163	5,265	0.9%
Henan	72.9	6,389	7,345	8.8%
Hubei	99.7	5,494	5,792	3.0%
Hunan	96.8	6,012	6,001	0.1%
Inner Mongolia	213.6	4,664	3,435	-18.4%
Jiangsu	95.5	6,534	6,640	0.8%
Jiangxi	103.0	3,980	3,675	4.7%
Jilin	178.6	4,482	3,809	8.5%
Liaoning	161.7	6,452	6,353	0.7%
Ningxia	260.2	1,249	803	-25.9%
Qinghai	292.3	1,327	831	-27.2%
Shaanxi	118.8	3,994	3,230	-11.4%
Shandong	81.8	7,014	7,343	2.3%
Shanxi	113.4	3,337	3,037	3.9%
Sichuan	80.4	8,757	10,438	10.3%
Tibet	609.3	1,377	1,377	0.0%
Xinjiang	247.5	3,849	3,530	6.1%
Yunnan	193.0	7,301	5,000	-20.8%
Zhejiang	93.9	4,021	3,787	2.4%

Notes:
(1) Tibet was excluded from the grant formula because of its very large fiscal gap, and its grant was set equal to its fiscal gap.
(2) The grant formula was: Grant = (58.4 x Population) + (229.9 x Nonagricultural Population) + (177.5 x MinorityPopulation) - (0.002 x National Income). The total cost of the grants is Y2.2 billion less than the total fiscal gaps. This represents a saving to the central government.
(3) The cost of compensating all the provinces that lose would be Y12.7 billion. This, minus the Y2.2 billion saving from the formula is less than 7 per cent of the revenue from the "three taxes" (Y160 billion).
(4) All data are for 1991.

The low degree of redistribution in the formula is a result of the attempt to reduce the size of losses to individual provinces. The formula could be made more redistributive by increasing the (negative) coefficient on national income or including a measure of the taxable capacity of each province (again with a negative coefficient). Such changes would increase the losses to some provinces, and so increase the costs of any compensation the government felt it had to provide.

There is currently an informal understanding that requires compensation to any province that loses from reform. However, this should not be applied to the reform of central-local relations. The provinces that would lose from greater redistribution are those that have been allowed to spend more than the average on services to their residents. It is wrong to argue that these provinces should keep this advantageous position, simply because they had achieved it at the time the "base figures" were established. It is only fair that their expenditures should be reduced towards the average in order to allow poorer provinces to increase their expenditures.

Other countries, including the UK, have reformed central-local relations in a way that has involved some local governments in large losses. The harmful effect of these losses have been reduced by introducing the reforms gradually, over three years, for example. This allows the local governments time to plan their expenditure reductions carefully and consider alternative sources of revenue. During periods of economic growth, such a gradual reform can mean that the absolute reductions of expenditure are small: the reform has simply meant that some local governments have not been able to receive the increase in resources that they would have expected without the reform.

To improve the provision of public services in its poor areas, the PRC has to be prepared to redistribute financial resources. If no province is allowed to lose, such redistribution will require substantial additional revenues for the central government. However, if some prosperous provinces are allowed to lose resources (or at least lose expected increases), this will reduce the budgetary costs of reform considerably.

Tax Administration

While the three study countries differ in their central-local fiscal arrangements, they show much greater similarity in tax administration. In each of them, as in almost all countries other than the PRC, the central government collects all of its own revenues. In addition, in Canada the central government collects the provinces' income taxes on their behalf, while the Indian federal government collects all of the shared taxes.

These arrangements have obvious administrative advantages in integrated economies, where many of the taxable transactions take place between provinces. It also means that the central government does not have to worry about local government officials allowing tax concessions that erode the central government tax base. The case for central administration is particularly strong for VAT, because tax paid on a product in one part of the country will be rebated when that product is used as an input in another part of the country. Tait (1988, pp.155-7) reports that only three countries other than the PRC have VAT administered at a subnational level. Two of these, Brazil and Mexico, have encountered difficulties in administration, including difficulties in ensuring adequate local tax effort. Only Germany, with a strict system of court rulings to enforce uniform treatment across the country, has been able to run a satisfactory VAT administered at a subnational level. The improvements that are needed in the PRC's administration of VAT can only be achieved by stronger central control.

For these reasons alone, the PRC government should strengthen central control over the tax collection system. Indeed, the particular situation in the PRC makes the case for this even stronger. At the moment, provinces have to be allowed large shares of each tax in order to motivate their tax collection efforts. But these large shares prevent the central government from collecting enough revenue to help the poorer provinces, and also provide a strong motive for local protectionism.[47] The redistributive system advocated in the last section requires the government to receive a much higher share of tax revenue, and preferably all

---

[47]   This protectionism can involve attempts to limit the movement of goods into the province from elsewhere in the PRC as well as granting special tax concessions that were discussed in Chapter 2.

of the indirect taxes. The achievement of this requires, as a first step, the establishment of a national tax service that is given the clear responsibility to enforce tax laws on a uniform national basis.

Macroeconomic Management

All three of the study countries have an institutional structure that allows the identification of two separate aspects of macroeconomic management: fiscal policy and monetary policy. Fiscal policy relates to the size of government revenues and expenditures, and the resulting budget deficit. Monetary policy relates to the size and growth of monetary aggregates, such as the quantity of notes and coins or the total value of bank deposits.

There is clearly some relationship between these two areas of policy. If the government runs a budget deficit, it may require the central bank to finance the deficit by issuing notes and coins. However, when there is a properly functioning financial market, there are other methods of finance that do not involve increases in the money supply. Thus, fiscal and monetary policy can be thought of separately, and this separation plays an important role in the models that are used in market economies to make economic forecasts and evaluate alternative policies.

The institutional structure that allows this separation is the independence of the banking system, as illustrated by the three study countries. In these countries, the government may decide how much of the budget deficit should be financed by expansion of the money supply, and may try to influence interest rates, but leaves decisions about loans to the banks.

When left to themselves, banks will decide on loans in an attempt to maximize their profits. They will therefore only lend on projects that can be expected to yield good rates of return.

By contrast, many bank loans in the PRC are made as a result of direct instructions or the application of pressure from some level of government. These policy loans are made to enterprises in financial difficulties and to enterprises wanting to undertake investment. To support these policy loans, the central bank has supplied credits that allow the banks to extend loans beyond their deposits. These central bank credits have the same expansionary effect on the money supply as credits to finance the government budget deficit.

This means that the banks are effectively carrying out government fiscal policy. There is no separation between monetary and fiscal policy. The expansion of central bank credits to support these policy loans should be counted as part of the government budget deficit.

Another institutional requirement for the separation of monetary and fiscal policy is the existence of a market in government securities. Such a market exists in all three study countries, and allows governments to run budget deficits, in either the long term or the short term, without requiring the central bank to increase the money supply. The PRC should develop its financial markets by integrating the secondary markets for bonds nationally, by establishing a commercial paper market, and by establishing an enterprise bond market. A thriving government securities market requires that interest rates be decontrolled.

Finally, the application of standard macroeconomic models requires the proper accounting of such financing operations. As explained in Chapter 1, the money raised by the domestic sales of government securities must not be counted on the revenue side of the budget, but as a component in financing the deficit. All three of the study countries follow this international accounting convention.

Macroeconomic stability requires a limit to the rate of monetary growth. The restriction of M2 growth to less than 25 per cent a year for any three-year period would eliminate the risk of hyperinflation. For this purpose, the reduction of the hidden deficit is just as important as the reduction of the open budget deficit. Policy lending should be conducted explicitly through the budget and not through the banking system. This could be achieved by channeling policy loans through a development bank supervised by the Ministry of Finance, with annual loan volume decided by the government. The banking system could then be commercialized and could cease providing preferential credit. Bank lending rates should also be gradually freed.

Social Security Systems

Both Canada and the UK have social security systems that provide retirement pensions and unemployment insurance. Their systems are financed through contributions from both employers and employees, as a proportion of the wage bill.

These systems relieve enterprises from any responsibility for their workers after they have retired, and make it easier for workers to be dismissed. That pensions are not lost when workers change employers improves labor mobility. Because these are the advantages that the PRC is seeking from reforming its social security system, the Canadian and UK examples provide useful models.

One problem that Canada and the UK are experiencing, along with most developed countries, is the increased proportion of retired people in the population, which makes it difficult to finance all of the pensions from the payroll contributions made by workers who are currently employed. Current contributions are having to rise, and the sizes of pensions are being looked at carefully to see whether they can be reduced in some way. It is important that the PRC choose a level of pension that the payroll contributions will be able to afford as the population becomes older.

Both Canada and the UK provide a rather low level of state pension, and encourage individual workers to contribute to private pensions in order to obtain a better standard of living during their retirement.

Enterprises are not responsible for housing for their workers in any of the three study countries. Housing for poor people in Canada and the UK is provided by local governments, but this provision is often inadequate. It is clear that market economies cannot operate efficiently with housing tied to employment, as in the PRC.

State-Owned Enterprises

India is the only study country with a large-scale SOE sector. India's experience with it is similar to that of the PRC: the sector is causing fiscal problems because of the large losses made by some enterprises. The Indian government is also experimenting with alternative management techniques to improve the financial performance of these enterprises. Thus, India's experience reinforces the view expressed in this report: that SOE reform is essential to bring the budget deficit under control.

As explained in Chapter 4, the decentralization of decision-making power to the SOEs and state-owned banks without a hard budget constraint has allowed SOEs to overpay their workers and overinvest. The reduced profits increased the open budget deficit and the expansion of investment credits increased the hidden budget deficit. It is important to emphasize that incomplete market reform and not decentralization is the reason for the greater macroeconomic instability.

Price controls are sometimes a reason for SOE losses, and so remaining price controls should be eliminated. Also, loss-making SOEs that are unlikely to ever become profitable should be closed, but not before price liberalization has made profitability a genuine measure of economic efficiency.

The poor financial performance of SOEs is a worldwide phenomenon. Because SOEs do not naturally maximize profits, an external environment that forces them to do so must be created. One way is to use the financial markets to discipline the SOEs. The method chosen by Canada and the UK in the 1980s was to privatize most of their SOEs. The PRC government should adopt a new supervision mechanism to force the SOEs to maximize their profits. One possible method is to:

1. Set up state asset management corporations (SAMCs) to remodel the SOEs into corporations, control labor costs, and tie managerial compensation to the performance of investments (with negative managerial compensation as a possibility).
2. Set up nationally-linked stock markets to allow SOEs and nonstate enterprises to raise capital. The formation of independent (nonstate) investment companies such as mutual funds should be encouraged to promote wide participation in the stock markets. The price movements of the shares of a particular SOE provide objective criteria to the SAMCs to determine labor and managerial compensation.
3. Enhance SAMCs' monitoring of SOEs' activities by increasing the number of independent people tracking the SOEs' financial performance and the number of SOEs subject to tracking in the stock markets. This is done by the SAMCs selling a portion of every SOE in their portfolios to the general public.
4. Instruct the SAMCs to act like profit-maximizing institutional investors and reward the personnel of each SAMC by comparing the rate of return on its portfolio with the rate of return

achieved by nonstate investment institutions and other
SAMCs. (The agency supervising the SAMCs must be vigilant to collusion among SAMCs.)
5.   Close SOEs that have been chronically unable to cover variable (production) costs, after price reform and the implementation of the social security and housing reforms discussed
in Chapter 5.
6.   Reduce the role of SAMCs in deciding compensation of SOE
personnel after the stock markets have become more sophis-
ticated, and after the SAMCs' holdings of SOE shares have
declined significantly. At this stage, the SAMCs should be
remodeled into corporations and their shares offered to
society.

Trade liberalization and exchange rate unification should be
implemented quickly so that the deregulation of SOEs will not
produce monopolies. Furthermore, the government should replace
all tariff and nontariff barriers with a low uniform tariff to ensure that market forces are the primary determinant of the composition of SOEs' output.

Tax Structure

The tax structure in the three countries studied is more suitable
for an economy with different types of enterprise ownership.
PRC taxes used to be collected almost entirely from SOEs.
This is changing to some extent, with the spread of different forms
of enterprise ownership. However, industrial SOEs still face a
heavier tax burden than other types of enterprise. This is made
most obvious by the "two funds," which require contributions
only from SOEs. The differential taxation by ownership type has
two important harmful effects. First, it puts SOEs at a competitive disadvantage, and leads to a misallocation of resources.
Second, it reduces the ratio of tax revenue to GNP as SOEs become responsible for a smaller proportion of national output.
The three study countries and almost all market economies
avoid these problems by applying equal taxation to all ownership types. The PRC should follow suit as quickly as possible.
A related issue has to do with unequal tax treatment of different products and sectors. PRC's highly differentiated indirect

taxes bear much more heavily on some goods and services than others. For example, the tertiary sector produced 20 per cent of GNP in 1990 but accounted for only 13 per cent of total revenue. Unlike the agriculture sector, where low incomes may preclude levying more taxes, there is no distributional argument for the low taxation of the tertiary sector. Again, this misallocates resources and leads to a loss of revenue if highly taxed goods lose their share of national output. Many countries have moved to more broadly based taxes, such as VAT, to cover services as well as manufactured goods. They have also moved to simplify rates, and the PRC must do the same.

The detailed proposals listed at the end of Chapter 2 constitute the major changes that are required to bring the PRC tax structure up to international standards. Their implementation would have three major effects: (1) all goods and services outside agriculture would be taxed at the same rate, except for a few goods, such as alcohol, tobacco, and petroleum products, that are taxed more heavily in all countries; (2) all enterprises will have their tax liabilities calculated in the same way; (3) the personal income tax will be brought up to international standard, so that it can be applied properly as personal incomes grow.

SEQUENCING OF REFORM

When reforms are interrelated, it is always difficult to find the best order in which to carry them out. However, in the PRC, a fairly clear sequencing can be recommended as the prerequisites for some reforms are already satisfied (see Box 6.1).

The changes that can be carried out most easily without waiting for other reforms are the changes to the tax structure, recommended at the end of Chapter 2. The price system has become sufficiently liberalized to remove any argument for nonuniform indirect taxes. Therefore, there should be an immediate move towards a single rate VAT on all goods and services outside agriculture, with product tax used as a supplementary excise tax on alcohol, tobacco, and petroleum products.

Similarly, there should be a rapid move towards the harmonization of enterprise income taxes across ownership types, as soon as uniform accounting standards (including more realistic

Box 6.1: Implementation of Reforms: Recommendations on Sequencing

Immediate (within 1 year)	Short-term (1 to 3 years)	Medium-term (4 to 6 years)	Supplementary Notes
Issue 1: Reform of Tax Structure			
	single rate for VAT		should be in line with price reforms
	VAT to give credit for taxes on investment	VAT extended to construction, transportation, and services	
prepare for invoice method for VAT administration	introduce invoice method for VAT administration		
	VAT extended to commerce		
exemptions no longer granted			
product tax limited to alcohol, tobacco, petroleum, cosmetics and other luxury goods			
apply domestic turnover taxes to joint ventures and foreign enterprises			
enterprise taxation be applied equally to all enterprises based on current joint venture tax rules and rate	abolition of levies on extrabudgetary funds (the "two funds")		tax rates adjusted to make up for lost revenue of "two funds"
reform personal income taxes			
		abolish investment orientation tax	
	implement an enlarged resource tax		to be coordinated with price reform

Immediate (within 1 year)	Short-term (1 to 3 years)	Medium-term (4 to 6 years)	Supplementary Notes
increase central monitoring of tax administration			
start formation of National Tax Service			

Issue 2: Reform of Central-Local Relations

	centralize revenue from 3 taxes (product tax, VAT and business tax), with formula grants to provinces in place of current base numbers method		legal guarantees should stipulate that formula will not reduce total revenue of local government from current levels
	local government given more control over an expanded real estate tax, a new urban (independent) construction tax, and new capital gains tax on land transfers and stock market transactions		all existing minor taxes to remain local government revenue real estate tax to be paid by all enterprises

Issue 3: Reform of State-Owned Enterprises

	eliminate remaining price controls		
	restructure SOEs into corporations and establish SAMCs to manage them		
	speed up closure of selected loss-making SOEs	apply bankruptcy laws uniformly	
uniform accounting system across enterprises and across industries			

Immediate (within 1 year)	Short-term (1 to 3 years)	Medium-term (4 to 6 years)	Supplementary Notes
	establish stock exchanges in all major cities		
	eliminate exemptions to SOEs from participation in citywide pension pool		
	expand SOE pension pool from city national level, and centralize management to national level	a common national pension pool for SOEs and nonstate enterprises	
	extend pension coverage to nonstate enterprises in nonagricultural sectors		
	create a national SOE unemployment scheme	a common national unemployment insurance scheme for SOEs and nonstate enterprises	
	extend unemployment insurance coverage to nonstate enterprises in nonagricultural sectors		
	speed up rent increases to market level, put SOE housing under local government, and gradually sell public housing at market prices		

Issue 4: Strengthening Macroeconomic Management

Immediate (within 1 year)	Short-term (1 to 3 years)	Medium-term (4 to 6 years)	Supplementary Notes
adopt regulation that M2 growth rate cannot exceed 25 per cent annually for three consecutive years			

Immediate (within 1 year)	Short-term (1 to 3 years)	Medium-term (4 to 6 years)	Supplementary Notes
terminate "dual leadership" control of local branches of central bank and state banks			
interest rate consolidation, preferential credit, set short term interest rate below long term interest rate	free interest rate of working capital, then interest rate of investment capital		
	commercialize the state banks, and allow establishment of branches of foreign bank in more cities	convert the state banks to joint-stock companies	
	integrate secondary markets for government bonds nationally		the first step toward developing open- market operations capability
	establish a commercial paper market	establish an enterprise bond market	enhance open-market operations capability
	all policy loans channeled through Ministry of Finance supervised development bank, annual loans determined by State Council		Ministry of Finance will be responsible for profits and loss of development bank, no easy People's Bank of China credit to this bank
unify the exchange rate, eliminate foreign exchange certificates	replace nontariff barriers with equivalent tariffs, then reduce all tariffs to a uniform level compatible to those in the General Agreement on Tariffs and Trade	reduce tariffs to a lower uniform level	

depreciation rates) are implemented. This should be based on the experimental system of "separating profit and tax" (see p. 143). The possible loss of revenue that would result from abolishing the levies on extrabudgetary funds, should be met by slightly increasing the average VAT rate and eliminating tax concessions on indirect taxes.

The need to improve enforcement of the tax laws will require introducing stronger central control. This can start immediately by increasing the degree of central supervision, with the aim of eventually setting up a national tax service.

These tax changes will make it easier to use profits as a measure of enterprise efficiency. However, there is also a need to remove nonproduction costs from enterprises: the pensions and housing of retired workers, and the housing of current workers. Thus, social security and housing reform must also move ahead as fast as possible, and prices should be made more realistic by removing controls on all goods that are not subject to monopolies and liberalizing international trade. At the same time, SOEs should be restructured into corporation and stock markets should be developed.

Once these aims are achieved, it will be possible to start eliminating enterprise subsidies and closing enterprises that are not profitable: the artificial forces that could have been blamed for poor financial performance will have been removed and the social costs of unemployment will have been reduced.

Thus the steps to enterprise reform are:

1. tax reform, completing price reform, social security reform, and housing reform;
2. restructuring of SOEs into corporations and development of stock markets; and
3. removal of SOE subsidies and the introduction of bankruptcy.

Note that the first two steps should be taken simultaneously, but the last step cannot be fully implemented until the first two are complete.

The reform of the banking system can take place simultaneously with the first steps of enterprise reform. Policy loans to support favored enterprises should be abolished and replaced by explicit subsidies, which will be abolished when the prerequisites for SOE reform are fulfilled. Banks will be allowed to make their own loan decisions and compete with each other. Markets for government securities will be developed, which should aid social security reform by providing high quality financial assets.

The full reform of central-local fiscal relations requires the simplification of the tax system and the strengthened central control of revenue collection. However, the main obstacle here will be the need to agree on the formula that will be used to redistribute central revenues to the provinces. The experiences of all three study countries would be useful in reaching a decision on this difficult issue.

Although the logic behind the sequencing is clear, there still remains a major problem. Imposing bankruptcy on SOEs requires a number of preconditions and can therefore be expected to take considerable time. In the meantime, attempts to collect taxes more rigorously may simply result in the need for more policy loans or (preferably) budgetary subsidies. The budget deficit may still not be brought under control.

In these circumstances, it will be necessary to increase the incentives for enterprise managers to control costs and maximize profits, as discussed in Chapter 4. It may also be necessary to start closing some enterprises that are clearly going to make losses even after all the other reforms are carried out. The selection of these enterprises will be difficult, both economically and politically.

Appendix I

Extrabudgetary Revenues and Expenditures

Extrabudgetary funds (EBF) are a standard feature of Soviet-type fiscal systems, created to provide a supplementary source of funds outside of budgetary appropriations. These funds are assigned to local governments, administrative agencies, and enterprises. They are distinguished from budgetary funds by two features: (1) they come under decentralized management and allocation by different agencies and organizations, and (2) they are earmarked for specific uses. For example, in recent years road maintenance fees have been a major source of extrabudgetary revenues in the PRC, generating over Y15 billion in 1990. The funds are collected by highway departments and used for road construction and maintenance. Similarly, until it was transferred to the budget in August 1990, the educational surcharge was a 1 per cent additional levy on turnover taxes that was collected by educational departments and earmarked for use on educational outlays.

In the PRC, EBF were first created in the early 1950s, when local governments were allowed to levy some tax surcharges to provide small amounts of resources for local use outside the budget. As enterprise bonus funds and major repairs funds were set up in 1955, they too were added to the category of EBF. Rental incomes from publicly owned housing, users' fees, surcharges for public utilities, etc. were also brought under the category of EBF, to which government regulations were applied to govern their sources and uses.

The size of EBF rose and fell with cycles of decentralization and recentralization. After growing rapidly during the Great Leap Forward (1958-1961), they were drastically cut back during the 1960s. With the onset of the Cultural Revolution (1966), however, EBF experienced another round of sustained growth. Through the 1970s, EBF under the management of enterprises grew especially rapidly (at an average annual rate of 13.7 per cent per annum from 1965 to 1978). The growth was due primarily to the decentralization of depreciation funds to enterprise control in 1967, a 0.5 per cent increase in depreciation rates, and the rapid growth of fixed assets in the 1970s. It also benefited from the addition of enterprise welfare funds (of 11 per cent of the total wage bill). By 1978, EBF under enterprise control had grown to over Y25 billion. On the eve of reform in 1978, total EBF were Y34.7 billion, equal to more than 30 per cent of the size of budgetary revenues. During the reform of the 1980s, EBF grew even more rapidly: in 1990 they totaled Y271 billion, equal to 80 per cent of budgetary revenues and 15.6 per cent of GNP.

Appendix Table I.1 presents the main sources of EBF for 1981-1990. The local government portion comprises only 2.9 per cent of total EBF in 1990. The EBF come from 11 sources including surcharges of taxes and public utilities, along with incomes of extrabudgetary enterprises owned by local governments.[48] This is the slowest growing category of EBF, with an average annual rate of 5.7 per cent during 1978-1990, compared with 18.7 per cent in the growth of total EBF.

The portion of EBF under administrative agencies comprised 17.2 per cent of the total in 1990. The sources for this portion include over 70 types of incomes including road maintenance fees, the educational surcharge on turnover taxes, rental incomes of public housing, market management fees, and management fees collected from individual and private enterprises. In addition, this category includes incomes from enterprises run by administrative agencies, such as workshops and factories owned by schools, hotels, and restaurants run by industrial exhibition halls, etc. This category has grown at an average annual rate of 20.2 per cent during 1978-1990, because fees and income-generating enterprises run by administrative agencies have proliferated.

---

[48]   Extrabudgetary enterprises are those built with extrabudgetary resources of local governments. These enterprises were initially distinguished from state-owned enterprises (SOEs) in that they did not remit profits to the government, and were thus "extra, or outside of the budget." In that sense, they were treated much like collective enterprises. This category was first introduced in 1958. In the early 1980s, with decentralization and the growth of locally managed funds, many extrabudgetary enterprises were built. However, with the introduction of income taxes for SOEs in 1983 and profit-contracting in 1986, the distinction between extrabudgetary and in-budget SOEs was eroded, and extrabudgetary enterprises are no longer a growing category.

The portion of EBF under enterprises comprises about 80 per cent of the total, and their sources are relatively few and straightforward. Retained profits, depreciation, and major repairs funds are the three big pieces that make up over 90 per cent of the total. These have grown at 19.2 per cent per year since 1978, as a result of enterprise reforms that sought to give enterprises more decision-making autonomy and to offer better incentives to motivate state-owned enterprises (SOEs) toward profit-maximizing behavior.

Appendix Table I.2 presents the uses of EBF. Summary statistics at the bottom of the table show the division of use: I, by governments including administrative agencies; II, by SOEs; and III, as contributions to the budget. Three trends stand out. (1) Overall expenditures fall short of revenues in the EBF accounts (unlike the budgetary accounts). (2) There is a surplus in even the "government" portion of EBF, which goes to cover budget deficits at the local level. (3) The share of expenditures by SOEs has fallen over time, from 81 per cent of total EBF expenditures in 1982 to only 61 per cent in 1990, much lower than the SOE share in EBF revenues. The difference is "contributions to the budget," which are taxes and fees levied on enterprise funds.

This trend in EBF expenditures by SOEs highlights a central problem in state-enterprise financial interaction. Over time, there has been a good deal of government indecision on how much enterprises should be allowed to retain as own funds. The introduction of the Energy and Transport Key Construction Fund in 1983 (whose rate was raised in 1987), the Budget Adjustment Fund in 1989, and the periodic compulsory purchases of treasury bonds, etc., have all been government attempts to recapture some of the enterprise funds. At the same time, other government regulations have aimed at increasing funds at the enterprises' disposal—the nearly 20 per cent increase in the enterprise share of EBF in 1991, for example, was due to regulations raising depreciation rates and the rate at which enterprises can draw major repairs funds. Contradictory policies such as these reduce incentives by increasing the degree of instability that hinders rational decision making by enterprises. From the perspective of economic efficiency, it would be better to harden the budget constraint on enterprises so that they are appropriately rewarded or punished for their performance. Having committed to a set of rules for enterprise profit sharing and withholdings to finance depreciation and tech-

Table I.1: Extrabudgetary Funds by Source
(Y100 million)

Item	1981	1982	1983
Total	601.07	802.74	967.68
I. *Local Governments*	41.30	45.27	49.79
Industrial-Commercial Tax Surcharge	5.22	5.72	6.12
Agricultural and Animal Husbandry			
Tax Surcharge	3.84	3.99	4.17
Urban Public Utility Surcharge	12.06	12.82	13.83
II. *Administrative Agencies*	84.90	101.15	113.88
Agency Development Funds			
Staff Welfare Fund			
Staff Bonus Fund			
Road Maintenance	29.35	35.96	40.94
Surcharge on Vehicle Purchase			
Transport Management Fee		0.80	1.32
Higher Education Fund			1.72
Middle and Primary School Fees	4.36	4.54	5.04
Incomes of Middle and Primary			
School Enterprises	5.76	5.31	5.51
Rural Education Surcharge			
Rental Income			
Market Management Fee		2.50	3.44
Individual Enterprise Management Fee			
Income From Tax Sharing			
III. *State-owned Enterprises and*			
Supervisory Departments			
Departments	474.87	656.32	804.01
Renovation and Reconstruction Fund	161.00	191.49	223.57
Profit Retention	168.11	206.43	317.71
Major Repairs Fund	113.39	129.49	143.25
Technical Development Fund			
Oil Field Maintenance Fee	19.55	24.36	23.53
Natural Gas Exploration Fund	6.10	9.72	21.82
Share of Fiscal Extrabudgetary Fund			
as Percentage of Total	21.00	18.24	16.91
Share of Enterprise Extrabudgetary Fund			
as Percentage of Total	79.00	81.76	83.09
As Percentage of Extrabudgetary Funds			
I. Local Governments	6.87	5.64	5.15
II. Administrative Agencies	14.12	12.60	11.77
III. State-owned Enterprises and			
Supervisory Departments	79.00	81.76	83.09

Source: Ministry of Finance.

1984	1985	1986	1987	1988	1989	1990
1188.48	1530.03	1737.31	2028.80	2360.77	2658.83	2708.64
55.23	44.08	43.20	44.61	48.94	54.36	60.59
7.07	1.07					
4.48	5.24	5.75	6.21	6.57	7.78	8.08
15.03	16.23	19.09	21.82	23.61	24.64	27.13
142.52	233.22	294.22	358.41	438.94	500.66	576.95
					31.99	36.70
					11.70	13.81
					10.03	11.72
51.51	79.68	92.42	105.66	120.82	136.92	151.65
	16.43	16.83	18.85	24.14	23.98	31.70
1.71	2.78	4.12	5.48	6.77	7.97	10.41
3.00	4.80	5.51	6.32	7.90	9.43	10.45
6.12	7.57	9.00	9.77	13.93	18.26	21.08
7.35	7.62	9.00	9.81	13.02	16.09	18.44
	1.54	13.42	22.98	29.86	42.22	39.84
	7.62	8.49	10.59	12.14	11.49	13.29
4.60	5.29	7.25	9.22	12.50	14.78	17.96
	2.41	3.75	5.23	7.17	9.20	11.48
		8.52	11.61	15.67	19.06	23.89
990.73	1252.73	1399.89	1625.78	1872.89	2103.81	2071.10
274.38	353.15	411.51	482.41	552.02	636.41	667.38
414.99	505.71	504.72	590.72	742.22	801.23	698.94
158.69	180.54	210.31	241.06	266.81	334.15	368.13
					18.12	18.71
22.19	29.57	32.02	31.21	39.61	41.34	46.35
38.19	66.25	67.44	67.11	50.08	35.05	18.00
16.64	18.12	19.42	19.86	20.67	20.87	23.54
83.36	81.88	80.58	80.14	79.33	79.13	76.46
4.65	2.88	2.49	2.20	2.07	2.04	2.24
11.99	15.24	16.94	17.67	18.59	18.83	21.30
83.36	81.88	80.58	80.14	79.33	79.13	76.46

Table I.2: Composition of Extrabudgetary Expenditures
(Y million)

Item	1982	1983
Extrabudgetary Expenditures	73,453	87,581
1 Investments in Fixed Assets	36,602	37,444
2 Technical Updating & Transformation	26,932	29,993
3 Capital Construction	9,670	7,451
4 Major Repair	10,562	11,988
5 Simple Construction	327	592
6 Welfare	6,899	7,732
7 Bonus	4,105	5,726
8 Road Use Fee	1,672	3,175
9 City Maintenance	2,439	2,862
10 New Product Trial	544	571
11 Increase in Circulating Funds	611	291
12 Sectoral Department Expenditures	3,746	3,298
13 Administration	669	586
14 Contribution to Government Funds for Development of Energy, Industry, Transport and Key Construction	0	6,955
15 Contribution to State Budget Adjustment Fund	0	0
16 Contribution to Shortfalls in Enterprise Contracts	0	0
17 Bonus Tax	0	0
18 Construction Tax	0	0
19 Others	5,277	6,361
20 I. Enterprises Expenditures[a]	58,495	63,482
% of Total Extrabudgetary Expenditures	79.64	72.48
21 II. Government Expenditures[b]	9,681	10,783
% of Total Extrabudgetary Expenditures	13.18	12.31
22 III. Contribution to Budget[c]	0	6,955
% of Total Extrabudgetary Expenditures	0.00	7.94
Expanded Government Expenditure[d]	144,681	163,783
% of GNP	27.86	28.19

a   Item 20 = 1 + 4 + 5 + 6 + 7
b   Item 21 = 8 + 9 + 10 + 11 + 12 + 13
c   Item 22 = 14 + 15 + 16 + 17 + 18
d   Expanded Government Expenditure = Budgetary Expenditure + Government Portion of Extrabudgetary Expenditure (Item 21)

Source: State Statistical Bureau 1990, Tables T6.14, T6.15; State Statistical Bureau 1991; Ministry of Finance 1989, p. 105; Ministry of Finance data.

1984	1985	1986	1987	1988	1989	1990
111,474	137,503	157,837	184,075	214,527	249,932	270,705
44,938	57,128	57,645	74,043	81,528	86,486	92,591
35,739	45,020	42,284	49,003	56,751	63,250	65,845
9,199	12,108	15,361	25,040	24,777	23,236	26,746
13,330	14,962	17,288	19,968	22,986	28,035	30,240
482	513	545	647	538	230	181
10,352	9,151	10,619	13,068	17,439	21,115	23,992
9,443	9,143	10,968	11,443	11,518	12,401	10,852
4,405	6,339	8,366	9,222	11,091	11,973	13,437
2,906	2,840	3,128	3,889	4,523	3,370	3,543
1,324	1,371	1,188	1,328	1,160	1,485	1,574
555	1,356	2,317	2,866	3,859	5,679	4,625
3,792	5,604	7,068	9,188	11,589	14,040	17,233
740	869	1,070	1,569	1,906	1,335	1,477
10,070	12,333	12,658	15,410	16,583	18,685	17,576
0	0	0	0	0	11,830	11,557
0	0	0	0	0	1,586	3,809
0	0	0	0	0	42	411
0	0	0	0	0	1,118	1,296
9,137	15,894	24,977	21,434	29,807	30,522	36,311
78,545	90,897	97,065	119,169	134,009	148,267	157,856
70.46	66.11	61.50	64.74	62.47	59.32	58.31
13,722	18,379	23,137	28,062	34,128	37,882	41,889
12.31	13.37	14.66	15.24	15.91	15.16	15.47
10,070	12,333	12,658	15,410	16,583	33,261	34,649
9.03	8.97	8.02	8.37	7.73	13.31	12.80
18,872	228,379	288,137	311,062	350,128	401,882	444,889
27.11	26.65	29.72	27.53	25.03	25.45	25.57

nical renovation, the government must live up to its promise in order to realize the intended incentive effects of enterprise funds.

The rapid growth in EBF under administrative agencies reflects the government's increasing willingness to levy users' charges to finance some operations — in 1991 these fees rose by another Y12 billion. This approach has some advantages, the main one being that it can promote a more realistic pricing of government services to encourage more economical use. Furthermore, the approach has the short-term advantage of allowing the government to avoid the political cost of raising taxes. Problems of the approach include a tendency toward unrestrained growth, which the Ministry of Finance and the Price Bureau must guard against. If fees proliferate in an unplanned way, they may lead to a structure of costs that is irrational in terms of resource allocation and income distribution. For example, using fees as a substitute for taxes has led to a phenomenon where parents in the poorest regions are saddled with the burden of having to finance a larger portion of their children's primary schooling than do parents in wealthier regions, a burden that is making basic education unaffordable to too many rural families (World Bank 1992b). Finally, shifting the burden of financing their operations to administrative agencies may create some dysfunctional incentives: in the PRC today one hears frequent criticisms that many agencies are so busy concentrating on profit-making activities that they neglect their public service functions.

Appendix II

The Evolution of Central-Provincial Revenue Sharing

THE PREREFORM FISCAL SYSTEM

The prereform fiscal system in the People's Republic of China (PRC) was directly modeled on that of the former Soviet Union and adopted during the early 1950s as an integral part of the system of centralized planning and allocation of resources. It shares two salient features with other Soviet-type fiscal systems: an overwhelming dependence on industry, and a reliance on profits of state-owned enterprises, along with taxes, for government revenue (Wanless 1985). Using administrative prices that systematically discriminated against agriculture and raw materials producers in favor of industry, surpluses from the agriculture and extractive sectors were transferred to the industrial sector, where artificially high profits were created. These were captured for government coffers through a combination of turnover taxes and profit remittances.

Through the 1970s, the composition of revenues in the PRC system followed the classic Soviet pattern. Industry was extremely profitable. In 1980, the average profit rate on capital was 15.1 per cent, with an average of 24.2 per cent in light industry and 12.4 per cent in heavy industry. Indirect taxes levied on turnover generated additional revenues for state coffers, making state-owned industry especially "revenue rich."

A key advantage of this fiscal system was high revenue buoyancy: during 1953-1978, government revenues grew at an average annual rate of 7.3 per cent, compared to national income growth of 6.0 per cent. Another advantage of the system was administrative expedience: with state ownership of the means

Note: Appendix II has been adapted from Wong 1992.

of production, profit expropriation and tax collection were straight-forward. From the late 1950s on, the growth of state-ownership in industry and commerce provided growing revenues under the heading of "enterprise incomes," which rose steadily to comprise 55 per cent of total revenues during the 1960s through the mid-1970s.

The PRC budget is "consolidated" and includes the bud-gets of all administrative levels. Despite substantial decentraliza-tion in many spheres, the budgetary process remained quite centralized through the Maoist period. The Ministry of Finance approved not only the consolidated budget, but also annual revenue and expenditure plans at the provincial level, and the Ministry set the amount of revenue transfers. Provinces in turn supervised formulation of budget plans at the municipal and county levels.

REVENUE-SHARING REFORMS

Revenue-sharing reforms began in 1980. To accommodate differ-ing local conditions and financial status, five types of revenue-sharing arrangements were introduced. Provinces were divided into four categories and put under different arrangements. While the specific forms of revenue sharing differed, the guiding prin-ciple was the same: all were designed to leave sufficient funds at the local level to cover approved expenditures (based on bud-geted figures for the base year 1979) while experimenting with different incentive schemes at the margin to reward revenue collection efforts.

In the first type, Guangdong and Fujian provinces enjoyed the most generous provisions, under which they remitted a lump sum to the center each year and retained the rest. With the lump sum fixed at the same level for 4-5 years, the remittance rate would fall, leaving progressively more resources in the provinces.

At the other end of the spectrum was the fiscal arrangement applied to the "cash cows" on whom the central government depended for a significant share of its revenues: Beijing, Shang-hai and Tianjin municipalities. Because of the importance of remittances to the central budget from the three cities, their revenue-sharing ratios continued to be set annually.

Under the third type of fiscal arrangement, Jiangsu Province remitted a fixed portion of all revenues collected, regardless of source.

REVENUE SHARING BY SPECIFIC SOURCES

The dominant form of revenue-sharing arrangements was the fourth and fifth types, which can be considered as one, and covered all the other provinces. Under this arrangement, revenues were distinguished by source and divided into central, local, shared, and adjustment incomes (see Figure II.1). Central and local "fixed incomes" came primarily from their respective enterprises— central enterprises remitted profits to central fixed income, while local enterprises remitted profits to local fixed income. Taxes were also divided by type: customs duties and industrial-commercial taxes collected by the Ministry of Railroad were designated as central taxes. The agriculture tax, salt tax, and income taxes on collective enterprises were assigned to local fixed income. The "fixed rate shared income" consisted of profits of large-scale enterprises under dual leadership by the central and local governments, which were shared at a fixed ratio of 80:20 between the central and local governments. Finally, revenues from the industrial-commercial tax, which comprised nearly 80 per cent of total tax revenues (and over 40 per cent of total budgetary revenues), were designated as "adjustment income."

Only "local" and "adjustment" income were subject to revenue sharing. With expenditures set at the 1979 base levels, the revenue sharing rates for local fixed income and adjustment income were set in a two-step process as follows:

(1) If $E^* \leq Y_f$, $a_2 = 0$, and a_1 was set such that
$E^* = a_1 Y_f$, where $0 < a_1 \leq 1$;

(2) If $E^* > Y_f$, $a_1 = 1$, and a_2 was set such that
$E^* = Y_f + a_2 Y_a$, where $0 < a_2 \leq 1$;

where E^* = base year local budget expenditures,
a_1 = local retention rate for local fixed income,
a_2 = local retention rate for adjustment income,
Y_f = local fixed income, and
Y_a = adjustment income.

Figure II.1: Flow of Funds under 1980 Revenue Sharing

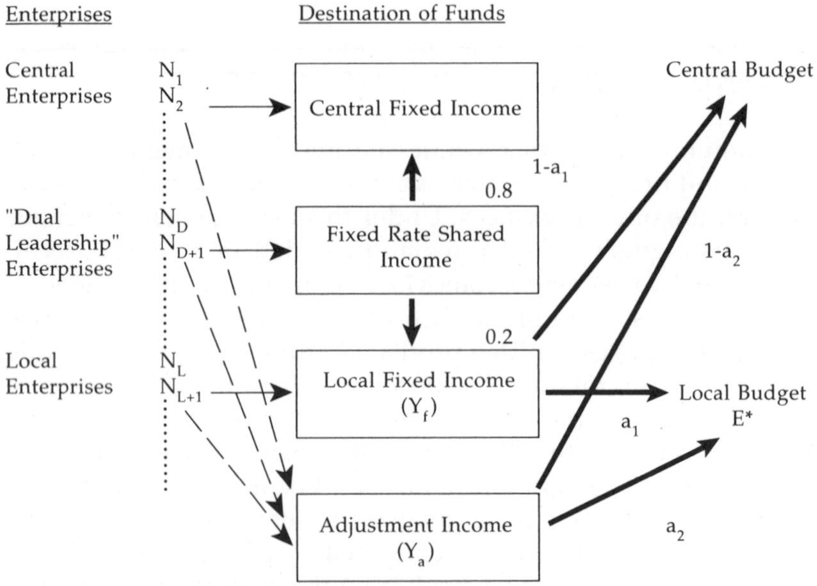

Enterprises   Destination of Funds

denotes profit remittances
denotes indirect tax payments
denotes revenue flows

Sources of Income:
Fixed rate shared income = profits of enterprises under dual leadership" of central and local governments (formerly central enterprises transferred to local management).
Local fixed income (Y_f) = profits remitted by local enterprises, plus all taxes other than industrial-commercial tax (agricultural tax, income taxes from local collective enterprises, salt tax, slaughter tax, etc.).
Adjustment income (Y_a) = receipts from industrial-commercial taxes.

Note: N_i = enterprises i, a_1 = local retention rate for local fixed income, a_2 = local retention rate for adjustment income, E^* = exogenously set local budget.

Source: Wong 1992, Figure 1.

Values for a_1 and a_2 are shown in Table II.1 for 13 of the 15 provinces that came under the fourth type of revenue-sharing arrangement in 1980. All but two of the retention rates for local fixed income (a_1) were set at 1. In all cases, they were greater than the retention rates for adjustment income $(a_1 > a_2)$.

The fifth type of revenue sharing was identical to the fourth, but where

Table II.1: **Revenue-Sharing Rates for Selected Provinces,
1980 and 1983**

		1980		1983
		a_1	a_2	b
1.	Anhui	1	0.581	0.762
2.	Gansu	1	0.532	1.000 +
3.	Hebei	< 1	-	0.635
4.	Henan	1	0.759	0.778
5.	Hubei	1	0.447	0.638
6.	Hunan	1	0.420	0.703
7.	Jilin	1	0.990	n.a.
8.	Liaoning	< 1	-	0.342
9.	Shaanxi	1	0.881	1.000
10.	Shandong	1	0.100	0.515
11.	Shanxi	1	0.579	0.826
12.	Sichuan	1	0.720	0.837
13.	Zhejiang	1	0.130	0.518

Notes:
a_1 = local retention rate for local fixed income
a_2 = local retention rate for adjustment income
b = local retention rate for total income

Source: Wong 1992.

$$E^* > Y_f + Y_a \; ;$$
then $a_1 = a_2 = 1$, and
$$E^* = Y_f + Y_a + S, \text{ where}$$
S = central subsidy.

This applied to eight provinces in 1980, all of which have significant non-Han populations: Guangxi, Guizhou, Inner Mongolia, Ningxia, Qinghai, Tibet, Yunnan, and Xinjiang.

The most significant changes under this system were the division of revenues by source and the recognition of local governments' rights to significant sources of revenue, along with the explicit commitment to linking up local revenue collections with local expenditures. With the promise to leave retention rates for local fixed and adjustment income (a_1 and a_2) unchanged for five years, the system offered a fixed marginal retention rate on local revenues, whereby increased revenue collections would increase local funds at a fixed rate.

An important feature of this division of revenues was the designation of enterprise incomes by ownership. This is a feature left over from the prereform system; what gave it new significance was the new system's avowed commitment to linking local expenditures to local revenue incomes. In the prereform system, since budgetary revenues were only weakly linked to expenditures, the frequent changes in enterprise ownership through the phases of centralization and decentralization did not significantly affect local expenditures. With the growing emphasis on self-financing at all levels, however, enterprise ownership acquired new importance.

Another new feature was the different treatment of enterprise incomes (profit remittances) and tax revenues: under this division of revenues, local governments were given a greater claim over profits generated by local enterprises than over the indirect taxes they paid (with $a_1 > a_2$). Together, these two features fundamentally altered the relationship between local governments and their enterprises and significantly decentralized the fiscal system: rather than acting solely as collection agents for the Ministry of Finance, local governments now collected taxes for the Ministry, but earned income from the enterprises under their ownership.

SHIFT TO SHARING OVERALL REVENUES

Despite promises to keep revenue-sharing ratios unchanged for five years, during 1982-1983, all provinces except Guangdong and Fujian, and the three cities (Beijing, Shanghai and Tianjin) were shifted to the Jiangsu-type revenue-sharing arrangement. This system altered the basis for revenue sharing by undoing one of the key features of the previous regime, eliminating the distinction between enterprise profit remittances and tax receipts. Industrial-commercial taxes paid by local enterprises were again pooled with enterprise incomes and other local revenues, with a single retention rate (b) set for the total (see Figure II.2):

$$Y_t = Y_f + Y_a$$

If $E^* \leq Y_t$, then b would be set at a level such that
$$E^* = b \, Y_t, \text{ where } 0 < b \leq 1.$$
If $E^* > Y_t$, then b would be set equal to 1, and
$$E^* = Y_t + S.$$

Figure II.2: Flow of Funds under 1982 Revenue Sharing

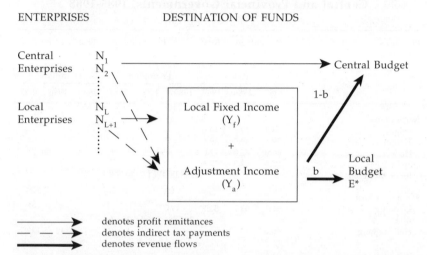

ENTERPRISES   DESTINATION OF FUNDS

	denotes profit remittances
	denotes indirect tax payments
	denotes revenue flows

Note: N_i = enterprises i, b = local retention rate, E* = exogenously set local budget.

Source: Wong 1992, Figure 2.

where
> E^* = base year local budget expenditures;
> Y_t = total local revenues;
> Y_f = local fixed income, as defined in 1980 revenue

sharing system;
> Y_a = adjustment income comprising revenues;
> b = revenue sharing rate; and
> S = central subsidy

After 1983, revenue-sharing arrangements changed two more times. In 1985 in the wake of the "tax-for-profit" reform, profit remittances were shifted into tax categories, requiring new definitions for "fixed" and "shared" revenues (See Table II.2). In 1988, the arrangements were again changed under fiscal contracting. While these changes altered the scope and definition of the basis for revenue sharing—whether it is Y_f, Y_a, or Y_t, or which taxes went into each pool (see Box II.1 and Table II.3)—the principles remained the same: that central revenues were not subject to sharing, allowable expenditures were driven by base year levels, and the central government determined the sharing formula.

Table II.2:   Revenue-Sharing System between the Central and Provincial Governments, 1985-1988

Provinces and Regions	Percentage of Total Collections Retained by Province (%)			Province Receives Subsidy from the Center (Y million)			Fixed or Contract Delivery to the Center (Y million)		
	1985	1986	1987	1985	1986	1987	1985	1986	1987
North China									
Beijing	48.2	49.6	49.6						
Tianjin	39.5	39.5	39.6						
Hebei	69.0	72.0	72.0						
Shanxi	97.5	97.5	97.5						
Inner Mongolia				1783.0[a]	1961.7	2059.8			
Northeast China									
Liaoning	51.1	52.7	52.7						
Jilin				397.0	396.6	396.6			
Heilongjiang	96.0							142.7	142.7
East China									
Shanghai	26.0	23.5	23.5						
Jiangsu	39.0	41.0	41.0						
Anhui	80.1	80.1	80.1						
Fujian				235.0				234.9	234.9
Jianxi				239.0				239.5	239.5
Shandong	59.0	77.5	75.0						
Central/South China									
Henan	81.0	81.0	87.1						
Hubei	66.5	100.0	100.0						
Hunan	88.0	88.0	88.0						
Guangdong							772.1	778.1	778.0
Guangxi				716.0[a]	788.0	827.4			
Southwest China									
Sichuan	89.0	100.0	100.0						
Guizhou				743.0[a]	817.6	858.5			
Yunnan				637.0[a]	925.9	972.2			
Tibet				750.0[a]	825.3	866.6			
Northwest China									
Shaanxi				270.0	270.3	270.3			
Gansu				246.0	245.6	245.6			
Qinghai				611.0[a]	671.9	705.5			
Ningxia				494.0[a]	543.1	570.3			
Xinjiang				1450.0[a]	1594.9	1674.6			

a Subsidies were to increase by 10 per cent per year after 1985.

Source: Bahl and Wallich 1992, p. 13.

Box II.1. Principles of Revenue Allocation and Tax Sharing, 1985

I. *Central Fixed Revenues*

1. Income and adjustment tax of all central government enterprises
2. Business tax from railroads, bank and insurance company headquarters
3. Profit remittances by all enterprises producing arms
4. Price subsidies paid to producers of grain, cotton and oil (treated as a negative revenue of the central government)
5. Fuel oil special tax
6. Income taxes, sales taxes, and royalties from offshore oil activities of foreign companies and joint ventures
7. Treasury bond income
8. 70 per cent of the three sales taxes collected from enterprises owned by the Ministry of Petrochemical Industries, the Ministry of Power, SINOPEC (Petroleum), and the China Nonferrous Metals Company
9. All customs duty and all VAT and product taxes collected at customs
10. Tobacco tax and business tax on tobacco
11. Product tax on liquor and tobacco

II. *Local Fixed Revenues, 1985-1987*

1. Income tax and adjustment tax of locally-owned enterprises
2. Income tax from collectively owned enterprises
3. Agriculture tax
4. Rural market trading tax levied on private sector traders

---

5. Local government grain trading loss (a negative tax)
6. Fines for delinquent taxes
7. The Urban Maintenance and Construction Tax[a]
8. Housing tax
9. Vehicle utilization tax
10. 30 per cent of the three sales taxes collected from enterprises owned by the Ministry of Petrochemical Industry, the Ministry of Power, SINOPEC, and the China Nonferrous Metals Company
11. Individual income tax
12. Wage bonus tax
13. Self-employed Entrepreneurs Tax
14. Slaughter Tax
15. Cattle Trading Tax
16. Contract Tax

III. *Taxes Shared Between the Central and Local Governments*

1. All sales taxes (value-added, business, and product) revenues from all enterprises, except those expressly excluded as described above under I:6, 9 and 10
2. Natural resource taxes
3. Construction tax
4. Salt tax
5. Industrial and commercial tax, and income tax, levied on foreign and joint venture enterprises
6. Energy and transportation fund tax

---

[a] The urban maintenance and construction tax is set at 7 per cent of total sales tax liability for municipalities (5 per cent for towns and 1 per cent everywhere else).

Source: World Bank (1990c), Box 3.2.

Table II.3.: Sharing Arrangements in 1987 by Type of Tax
(per cent)

Tax Category	Shared	Fixed Central	Fixed Local
Industrial-Commercial Taxes			
1.Product and VAT:			
a. Enterprises owned by four Ministries[a]	30	70	0
b. Tobacco products produced by centrally owned enterprises	0	100	0
c. Other general taxes	100	0	0
d. Product tax and VAT on imported goods	0	100	0
e. Refund of product tax and VAT to central government foreign trade company	0	100	0
f. Refund of product tax and VAT on export goods, to industrial enterprises and local foreign trade companies	100	0	0
2. Business Tax			
a. Enterprises owned by four Ministries	30	70	0
b. Railway, central tobacco enterprises, bank headquarters	0	100	0
c. General business tax	100	0	0
d. Self-employed urban and rural households in industry and commerce	100	0	0
3. Consolidated Industry and Commerce Tax			
a. Offshore oil enterprises	0	100	0
b. Other enterprises	100	0	0
c. Imported products	0	100	0
Other Taxes			
4. Special Adjustment Tax	0	100	0
5. Collective Enterprises Income Tax	100	0	0
6. Self-Employed Households in Industry and Commerce	100	0	0
7. Individual Income Tax	100	0	0
8. Individual Income Adjusted Tax	100	0	0
9. Joint Venture Income Tax			
a. Offshore oil	0	100	0
b. All others	100	0	0
10. Foreign Enterprise Income Tax		10	
a. Offshore oil	0	100	0
b. All others	100	0	0

a   Ministry of Petrochemical Industries, Ministry of Power, SINOPEC, and Ministry of Non-ferrous Metals.

Source: World Bank 1990c, p.256.

Tax Category	Shared	Fixed Central	Fixed Local
11. Urban Construction and Maintenance Tax	0	0	100
12. Vehicle Utilization Tax	100	0	0
13. Local Vehicle Utilization Tax	0	0	100
14. House Tax	100	0	0
15. Slaughter Tax	100	0	0
16. Animal Trading Tax (livestock transactions)	100	0	0
17. Free Market Transaction Tax	100	0	0
18. Natural Resource Tax	100	0	0
19. Central Resource Tax	0	100	0
20. SOE Bonus Tax	100	0	0
21. Wage Adjustment Tax	100	0	0
22. Institutions Bonus Tax	100	0	0
23. Collectives Bonus Tax	0	0	100
24. Construction Tax	100	0	0
25. Special Fuel Using Tax (crude oil burning tax)	0	100	0
26. Deduction and Refund of Fuel Tax	100	0	0
27. Salt Tax	100	0	0
28. Revenue from Penalties and Fines: customs duty categories)	0	100	0
29. Agriculture Taxes			
a. Animal husbandry	100	0	0
b. Forestry and special products	100	0	0
c. Central land occupation tax	0	100	0
d. Local land occupation tax	0	0	100
30. Income Tax			
a. SOE income tax	100	0	0
b. SOE adjustment tax	100	0	0
c. SOE profit remittance	100	0	0
d. Subsidies for planned losses	100	0	0
31. Contribution for Energy Transportation Projects			
a. Paid by central SOEs	0	100	0
b. Paid by local SOEs	0	100	0
32. Interest Income	n.a.	n.a.	n.a.
33. Earmarked Revenue	n.a.	n.a.	n.a.
34. Revenue from Loan Repayment for Capital Construction	n.a.	n.a.	n.a.
35. Revenue from Other Sources: other revenue joint ventures	100	0	0

Appendix III

The Shenzhen Approach to Supervision of the SOE Sector

Shenzhen, which has probably the most market-oriented economy in the PRC, has embarked on an innovative method of enterprise management. Shenzhen established the Shenzhen Investment Management Company (SIM) in 1987 to oversee the performance of Shenzhen's state-owned enterprises (SOEs). SIM supervises 100 holding companies that are called "first-level companies;" and the 100 first-level companies, in turn, supervise the operations of 1419 second-level enterprises (which produced Y34 billion in output value and Y9 billion in net output value in 1991).

SIM practices an indirect approach in the management of SOEs in order to separate its ownership and management obligations. SIM appoints a board of directors for each company, and the salary of a company director depends on the change in the value of the company's assets. There is no ceiling on a director's salary.

At the beginning of the year, SIM sets for each company a target amount of profits to be remitted and a formula for sharing profits above target. In 1991, SIM received Y190 million in after-tax profits. (It is puzzling that SIM's profits do not appear in the city government's budget even though SIM is a branch of the city government.)

SIM plans to use its accumulated profits to establish three funds for its enterprises: (1) a circulating capital fund, (2) an investment fund, and (3) a technology upgrade fund. Loans from the three funds will be extended at below bank rates.

To encourage prudent investment, SIM requires that the directors guarantee the investment loans with their personal savings. (Full collateral is, of course, not possible given the scale of most investment projects.) If the profit performance of an investment turns out to be worse than the forecast in the project application, then the directors suffer a loss proportional to the profit shortfall. If the profit performance is higher than forecast, then a proportional reward is given.

To further tighten the budget constraint perceived by SOEs, SIM will convert the first-level companies into limited liability companies in 1993, and the second-level companies into limited liability companies in 1994. With limited liability, SIM will no longer have to automatically bail out firms rendered unprofitable by mismanagement. Such firms can be allowed to go bankrupt.

The use of profits retained at SOEs has to be approved by SIM. SIM in effect decides the dividend and bonus practices of Shenzhen's SOEs. The general guidelines for disposing of retained profits are: (1) 35-60 per cent for dividends, (2) 35-55 per cent for accumulation fund, and (3) 10-20 per cent for the welfare fund.

The Shenzhen Petrochemical Company is one of the first-level companies supervised by SIM. Its name is misleading because many of the 33 enterprises in which it has holdings are not related to petrochemical activities. Forty per cent of Shenzhen Petrochemical Company's profit comes from real estate investment, 45 per cent from industrial operations, and 15 per cent from trading activities.

In 1991, the company had after-tax profits of Y44 million and remitted Y0.8 million to SIM. In 1992, the company had after-tax profits of Y63 million and remitted about Y26 million to SIM. The big jump in the remittance rate from 2 per cent to 41 per cent clearly shows the bargaining element in setting target profits.

In 1992, SIM converted the Shenzhen Petrochemical Company to a joint-stock company. SIM held 72 per cent of the shares, domestic agents held 15 per cent, foreign agents held 11 per cent (in the form of B shares), and employees held 2 per cent.

The Shenzhen Real Estate Company is also a first-level company (it was a second-level company in 1991). Its start-up capital was land granted by the city. It now manages 42 companies with capital of Y1.4 billion. It has substantial real estate investments abroad, particularly in Los Angeles, Melbourne, Moscow, and Vancouver. In 1991, the company generated sales of Y300 million and profits of Y50 million; in 1992, sales were Y500 million and profits Y100 million. It remitted Y15 million to SIM in both years.

The operations of the Shenzhen Real Estate Company are of a mixed welfare-commercial nature. It builds welfare housing that is sold below cost to government officials, low profit housing that is sold at a low markup over cost to SOE employees, and commercial housing that is sold at market prices to the general public.

Sufficient information was not available to allow a conclusion of how effective SIM's innovative financial arrangements have been in fostering prudent risktaking by its managers. However, SIM's enterprises still display two flaws associated with the SOE system. The first is that SIM required its SOEs to occasionally act in a manner contrary to profit maximization. The SOEs still performed tasks that should be done only by the state (e.g., providing housing at below market prices to civil servants and SOE employees). The second flaw is the absence of well-defined financial arrangements between SIM and its enterprises (e.g., bargaining over profit remittance-continues).

SIM's intention to provide below market rate loans to its enterprises reveals a greater concern for the welfare of its constituents (which increases with the expansion of production) than for the financial welfare of its owner, the state. One might rationalize SIM's intention as the result of its industrial policy of picking winning products. However, there is no indication that SIM can do a better job picking winners than a market-oriented financial system such as the stock market.

References

Anhui Tongji Nianjian (Anhui Statistical Yearbook), 1988.

Bahl, R. and C. Wallich, 1992. "Intergovernmental Fiscal Relations in China." World Bank WPS 863.

Cai Derong, ed., 1991. *China's Urban Housing—Theory, Practice and Reform Proposals* (in Chinese). Beijing: Chinese Statistics Press.

Caizheng (Finance), 1991, 1990. Beijing, Chinese Finance and Economics Press (monthly), (8):38-39; (6):20.

Chen Rulong, 1988. *Contemporary Chinese Finance (Dangdai Zhongguo Caizheng)*, two volumes. Beijing: Chinese Academy of Social Sciences Press.

China Daily, 23 September 1992.

China Daily, 24 November 1992.

China Daily, 5 December 1992.

China Daily, 28 December 1992.

China Daily, 19 May 1993.

China Society for Finance, 1991. *Almanac of China's Finance and Banking*. Beijing: China's Financial Publishing House (English edition).

China Statistical Yearbook (see State Statistical Bureau).

Chongqing Municipal Housing Reform Office, 1992. "Key Points for Advertising the Collection of Housing Deposits." Document No. 46.

Chongqing Municipal Housing Reform Office, 1992. "Detailed Rules for Implementing Housing Deposits in Chongqing." Chongqing Housing Reform Document No. 33.

Chongqing Municipal Leading Group on Housing Reform, 1992. "Temporary Methods for Managing Cooperative Housing Construction in Cities and Towns in Chongqing Municipality." Chongqing Housing Reform Document No. 14.

Chongqing Municipal Leading Group on Housing Reform, 1992. "Temporary Methods for Managing the Sale of Public Housing at Preferential Prices in Chongqing." Chongqing Housing Reform Office Document No. 13.

Chongqing Municipal People's Government, 1992. "Notification on the Temporary Methods for Managing Housing Deposits in Chongqing Municipality." Chongqing Municipal Government Document No. 119, June 24.

Clarke, D. C., 1989. "The Legal Background to the Behavior of State-owned Enterprises." December, mimeo.

Deng Yingtao, Yao Gang, Xu Xiaobo, and Xue Yuwei, 1990. *Zhongguo Yusuanwai Zijin Fenxi* (The Analysis of China's Extrabudgetary Funds). Beijing: China People's University Press.

Donnithorne, Audrey, 1981. "Centre-Provincial Economic Relations in China." Contemporary China Papers, No. 16, Contemporary China Centre, Research School of Pacific Studies, Australian National University.

Easson, A. J. and Li Jinyan, 1987. "The Evolution of the Tax System in the People's Republic of China." *Stanford Journal of International Law*, pp. 339-447.

Fan Gang and Wing Thye Woo, 1992. "Decentralized Socialism and Macroeconomic Stability: Lessons from China." Working Paper No. 411, September, Economics Department, University of California at Davis.

Furusawa, K., 1990. "Rural Enterprises under Reconsideration." JETRO, *China Newsletter* No. 88, Sept.-Oct.

Guangdong Jingji Nianjian (Guangdong Economic Yearbook), 1986.

Guangxi Nianjian (Guangxi Yearbook), 1986.

Heady, C., 1992. "Modelling Price Reform in China." School of Social Sciences, University of Bath, processed.

Hebei Jingji Tongji Nianjian (Hebei Economic and Statistical Yearbook), 1991, 1992.

International Monetary Fund, 1992. *International Financial Statistics Yearbook*.

Kornai, J., 1980. *Economics of Shortage*. New York: North Holland.

Lee, Hong Yung, 1990. "China's New Bureaucracy?" Paper presented at the conference "State and Society in China: The Consequences of Reform, 1978-1990," 16-17 February, Claremont McKenna College.

Liu Keqiang and Xia Guang, 1991. "A Few Points on Strengthening County-level Finance." *Caizheng* (3):47-48.

Ma Shaoqiang, 1992. "Value of Policies: An Evaluation of China's Special Treatments to Guangdong Province in the 1980s." M.A. thesis, June, University of California, Santa Cruz.

Ministry of Finance, 1992. "Fiscal Reform and Banking, Social Security and Price Reform." Background paper prepared for the ADB TA for MOF, December.

Ministry of Finance, 1992. *Zhongguo Caizheng Nianjian* (Chinese Fiscal Yearbook).

Ministry of Finance, General Planning Office, 1992. *Zhongguo Caizheng Tongji, 1950-1991* (Chinese Financial Statistics). Beijing: Science Press.

Ministry of Finance, General Planning Office, 1989. *Zhongguo Caizheng Tongji, 1950-1988* (Chinese Financial Statistics). Beijing: Chinese Finance and Economics Press.

Oates, W., 1972. *Fiscal Federalism.* New York: Harcourt, Brace, Jovanovich, p. 55.

Oi, Jean, 1992. "Fiscal Reform and the Economic Foundations of Local State Corporatism in China." *World Politics* 45:1, pp. 99-126, October.

Oksenberg, M. and James Tong, 1991. "The Evolution of Central-Provincial Fiscal Relations in China, 1953-1983: The Formal System." *China Quarterly.*

People's Bank of China, 1991. *Annual Report.*

Prime, P., 1991. "Regional and Developmental Implications of China's Tax Reform: Interprovincial Comparisons of Revenue Collection and Distribution." Mimeo, October, Center for International Research, Bureau of the Census, U.S. Department of Commerce.

Reynolds, B., ed., 1987. *Reform in China: Challenges and Choices.* Armonk, New York: M. E. Sharpe.

Shah, Anwar, 1991. "Perspectives on Intergovernmental Fiscal Relations." World Bank Country Economics Department Working Paper No. 726, July.

Shen Fuquan, 1985. "Use Subsidy Grants Well to Fight the Battle of Self-Renewable." *Caizheng* (12):8-9.

Shenzhen Municipal Government, May 1992. "The Temporary Provisions on Social Insurance of Shenzhen City."

Shenzhen Tongji Nianjian (Shenzhen Statistical Yearbook), 1992.

Sichuan Jingji Nianjian (Sichuan Economic Yearbook), 1986.

Sichuan Provincial People's Government, 1991. "The Appraisal by the Sichuan Provincial People's Government of the Chongqing Municipal Housing Reform Design." Provincial Government Document No. 628.

State Council Leading Group on Housing Reform, 1992. "The Appraisal by the State Council Leading Group on Housing Reform of the Liaoning Provincial Comprehensive Design for Urban Housing Reform." Housing Reform Document No. 3.

State Statistical Bureau, 1991. *China Statistical Yearbook 1991* (English). Beijing: China Statistical Information and Consultancy Service Center.

State Statistical Bureau, 1992. *China Statistical Yearbook 1992* (English). Beijing: China Statistical Information and Consultancy Service Center.

State Statistical Bureau, 1986, 1987, 1988, 1989, 1991, 1992, 1993. *Zhongguo Tongji Nianjian* (China Statistical Yearbook), annual. Beijing: Chinese Statistical Press.

Sun Tanzhen, Wang Chaocai, Yao Gang and H. Yamamoto, 1991. *Chinese Economic Development and Rural Public Finance.* Institute of Developing Economies, Joint Research Program Series No. 92, p. 104, March.

Tait, A., 1988. *Value Added Tax: International Practice and Problems.* Washington, D.C.: IMF.

Tam On Kit, 1991. "Capital Market Development in China." *World Development*, Vol. 19, No. 5, May.

Tidrick, G. and Chen Jiyuan, 1987. *China's Industrial Reform.* Oxford.

Tong, James, 1989. "Fiscal Reform, Elite Turnover and Central-Provincial Relations in Post-Mao China." *The Australian Journal of Chinese Affairs*, No. 22, July, pp. 1-28.

U.S. Department of Health and Human Services, Social Security Administration, 1987. *Social Security Programs Throughout the World.*

Walder, A., 1989. "Factory and Manager in an Era of Reform." *China Quarterly*, No. 118, June.

Wang Bingqian, 1986. "Maintain Budgetary Balance to Serve Economic Development and System Reform." *Caizheng Yanjiu* (9), pp. 1-6, reprinted in *Caizheng, Jinrong* (12).

Wang Bingqian, 1989. "Report on the Implementation of the 1989 State Budget." Seventh National People's Congress, 31 August, *Caizheng* (10), pp. 33-36.

Wang Bingqian, 1990. "Report on the Implementation of the 1989 State Budget and the 1990 Draft Budget, at the Third

Plenary Session of the Seventh National People's Congress, March 21, 1990." *Renmin Ribao* 8 April.

Wang Yukun, 1992. "On Our Country's Urban Housing System Reform." *Jingji Yanjin* 1, pp. 75-80.

Wang Yukun, 1991. "The Size of China's Housing Subsidies." *Review of Urban and Regional Development* (Tokyo, Japan), Vol. 3, No. 1, pp. 103-116.

Wanless, P. T., 1985. *Taxation in Centrally Planned Economies.* New York: St. Martin's Press.

Wong, Christine, forthcoming 1994. *Economic Reform in the People's Republic of China*, Hong Kong: Oxford University Press.

Wong, Christine P. W., 1992. "Fiscal Reform and Local Industrialization: The Problematic Sequencing of Reform in Post-Mao China." *Modern China*, v.28, n.2, April.

Wong, Christine P. W., 1991. "Central-Local Relations in an Era of Fiscal Decline: The Paradox of Fiscal Decentralization in Post-Mao China." *China Quarterly* (128), December.

World Bank, 1992a. *China: Budgetary Policy and Intergovernmental Relations.* Report No. 11094-CHA, October 30.

World Bank, 1992b. *China: Education Development in Poor Provinces.* Staff Appraisal Report, Report No. 10010-CHA, February 11.

World Bank, 1992c. *China: Implementation Options for Urban Housing Reform.*

World Bank, 1990a. *China: Macroeconomic Stability and Industrial Growth under Decentralized Socialism.* Washington, D.C.

World Bank, 1990b. *China: Reforming Social Security in a Socialist Economy.*

World Bank, 1990c. *China: Revenue Mobilization and Tax Policy.* Washington, D.C.: World Bank.

World Bank, 1988. *World Development Report 1988.* Oxford: Oxford University Press.

World Bank, 1992. *World Tables 1991.* Baltimore: Johns Hopkins University Press.

Xinjiang Caizheng Nianjian (Xinjiang Financial Yearbook), 1986.

Xu Riqing, 1988. "Some Thoughts on Local Government Fiscal Contracting." *Caimao Jingji* (Finance and Trade Economics), (11) pp. 53-54.

Yang Zhaoming and Fang Hesheng, eds., 1990. *Difang Caizheng Guanli* (Local Fiscal Management). Beijing: Chinese Financial Economics Press.

Yun Zhiping, Bai Yihong, and Tan Chunlin, 1991. *Explorations on Our Housing System Reform*. Beijing: Chinese Finance and Economics Press, pp. 204-209.

Zhang Hongbing, 1990(1). "Brief Introduction on National Township (and Town) Budgetary Accounting Forms." *Caizheng*.

Zhang Shuguang, 1990. "Personal Income in Kind." *Jingji Yanjiu* (Economic Research), Issue No. 12.

Zhao Bokun and Zhang Hongbing, 1985(2). "From Investigating the Situation in Anhui and Jiangsu Provinces to Discussing Some Issues in Building Xiang(zhen) Fiscal Organs." *Caizheng*, pp. 22-3.

Zhao Renwei, 1989. "Income-in-Kind in the Process of Economic Reform." *Jingji Yanjiu* (Economic Research), Issue No. 4.

Index